1308

THE REFERENDUM EXPERIENCE
Scotland 1979

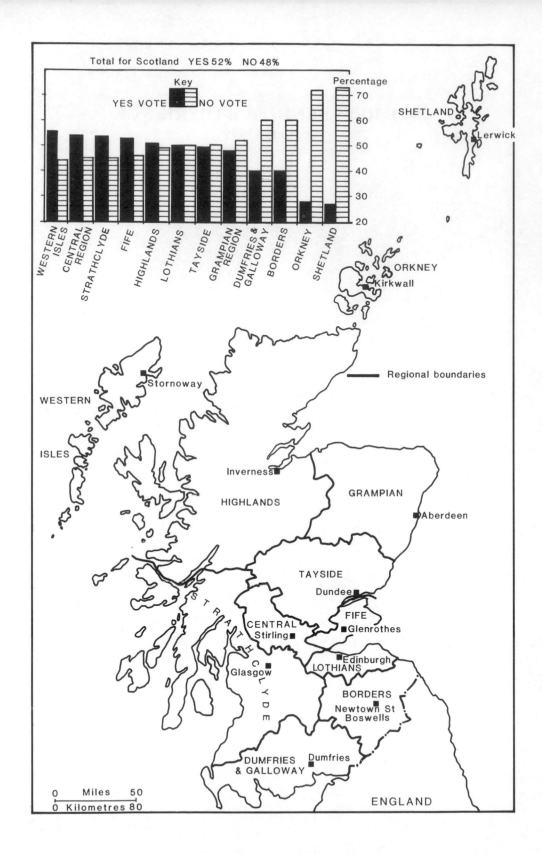

REGIONAL MAP OF SCOTLAND
Yes-No Voting in Referendum

THE REFERENDUM EXPERIENCE

Scotland 1979

editors

John Bochel

David Denver

Allan Macartney

With Foreword by
David Butler

ABERDEEN UNIVERSITY PRESS

First published 1981
Aberdeen University Press
A member of the Pergamon Group

British Library Cataloguing in Publication Data

The Referendum experience, Scotland 1979
1. Referendum—Scotland
2. Decentralization in government—Great Britain
I.   Bochel, John   II. Denver, David
III. Macartney, Allan
328'.2   JF493.G/

ISBN 0 08 025734 8

Typescript by Publication Preparation Service, Penicuik

PRINTED IN GREAT BRITAIN AT
THE UNIVERSITY PRESS, ABERDEEN

FOREWORD

This study of a massive event in the history of Scotland, and indeed of the United Kingdom, is itself on a grand scale. But there is every justification for so comprehensive a record of how, in a quite new fashion, a part of the British public was asked to decide the way in which it was to be governed. A referendum is a deviant species of election and an election always provides a challenge to historians and political scientists: it involves the whole polity; it takes up a compact period of time; it has a specific and measurable outcome; and, most of all, it has an outcome that represents a landmark in a nation's story, a verdict on how affairs have been managed and a decision on how they are least likely to be mismanaged in the future. To describe how the politicians and the media have tried to influence the electors and to analyse what has determined the final casting of the votes is plainly worth the effort. Therefore in recent years most national elections have received full academic treatment. All too often, alas, the approach has been rather derivative and formula-bound.

This book, however, seems to me a model of its kind. A diversity of authors and approaches have been edited into a single absorbing account of a nation involved in a new kind of decision making. The Referendum cut across traditional party loyalties and challenged many people to think afresh about the rules of the political game. Referendums by-pass established institutions and require ordinary electors to make individual decisions. Parties, politicians, newspaper editors and, above all, broadcasting authorities find that they cannot solve their problems by following the routine arrangements of party politics. New forms of communication and new guidelines of fairness have to be devised. Scotland in 1979—like Quebec in 1980—provides a classic case study of the dilemmas involved and of how intelligent and conscientious believers in democracy sought to solve them.

Analogous situations will recur. Therefore it is important that past experience should not run to waste. This book offers an invaluable record for politicians and administrators in Britain, and farther afield, to draw upon, as they decide how to tackle future references to the people, when great problems have to be decided by mass suffrage.

As one who has written extensively about elections and about referendums, I was flattered to be asked to provide a preface to this volume. Having now read it, I feel honoured to be associated with so enlightening a work of reportage and of scholarship.

NUFFIELD COLLEGE   DAVID BUTLER
OXFORD

APRIL 1981

CONTENTS

TABLES

MAPS AND DIAGRAMS

PREFACE

The Referendums on devolution held in Scotland and Wales on March 1, 1979 were significant political events. They were the culmination of many years of debate and the second major experiment with referendums in recent British history; their results led directly to the downfall of the Callaghan Government and to a General Election which returned the Conservatives to power and put Mrs Thatcher into 10 Downing Street. Although these last developments could not have been foreseen before the event, it was clear to the three Editors that the Referendums were going to have important consequences not only for the Scottish and Welsh peoples but also for the British Constitution and for the future shape of British politics.

Given this, we felt that a study of the Scottish Referendum should be undertaken in some detail. It was predictable that other political scientists would produce articles and papers dealing with the Referendum, but we could discover no plans for a comprehensive and detailed account. We therefore took the initiative in designing this study and invited contributions from colleagues interested in various aspects of Scottish politics. Although we determined the substantive area of concern of each contribution and suggested guidelines, no attempt was made to standardise them or to impose a "line". Each contribution, therefore, is the distinctive product of the author(s) concerned. The book thus contains a range of approaches and methodology from formal surveys of campaign organisations and content analysis of the local press through observational and impressionistic accounts of campaigns in the city-regions to a frankly personal view of one campaign.

Our hope is that the book will not only provide an enduring record of the Referendum but will convey something of the variety and flavour of this particular chapter of our political history.

ACKNOWLEDGMENTS

The production of a volume of this kind inevitably gives rise to debts to numerous individuals and institutions and these we would like to acknowledge.

The Nuffield Foundation generously provided funds to enable the contributors to meet on several occasions, and for other aspects of the study. The Universities of Dundee and Lancaster provided funds for specific pieces of research, as did the Open University Social Science Faculty, while the Open University in Scotland provided a great deal of material assistance. We are most grateful for their help.

The contributors were most encouraged by the willingness of a large number of people involved in Referendum campaigning to give information and interviews and reply to lengthy questionnaires. These are too numerous to thank individually but only their co-operation made the whole exercise possible.

Our thanks are due to the following for sending in campaign monitoring reports: Dave Allen, Malcolm Bain, Billy Ballantyne, Hugh Blackwood, David Boddy, Des Bonnar, Ken Bratton, Andrew Brown, Crawford Brown, Fiona Brown, Robert Corrins, Jean Cox, Morag Craig, Jim Cumming, Gordon Dickinson, Pat Edwin, Iain Forbes, Dan Gunn, Joe Harkins, Elizabeth Hogg, Ron Kaye, Ian Kinnaird, Marian Lever, Colin Luckhurst, Donald Macdonald, Jim McDonald, Ann MacInnes, Joyce MacInnes, Anne MacIver, John McKenzie, Alan McLay, Archie Morton, Ian Murray, Murray Normand, Tommy Rendall, Branislav Sudjić, Julian Tennant, Sylvia Thorne, David Wilson, George Wilson and Fergus Young.

We would like to thank the following (all of Dundee University): Val Baker for coding a survey of parties; Moira Bell for coding and computing a survey of campaign groups; Doris Tindal for much secretarial assistance.

We are most grateful to David Butler, author of many studies of elections and referendums, for agreeing to write a foreword to the book. To John Hunt, cartographer with the Open University, we acknowledge our indebtedness for the maps he drew specially for this book. For helping to provide illustrative material from the other referendums held in 1979/80 (in Catalonia, Euzkadi, Greenland, Quebec and Wales) we would like to thank David Cameron, Michael Hughes, Barry Jones, Chris Ross, Irma Tubella, Rick Wilford, Ebbe Anderson, the Electoral Officer of Quebec, Grønland, the Danish Institute (Edinburgh), the Délegation générale of Quebec in London and the Director-général du Financement des partis politiques. To Alan Grant we express our thanks for taking on the onerous task of compiling the index.

For meticulous proofreading and many suggestions for stylistic improvements we are greatly indebted to Jay Macartney. Thanks are also due to Riet Cannell (of Publication Preparation Service, Penicuik) not only for admirable typing of the camera-ready copy but for many suggestions for editorial improvements and correction of anomalies.

Last, but not least, we wish to thank Aberdeen University Press not only for publishing this book but for the helpful yet businesslike advice afforded the editors.

This formidable list of those who helped us in various ways emphasises the extent to which detailed study of an event as complex as a referendum requires the assistance of people far removed from the academic's study. We hope we may have produced a volume worthy of their efforts on our behalf.

J.M.B. D.T.D. W.J.A.M.

NOTES ON TERMINOLOGY

As far as possible we have used **Referendum** with a capital "R" to refer to March 1, 1979, while other referendums appear in lower case.

Our choice of the **plural** form of referendum was made in deference to the combined authority of Butler and Ranney and the Oxford English Dictionary. A footnote quotes the editor of the dictionary as follows:

> Usage varies, even in high places, and both *referendums* and *referenda* are found in print. My own view is that *referendums* is logically preferable as a plural form meaning ballots on one issue (as a Latin gerund, *referendum* has no plural). The Latin plural gerundive *referenda* meaning "things to be referred" necessarily denotes a plurality of issues. A note to this effect is being added to our entry for the word in the forthcoming third volume of *A Supplement to the Oxford English Dictionary*.
>
> (D. E. Butler and A. Ranney, *Referendums* [American Enterprise Institute, Washington, D.C., 1978], pp. 4-5)

In the light of the complexities of the legislation on devolution and the sometimes inaccurate references thereto, it may be helpful to remind readers that a **Bill** is a piece of draft legislation before Parliament; it becomes an **Act** or Statute when it has been passed by both Houses of Parliament and received the Royal Assent.

ABBREVIATIONS

AFA   Alliance for an Assembly
ASW   Amalgamated Society of Woodworkers
AUEW   Amalgamated Union of Engineering Workers
BBC   British Broadcasting Corporation
BIE   Britain in Europe
CATOR   Conservatives Against the Treaty of Rome
CBI   Confederation of British Industry
Cllr   Councillor
CLP   Constituency Labour Party
Con.   Conservative
CPGB   Communist Party of Great Britain
CPPB   Committee on Party Political Broadcasting
CYC   Conservative Yes Campaign
EEC   European Economic Community
GMWU   General and Municipal Workers Union
HTV   Harlech Television
IBA   Independent Broadcasting Authority
ITN   Independent Television News
ITV   Independent Television
KBU   Keep Britain United
Lab.   Labour
Lib.   Liberal
LMY   Labour Movement Yes
LVN   Labour Vote No
MORI   Market and Opinion Research International
MP   Member of Parliament
NAC   No Assembly Campaign [Wales]
NALGO   National and Local Government Officers Association
NOP   National Opinion Polls
NRC   National Referendum Campaign [1975]
NUFTO   National Union of Furniture Trade Operatives
NUPE   National Union of Public Employees
ORC   Opinion Research Centre
P&J   *Press and Journal*
PPB   Party Political Broadcast/Broadcasting
SCADA   Student Campaign Against the Devolution Act
SCARR   Scottish Campaign Against the Rigged Referendum
SIB   Scotland is British
SLP   Scottish Labour Party
SNP   Scottish National Party
SSN   Scotland Says No
STUC   Scottish Trades Union Congress
STV   Scottish Television Ltd
T&GWU   Transport and General Workers Union
UCATT   Union of Construction, Allied Trades and Technicians
WAC   Wales for the Assembly Campaign
YFS   Yes for Scotland

CHRONOLOGY

1973	October	Report of Royal Commission on the Constitution.
1974	February	General Election. Labour Government elected (H. Wilson, Prime Minister). W. Ross, Secretary of State for Scotland.
	June	Privy Council Paper "Devolution within the United Kingdom: some alternatives for discussion."
	September	Government White Paper "Democracy and Devolution: proposals for Scotland and Wales." (Cmnd 5732)
	October	General Election. Labour Government returned (H. Wilson, Prime Minister). W. Ross, Secretary of State for Scotland; E. Short, Lord President.
1975	November	Government White Paper "Our Changing Democracy." (Cmnd 6348)
	December	*Scottish Labour Party (SLP) formed.*
1976	January	*SLP launched*
	April	J. Callaghan appointed Prime Minister (resignation of H. Wilson). B. Millan, Secretary of State for Scotland; M. Foot, Lord President; J. Smith, Minister of State, Privy Council Office.
	May	*Keep Britain United (KBU) launched.*
	August	Government White Paper "Devolution to Scotland and Wales: supplementary statement." (Cmnd 6585)
	September	*Scotland is British (SIB) formed.*
	November 23	*SIB launched.*
	29	**Scotland and Wales Bill published.**
	Nov./Dec.	*Union Flag group formed.*
	December 8	*Shadow Cabinet decision to oppose Second Reading of Scotland and Wales Bill. Resignation of shadow Secretary of State for Scotland A. Buchanan-Smith and shadow Scottish Office spokesman M. Rifkind. T. Taylor appointed shadow Secretary of State for Scotland.*
	December 16	**Government announces intention of holding referendums in Scotland and Wales before implementation of the Bill.**
		Scotland and Wales Bill receives Second Reading.
1977	February	Guillotine (timetable) motion defeated. Scotland and Wales Bill dropped.
	March 21	*Alliance for a Scottish Assembly formed.*
	24	Government reaches agreement with Liberal Party (Lib.-Lab. Pact).
	April	J. Smith takes over responsibility for devolution.
	July	Government announces intention of introducing separate Bills for Scotland and Wales.
	November 4	**Scotland Bill published.**
	November 27	*Labour Party (Scottish Executive) decides to go it alone in campaigning for a Yes vote in the Referendum.*

1978	January	25	**Cunningham amendment (40 per cent rule) passed.**
		26	*Yes for Scotland (YFS) launched.*
	March		*Labour Party (Scottish Council) Conference endorses Scottish Executive line on Referendum campaigning.*
	July	31	**Scotland Bill receives Royal Assent as The Scotland Act 1978.**
	November	1	**Date of Referendum announced.**
		11	J. Smith appointed Minister of Trade.
		13	*Labour Party Scottish Secretary rules out cross-party co-operation in Yes campaign.*
		14	*First leaflet published by Labour Vote No (LVN).*
		26	*Liberal Leader warns against proliferation of Yes groups.*
		27	*Alliance for an Assembly (AFA) launched.* *LVN launched.*
		30	*Scotland Says No (SSN) launched.* *Labour Movement Yes (LMY) campaign plans announced.*
	December	20	**Referendum Order (No. 1912) published.**
1979	February	12	*LMY campaign launched by Prime Minister.*
	March	1	**Referendum Day.**
		2	Results announced.
		28	Government defeated on No Confidence motion in House of Commons.
	May		General Election. Conservative Government elected (Mrs M. Thatcher, Prime Minister). G. Younger, Secretary of State for Scotland.
	June	20	**Repeal of The Scotland Act 1978.**

CHAPTER 1

THE BACKGROUND TO THE REFERENDUM

John Bochel, David Denver and Allan Macartney

INTRODUCTION

On March 1, 1979 electors in Scotland went to the polls to record their answers to
the question "Do you want the provisions of the Scotland Act 1978 to be put into
effect?". On the face of it this seems an obscure question to ask voters but
lengthy public debate must have ensured that relatively few of them could be in ignorance of its point. They were being asked to vote on a major constitutional
change, the creation of an elected Scottish Assembly with legislative powers over a
wide range of subjects and with an Executive to give effect to the legislation. The
Referendum was the culmination of more than 10 years of discussion, manoeuvre and
debate over the issue, which had, according to most commentators, been sparked off
and sustained by the electoral success of the Scottish National Party (SNP) and had
involved the appointment of a Royal Commission, two official consultative papers,
three White Papers, a great deal of Parliamentary time, divisions within parties
and much scheming, arm-twisting and inter-party negotiation.

The story of the devolution issue over those years has been recounted fully elsewhere (see, for example, Bogdanor, 1979, Chapters 4-7; Drucker and Brown, 1980; and,
for a useful chronology, Drucker and Drucker, 1978, pp. 204-207), and so here we
need confine ourselves only to the barest outline.[1] Following the electoral success
of the SNP (and Plaid Cymru, the Welsh Nationalist Party) in Parliamentary by-elections and local elections in the period 1966-1968, the then Labour Government
appointed a Royal Commission "to examine the present functions of the central
legislature and government in relation to the several countries, nations and regions of the United Kingdom, to consider ... whether any changes are desirable in
those functions or otherwise in present constitutional and economic relationships
..." (Kilbrandon, 1973, pp. iii and iv). The report of the Commission was published
in October 1973 and a majority of its members recommended the creation of elected
Assemblies in Scotland and Wales. The view of the Commission was that there was a
clear demand for some form of devolution in these countries as evidenced by opinion
polls and the continuing electoral success of the Nationalist parties. Following
the General Election of February 1974, at which the Nationalists had made further
advances, the new minority Labour Government produced a consultative document,

---

[1]For an exhaustive bibliography on devolution, the Referendum and other aspects of
 Scottish politics see the reference section of successive *Scottish Government
 Yearbooks* and in particular Allen (1979).

Devolution within the United Kingdom: some alternatives for discussion, which outlined the main schemes recommended by the Royal Commission. Following consultations
based on this document the Government issued, in September, a White Paper, *Democracy and Devolution: proposals for Scotland and Wales* (Cmnd 5732); but a month
later there was another General Election. In the two years following this election,
at which the SNP won 11 seats and took 30.4 per cent of the Scottish vote, making
it second only to Labour in terms of popular support in Scotland, the Government
brought out two further White Papers on the subject, *Our Changing Democracy* (Cmnd
6348) in November 1975 and *Devolution to Scotland and Wales: supplementary statement* (Cmnd 6585) in August 1976. In November 1976 the Scotland and Wales Bill was
published and it received its Second Reading in December. Following slow progress
at the Committee stage (see Jordan, 1979), the Government moved a guillotine (timetable) motion but this was lost, partly because of defections and abstentions
amongst Labour MPs. This meant, effectively, that the Bill was lost and in November 1977 separate Bills for Scotland and Wales were introduced. After the Second
Readings guillotine motions were carried, thanks to Liberal support this time and
the return of the bulk of Labour defectors who realised that the life of the minority Government was at stake. Finally, with some important amendments, the Bills
were passed by Parliament and received the Royal Assent in July 1978 (for a detailed examination of the Scotland Act 1978 see Bradley and Christie, 1979).

This briefest of histories of the modern devolution issue omits much, of course -
the heart-searchings in all parties, the manoeuvrings amongst parties inside and
outside Parliament, the ebbs and floods of support for the SNP, the fate of a
government and so on. Our concern here and throughout this volume is, however, very
specifically with the Referendum and not with the devolution issue nor with the
circumstances which brought it to the forefront of British political discussion and
kept it there for more than 10 years.

Wide variations obtain in the extent to which referendums have been, and are, used
in democratic political systems as a means of allowing the electorate a direct say
on some specific policy or constitutional issue. In some states of the USA, for
example, voters are regularly called upon to make judgments on proposed laws, constitutional amendments and so on at state and local level. Thus, in San Mateo
County, California in November 1976 voters, in addition to choosing between candidates for numerous public offices from the Presidency down, were also asked to vote
for or against 15 propositions affecting the state as a whole, ranging from a
Housing Finance Bond Law and an Agricultural Labor Relations statute to a proposal
to license greyhound racing, and on five proposed amendments to the San Mateo
County Charter. For each proposition each voter was supplied with the text of the
proposal, arguments in favour, arguments against, rebuttals to these two statements
and an analysis by a "Legislative Analyst".

Switzerland and Australia are two democratic societies which have made frequent use
of nationwide referendums. Butler and Ranney record 297 of these in Switzerland and
39 in Australia up to September 1, 1978 (Butler and Ranney, 1978, p. 6). Although
a majority of countries in Europe have experimented with referendums since 1900,
most have made very sparing use of them. The topics upon which electors were asked
to vote have been more often than not constitutional. Of 58 nationwide referendums
in Europe, excluding Switzerland, 32 were on constitutional matters (Butler and
Ranney, 1978, Chapter 1).

Butler and Ranney point to the difficulty of making simple generalisations about
why referendums are held in particular countries on specific issues but after a
comprehensive study of all those they knew to have been held they claim to have
detected certain common elements. Firstly, in some countries referendums are, for
certain purposes, a constitutional requirement. The constitutions of Australia and
Switzerland, for example, cannot be amended without the approval of the voters,
expressed in a referendum, for the changes proposed. Secondly, referendums are

sometimes used to legitimise certain actions or decisions of the government, or
even sometimes to legitimise a new régime. In parliamentary democracies governments
usually claim that winning an election on a manifesto gives them a mandate for
their actions and so referendums are seldom required. Thirdly, referendums are
sometimes used when governments or parties are divided on an issue and it is expedient to transfer decision-making to the electorate so that the government is
not embarrassed and the party remains nominally united.

There have been only three (four, if we consider the Scottish and Welsh ones as
separate) major referendums in the United Kingdom.[2] The British constitution, such
as it is, did not either sanction or forbid their use. When the time came to have
the 1975 EEC referendum, a simple Act of Parliament was all that was required to
permit it. Governments and politicians have tended to oppose the use of referendums
in the UK on the grounds that they constitute an abrogation of government responsibility and would contribute to an undermining of Parliamentary supremacy. In 1975,
however, these misgivings were overcome and the first national referendum, on the
question of Britain's continued membership of the European Community was held.
Government spokesmen justified the holding of this referendum by reference to the
unique constitutional importance of the issue but it is generally agreed that it
was essentially a political expedient. Both the Labour Government and the Party in
the country were deeply divided on the matter of continued membership of the EEC
and a referendum provided, as James Callaghan anticipated it might, "a rubber life-
raft in which the whole party may one day have to climb" (Butler and Kitzinger, 1976,
p. 11). It was a device which enabled individuals to agree to differ on a specific
issue whilst preserving collective responsibility and support for the Government
on others. The maintenance of the Government was one objective but many anti-EEC
politicians also saw in the referendum their last chance of getting out of the
Common Market.

From our perspective what is important is that a referendum was held. Despite what
had been said about the uniqueness of the EEC issue governments could never again
claim that it was impossible to hold a referendum because it was contrary to
British constitutional practice. A precedent had been set, and precedents contribute to making the British constitution what it is. And polls found that the majority of electors approved of the idea of referendums. At the time of the EEC referendum in 1975 an ORC poll showed that 61 per cent of respondents thought that it
had been right to hold a referendum (Barker and Spencer, 1975). In October 1977 and
October 1978 Gallup found substantial majorities of the electorate believing that
there should be referendums on capital punishment, the role of trade unions, immigration and nationalisation. Oddly enough, the idea of a referendum on devolution
received lowest support in 1977 when 57 per cent approved of one on this issue, and
less than majority support in 1978 when only 49 per cent approved. It seems likely,
however, that devolution would be of minimal concern to the majority of Gallup's
respondents who were English.

The Government's original Scotland and Wales Bill contained no provision for referendums. In the extensive Commons debates on the Bill, however, the Government
quickly came under pressure, mainly from its own backbenchers, to hold a referendum
on the issue. Demands were made in speech after speech during the Second Reading
debate and finally the Government capitulated. On December 16, 1976 the Prime Minister was asked by Norman Buchan, Labour MP for West Renfrewshire, whether he had
had an opportunity "to take note of the pressure from all sides of the House for a
referendum? Has he yet given any further consideration to that?" Rather coyly
Callaghan replied: "Yes, Sir, the Cabinet considered this matter at its meeting

---

[2]There was one in Northern Ireland on March 8, 1973, on the question of whether
Northern Ireland should remain part of the United Kingdom.

this morning. It reached its conclusions. I heard the speech made by Mr Buchan on this subject at Blackpool. It may be that he will not be disappointed at the end of the day" (Hansard, Fifth Series, Vol. 922, cols 1725-6).

Later, John Smith, the Minister mainly responsible for piloting the devolution legislation through the House, confirmed that the Government's proposals would be submitted to the electors of Scotland and Wales in a referendum. The Referendum would be introduced as a new clause in the Bill at the Committee stage. This was duly done on February 10, 1977.

There were clearly two sides to the argument on a referendum. The Labour Party had fought and won an election in which it had promised to legislate on devolution. By the standards of British political practice it had a "mandate" for its Bills and was entitled not to think a referendum necessary under these circumstances. On the other hand a major constitutional change was proposed and it could be argued that the electorate (albeit only the Welsh and Scottish electorate) should be consulted. In addition the main argument deployed by the Kilbrandon Commission to justify its proposals had been that there was a clear and demonstrable demand for some form of devolution in Scotland and Wales. Why not, then, proponents of a referendum argued, test the strength of such demands directly by means of a referendum, especially given the precedent of the Common Market referendum?

It has to be emphasised that the initiative for a referendum did not come from the Government: pressure for the holding of a referendum came mainly from *opponents* of Government policy. Anti-devolutionists saw it as a last chance to defeat devolution proposals. Given a referendum they could vote for the Bill, thus preserving the Government in power, and then campaign against the implementation of the legislation. Some pro-devolution Labour MPs supported a referendum on the grounds that, as well as asking voters for their verdict on the Government's proposals, they could at the same time be asked to express their views on independence for Scotland. The result of this further question would, it was thought, greatly embarrass the SNP. Norman Buchan was one of those who advocated an additional question.

It seems clear that few of the advocates of a referendum were motivated by democratic ideology and it is equally clear that the Government's concession was made in order to save its Bill, its life and its future electoral prospects in Scotland. Most recalcitrant Labour backbenchers were persuaded to support it only by the promise of a referendum. Had the Government had a larger majority in the Commons then it is possible (given tighter control over its backbenchers) that this concession would not have been necessary to secure the passage of the Bill. Ultimately, then, as in the case of the EEC, a referendum was resorted to as an expedient because of divisions of opinion within the Labour Party.

REFERENDUM RULES

From the time, back in December 1976, when the Government made the concession of referendums in an attempt to get the Scotland and Wales Bill through Parliament (Drucker and Drucker, 1978, p. 208), thought had to be given to the rules for the conduct of each Referendum. Various existing models could have been considered (see Butler and Ranney, 1978; see also Canada, 1978), or a brand new model could have been designed, as was done in Quebec (Quebec, 1980a, 1980b), Catalonia and Euzkadi, not to mention the Danish-held referendum in Greenland in early 1979 (see Hvidt, 1980).

It is, however, hardly surprising, given the strength of pragmatism in British government, that the only previous referendum in Great Britain (see Butler and Kitzinger, 1976) should have been most frequently cited as the model on which the 1979 Referendums were to be based. Thus, Secretary of State for Scotland Bruce

Millan, piloting the Scotland Act 1978 Referendum Order 1978 through the Commons, stated: "It follows substantially the precedent of the order made for conducting the E.E.C. referendum held on 5 June 1975" (Hansard, 958, col. 1270), while in the same debate his junior Minister, Harry Ewing, said: "We have a precedent here, because during the E.E.C. referendum campaign ..." (*ibid.*, col. 1332). This was also the view of John Smith, popularly known as the Devolution Minister, who stated that the Government had tried to follow the precedent of 1975, *mutatis mutandis*.

If in fact that precedent had been followed precisely in 1979, it would have gone far towards establishing a constitutional convention on the holding of referendums in the United Kingdom. The fact that the 1979 practice followed the 1975 precedent only in some respects, but diverged markedly in others, is something that will be considered in its various implications in the concluding chapter. But first it is necessary to detail the respects in which 1979 followed the 1975 precedent or otherwise, and at least attempt to explain why these variations occurred.

Some provisions caused somewhat less controversy than had been the case with the Euroreferendum. The wording of the question on the ballot paper was one example (see Butler and Kitzinger, 1976, Chapter 3, *passim*). The same was true for the arrangements for the count (*ibid.*): it was readily agreed that the votes should again be counted on the basis of the Regional and Island Councils. The amendments made by the appropriate Orders to the application of the Representation of the People Acts were virtually identical, with the symbolically important difference that there was no provision for umbrella or non-party groups to send observers to the count or to be represented at polling stations. As a Government spokesman put it, "there is no intention of having consultations with any umbrella organisations which might spring up during the campaign" (Hansard, 958, col. 1334).

This issue, which led to protests from Scotland Says No and Yes for Scotland spokesmen alike, points up an important difference between 1975 and 1979 and one which was to have spillover effects on broadcasting and information policy. It should be understood that the basic reason for this attitude has its origins in the decisions within the ruling Labour Party to go it alone in an official Labour Movement Yes campaign (see Chapter 2): the Cabinet were, on this issue at least, merely accepting and implementing Party policy.

The effect on arrangements for broadcasting are discussed extensively in Chapter 7 but the implications for information policy were equally important. Whereas in 1975 "it was readily agreed that there should be a nationwide distribution of leaflets giving the Government's position and the pro and anti cases" (Butler and Kitzinger, 1976, pp. 55-56), in 1978 the idea was apparently abandoned early on because the Government Whips warned that the backbenchers would not accept it.

As these backbench rebels were presumably the same ones who had successfully backed the 40 per cent amendment (for which see below), the decision, or non-decision, was criticised by Yes spokesmen as a deliberate attempt to keep down the turnout as well as the general level of understanding of the provisions of the Scotland Act. Even the provision of an explanatory pamphlet in post offices in Scotland and Wales (as was done for the White Paper in 1976) was not attempted. It was thus left to "private enterprise" to fill this information gap. The efforts were paltry. The Citizens' Advice Bureau, for instance, distributed between 5,000 and 10,000 copies of an explanatory leaflet, while the Labour Movement Yes campaign sold around 4,000 copies of a pamphlet to interested members of the public (see Chapter 4, part V); the Conservative and Labour Parties likewise produced explanatory booklets, mainly for members. HM Stationery Office in Scotland sold approximately 750 copies of the Act, and at most a few hundred copies of an academic book (Bradley and Christie, 1979) were purchased by those interested. It is obvious that this does not match the nationwide distribution of leaflets as in 1975 (or the free distribution of an electoral address by each candidate at a Parliamentary election), and it is known that some voters received no communication at all through their letterboxes. The party political broadcasting ban was another factor tending marginally to reduce the publicity given to the Referendum. Against this has to be set the extensive advertising of arrangements for postal votes, undertaken officially.

The efficacy of backbench rebellion can again be seen in the question of the timing of the poll - something which the Government were able to control in 1975. An amendment inserted by the No side in Parliament meant that it was impossible to synchronise the Referendum with a general election; instead a delay of about four months would have had to follow the dissolution of Parliament before the Referendum could have proceeded. Presumably the calculation was that the effect of the 40 per cent rule would have been largely negatived by the high turnout which normally attends a general election.

In 1975 campaign organisations each received a sum of money of £125,000 (in addition to the free printing and distribution of their respective leaflets); this time no public funds went to either side. In the EEC case, "the problems of financing the campaigns attracted oddly little attention" (Butler and Kitzinger, 1976, p. 57); in the case of the devolution Referendum it was never seriously attempted but this decision again attracted little attention - it was presumably accepted as a consequence of the ruling party's attitude towards umbrella organisations.

The story on campaign expenditure is somewhat different. In 1975, although it was decided not to restrict expenditure by each side (it was considered too late for this to be feasible), it was nevertheless belatedly decided to oblige the campaigning organisations to publish accounts (Butler and Kitzinger, 1976, p.59). In debates on the devolution Referendum it was even suggested by a Conservative backbench opponent of the Scotland Act that there should be limits on expenditure by each side. What Sir John Gilmour described as a "loophole in the arrangements for the referenda" (Hansard, 958, cols 1321-1322), however, remained unplugged. As a result the public will never know precisely how much was spent on the campaign, where it all came from, nor how the expenditure was broken down. Jim Sillars, MP, leader of YFS, described this decision not to restrict expenditure as a further deliberate move by Labour backbench rebels to give the business community an advantage in the campaign; Parliament, however, remained indifferent.

The 40 per cent Rule

The biggest difference between the two referendums, however, concerned the interpretation and implementation of the result. In 1975, "Mr Wilson's reiteration of the White Paper assertion that a one-vote margin would be enough for him 'a simple majority - without qualifications or conditions of any kind' (see Cmnd 5925, para 3) was not really challenged" (Butler and Kitzinger, 1976, p. 65, footnote 14). The then Prime Minister might indeed have been applauded had he quoted in support of his position this classic statement of the referendum as the ultimate authority: "In countries with democratic governments the popular will is ordinarily deemed equivalent to the will of a majority. Hence the plebiscite or referendum, when resorted to in matters of internal affairs, is employed as the means of establishing which side of the argument is represented by the majority and as such entitled to prevail" (Mattern, 1921, p. 151). Certainly, the House of Commons gave short shrift in 1975 to the attempt to introduce a threshold or qualified majority provision. "There was, in fact, little argument over the question of whether a simple majority of those who bothered to vote would be adequate for a decision. When, citing the Danish precedent, Peter Emery finally moved that only a 60 per cent majority on a two-thirds turnout should be a mandate for leaving the Market, his amendment was negatived without a division" (Butler and Kitzinger, 1976, pp. 64-65, footnote 14).

The position was very different in the case of the 1979 Referendums. The House of Commons celebrated Burns Nicht 1978 by passing an amendment tabled by a Scotsman who represented the London seat of Islington South & Finsbury, George Cunningham. The Cunningham amendment, or 40 per cent rule as it was generally termed, stated: "If it appears to the Secretary of State that less than forty per cent of the persons entitled to vote in the referendum have voted 'yes' ... he shall lay before Parliament the draft of an Order-in-Council for the repeal of this Act" (Section 85(2) of the Scotland Act 1978).

As Bogdanor, in a commendable article, has put it: "The genesis and constitutional status of this provision are of great interest for a number of reasons. Resulting from an amendment by a backbench MP on the Government side of the House, it has some claim to be the most significant backbench initiative in British politics since the war for it played a crucial part in securing the repeal of the Scotland Act, depriving the Scots of an Assembly for which a majority had voted" (Bogdanor, 1980, p. 249). As the provision was one of the most contentious issues of the campaign and as its implications remain controversial, it deserves elaboration.

The Cunningham amendment was the outcome of a determined backbench opposition to the Scotland Bill in which both Labour rebels and the Conservative Union Flag group (see Jordan, 1979, p. 7 and *passim*) were involved. In one sense the 40 per cent rule was accidental: various other figures were suggested but in the end support coalesced round the 40 per cent (of *electors* rather than voters) threshold. Such a provision is unusual but not unique. Butler and Ranney (1978, p. 17) list Denmark (until 1953, 45 per cent of electors), the Weimar Republic (50 per cent of electors) and Uruguay (35 per cent of electors), while The Gambia (two-thirds of *voters*) and New Zealand (1908-1914, 60 per cent of voters) are two examples of unitary states where a simple majority was not enough. It should be recorded that the Danish precedent was not known to George Cunningham when he proposed his amendment, though subsequently used to defend it. There are, in any case, two reasons for querying the relevance of the present Danish model[3] (Section 88 of the Constitution, for which see Miller, 1968, pp. 284-294). One is that Denmark did not seek to apply the provisions of Section 88 to the Greenland Home Rule referendum of 1979 - an advisory referendum in which the turnout, as it happened, was very similar to the Scottish Referendum turnout six weeks later (Hvidt, 1980, p. 317). The other is that the Danish *Folkeregister* is much more accurate than the British electoral register. The *Folkeregister* is in effect a register of all residents in the locality. There is an obligation to notify changes of address and the register is usually kept up-to-date; registration is also aided by the *personnummer* system which allocates a 10-digit identity number to each person. This greater accuracy is reflected in the almost 10 per cent higher average turnout at Danish elections.[4] Indeed there are other difficulties about citing Denmark, since Sections 20 and 42 of the constitution could arguably be invoked, in which case a 30 per cent vote of all electors *against* the relevant Act would be required to prevent its implementation.

However, all of this was in a sense unimportant for the Cunningham amendment, the rationale for which was not the following of any particular foreign precedent; instead, the amendment took as its starting point the assertion that devolution was what the Scots wanted. In a word, a sceptical Parliament said to the Government: prove it, and prove it conclusively. The implication that abstainers were deemed

---

[3] The writers wish to acknowledge the invaluable assistance of Alastair R. Thomas in this section. He is not, of course, responsible for the views expressed.

[4] It averaged 86 per cent in the last 12 elections. The Scottish turnout at general elections over a comparable period was in the range 76.2 per cent to 76.6 per cent, depending on how it is calculated. Turnout in Danish referendums this century has averaged 63.4 per cent.

to be satisfied with the *status quo* was the justification for making the 40 per
cent hurdle apply to only the Yes side and not the Noes. As will be seen, it was
this aspect which gave rise to some of the most bitter exchanges during the course
of the campaign.

But first the important constitutional point has to be considered as to whether the
40 per cent rule in effect broke new ground by making the Referendum mandatory (if
the 40 per cent hurdle were surmounted), thus fracturing that cornerstone of the
British constitution, Parliamentary sovereignty. In one sense it can be argued that
it did not: that theoretically and legally Parliament could have refused to pass a
Commencement Order no matter what the voting figures turned out to be. Likewise
it was theoretically possible that a No majority in the Referendum could have been
overridden by a Parliamentary vote. Theoretically, then, Parliamentary sovereignty
remained intact. But if this argument looks unrealistic then it follows that the
40 per cent rule made certain results virtually mandatory. What the 40 per cent
rule really did was justify Parliament in its own mind in exercising its discretion
if the result was close - in this case in a debate on a Repeal Order rather than a
Commencement Order. But those niceties were lost on the man in the street to whom
the 40 per cent hurdle appeared more solid than theoretical Parliamentary sovereignty. In essence, then, the 40 per cent rule was a Parliamentary declaration of intent.

The Government's embarrassment at having to live with the threshold provision was
made more acute by the difficulties involved in assessing the meaning as well as
the numbers of "the persons entitled to vote in the referendum". In the end the
Secretary of State went for a "minimalist" strategy, deducting from the register a
figure to take account of deaths (26,400), those under age on polling day (49,802),
convicted prisoners (2,000) and only two categories of double-registered voters
(11,800). This then produced an "adjusted" electorate. The official figure did not,
however, state in advance any estimate for others who were double-registered (who
could not legally vote twice), for the "recent" sick, or for other inaccuracies.
Bogdanor compares Secretary of State Millan's deductions (90,002) with "the maximum
possible number which he could have made if he had taken account of all the main
categories of unavoidable non-voting", on which he puts a figure of a further
587,226. The target for a 40 per cent Yes vote then (allowing for the 52,000 valid
postal votes cast) would have been not 1,498,845 but 1,284,754 (Bogdanor, 1980,
pp. 254-255). That said, it has to be borne in mind that the maximum allowance
could presumably have been cited by the Secretary of State in a Repeal Order debate
in the House of Commons.

The lasting effects of the 40 per cent rule on the British constitution will be
considered in the concluding chapter. But next an account must be given of the role
it played in the Referendum campaign.

The Yes side made a great deal of play of the 40 per cent rule, describing it as a
gerrymandering device, a rigging of the Referendum, an anti-democratic measure, and
so on. An SNP spokesman described this as one of the most successful themes in their
campaigns. Others on the Yes side were afraid of going on too much about the rule
lest it appear a sign of weakness, and expressed confidence in the voters' ability
to leap over the hurdle. In other words there was ambivalence on the Yes side
about whether or not they implicitly accepted the rule. The No side when challenged
tended to reply that if the Scottish people really wanted devolution the 40 per
cent rule was not unreasonable and that indeed 50 per cent would not be unjust,
given the dangers they saw as attendant on the implementation of the Act. The
electoral register likewise provided (see Chapter 6) a long-running story with the
endless production of anomalies of various kinds which pointed up how ill-suited
the British system of permissive electoral registration was for the task it was now
asked to perform.

The No side in turn became increasingly heated about the way the 40 per cent rule was being interpreted by the Yes side. The basis for misunderstanding can best be understood by the following reconstructed and fairly typical doorstep conversation between a Yes canvasser and an elector.

"I'm calling about the Referendum - you know, the Scottish Assembly."

"Oh, aye."

"I wanted to ask if you're going to vote Yes or No."

"I'm not sure, son, I haven't given it much thought."

"Well, you know that if you don't vote they'll say you don't want the Assembly."

It was a short step from such conversations to shorthand statements that an abstention equalled a No vote, a statement which appeared in many publications, on the Yes side and elsewhere. It now appeared to the No side that the Yes side were deliberately embarking on a campaign to persuade No voters not to vote, rather than campaigning to bring out the assumed Yes majority on polling day.

Ironically, therefore, at the end of the day almost equal dislike for the complications of the 40 per cent rule was being expressed by both sides. The implications of this for the future are considered in the concluding chapter.

Conclusion

As a last comment before leaving the subject of the ground rules for referendums, this composite quotation from Butler and Kitzinger goes a long way towards explaining the differences which emerged as between 1975 and 1979:

> Many of the fears about the debate on the Referendum Bill
> were belied by events. In January sources close to Mr Heath
> had indicated that there would be all out opposition to it -
> but gradually the pro-Marketeers came to realise that that
> would be counter-productive. The polls began to indicate
> that they were going to win and win handsomely and the de-
> sire both to arouse anti-referendum feeling and to quibble
> about the detailed rules of the game evaporated ... .

> The committee stage, since it was a major constitutional
> measure, was taken on the floor of the House. It was thought
> ambitious of Mr Short to plan to get it through in three
> days - but in fact with late sittings the committee only
> took two and the report stage and Third Reading only one.
> The chair was fairly ruthless in selecting amendments for
> debate but no major points were omitted, even though a pro-
> cedural muddle meant that the issue of a conditional ma-
> jority was only dealt with at the report stage ... In fact,
> the Conservative tactics were to make clear their opposition
> to the principle of a referendum by voting against the White
> Paper on March 11 and against the Second and Third Readings
> of the Bill, but otherwise to do what they could to speed
> its passage. Only on a central count did a majority of MPs
> go against Mr Short's advice ... . The opposition virtuously
> resisted the temptation to consume by obstruction three or
> four extra days of government time in an overloaded session
> and the Conservative Whips had worked on some of their more
> determined MPs ... .

> The Bill passed rapidly through the House of Lords on April
> 29 and May 5-6. Only two amendments were pressed to a divi-
> sion ... .

....

Political considerations may explain why the Referendum Bill
had in the end such an easy passage, while the one-sided
nature of the battle and the clear outcome may have contributed to the absence of complaint about the way in which its
provisions operated ... .

But the real reason for the unexpectedly easy passage of the
Bill was political: pro-Marketeers were in an overwhelming
majority in the House of Commons and they had belatedly
realised that the referendum would go their way.

Sending the Bill on its way to the Royal Assent on May 7,
Mr Peyton, the Shadow Leader of the House, remarked: "I
must remind the Government of how much they are indebted to
the Opposition for the exceedingly reasonable, restrained
and sensible way in which they received a Bill which was
based on a rather unwelcome dodge and device adopted by the
Prime Minister in a moment of difficulty for himself".
(Butler and Kitzinger, 1976, pp. 64-67, *passim*.)

FINAL COMMENT

Possibly some of the sins of commission and omission which were a feature of the
Referendum campaign resulted from the *ad hoc* nature of the Referendum and the motives of expediency that produced it. Perhaps stock of our referendum experiences
should now be taken so that an informed debate may proceed about what place, if any,
that device should have in our political system (see Baur, 1979). Only when that
has been settled can the discussion move on to the formulation of an agreement on
conventions which would avoid the kinds of friction which detract from the substantive issues which the people are asked to decide. We return to this theme in
the concluding chapter.

In any event, after all the muddle and confusion, the scene was now set. After more
than 10 years of continuous and, at times, intensive debate the Scots and Welsh
were asked to determine themselves how they should in future be governed.

REFERENCES

Allen, C.H. (1979). The study of Scottish politics: a bibliographical sermon. In
    H.M. Drucker and N. Drucker (Eds), *The Scottish Government Yearbook 1980*.
    Paul Harris, Edinburgh.
Barker, P. and N. Spencer (1975). People and power: a *New Society* survey. *New
    Society*, 32, 661 (5.6.1975).
Baur, C. (1979). Time to lay down referendum rules. In H.M. Drucker and N. Drucker
    (Eds), *The Scottish Government Yearbook 1980*. Paul Harris, Edinburgh.
Bogdanor, V. (1979). *Devolution*. OUP, Oxford.
Bogdanor, V. (1980). The 40 per cent rule. *Parliamentary Affairs*, 33 (3), 249-263.
Bradley, A.W. and D.J. Christie (1979). *The Scotland Act*. W. Green & Son, Edinburgh.
Butler, D.E. and U. Kitzinger (1976). *The 1975 Referendum*. Macmillan, London.
Butler, D.E. and A. Ranney (1978). *Referendums*. American Enterprise Institute,
    Washington.
Canada, Government of (1978). *Understanding referenda: six histories*. Canadian
    Unity Information Office, Ottawa.
Drucker, H.M. and G. Brown (1980). *The Politics of Nationalism and Devolution*.
    Longman, London.
Drucker, H.M. and N. Drucker (1978) (Eds) *The Scottish Government Yearbook 1979*.
    Paul Harris, Edinburgh.
Hvidt, K. (1980) (Ed.) *Folketinget: håndbog efter valget den 23 oktober 1978*.

J.H. Schultz Bogtrykkeri, Copenhagen.

Jordan, G. (1979). The Committee stage of the Scotland and Wales Bill. *Waverley Papers*, Scottish Government Studies, Occasional Paper 1. University of Edinburgh.

Kilbrandon (1973). *Royal Commission on the Constitution: Report*. HMSO, Cmnd 5460.

Mattern, J. (1921). *The Employment of the Plebiscite in the Determination of Sovereignty*. The Johns Hopkins Press, Baltimore.

Miller, K.E. (1968). *Government and Politics in Denmark*. Houghton Mifflin & Co., Boston.

Quebec, Government of (1980a). *The ABCs of a referendum in Quebec*. Chief Electoral Officer of Quebec, Communications Service.

Quebec, National Assembly of (1980b).*Referendum in Quebec: the financing of national committees*. Assemblée National du Québec, Bureau of Finance and Parti Politique.

CHAPTER 2

THE PROTAGONISTS

Allan Macartney

Many factors helped to determine the outcome of the Referendum, as a reading of the rest of this book will demonstrate. Moreover the closeness of the result leaves scope for endless debate about the significance or otherwise of various factors. It is indeed one of the fascinations of a referendum that at the beginning of the campaign there is much more uncertainty than at a general election and thus opportunity for effective action by a variety of actors in the body politic. In a general election established political parties and voting habits make the result in many areas predictable. In a referendum there are no real equivalents of "safe seats". In the case of Scotland in 1979 (or more accurately 1978/79), however, the fluidity which did indeed emerge as the formal campaign progressed was not foreseeable in 1978 since opinion polls all forecast a convincing Yes majority.

Accordingly, the campaigning groups merit a central position in a study such as this, and one of the fascinating aspects of this experiment in direct democracy is the influence which can accrue to the self-appointed - the founders and leaders of groups, at all levels, to a large extent unaccountable except, ultimately, to the voters. One message of this chapter, however, is that the understandable concentration on group identities and boundaries, and on official pronouncements by leaders, needs to be modified by a study of some other factors in the whole campaign. Thus this chapter will, *inter alia*, examine not only the content but also the volume of campaign literature; the more colourful aspects of campaigning (again quantified as far as possible); central organisation; finance; the liaison system with branches and with other groups on the same side; the composition of groups and their morale. The interactive themes of the campaign also require a prominent place in an understanding of what was going on.

But first the structure (and to understand that, the origins) of the various groups must be set forth.

As an aid to clarity I have avoided as far as possible the use of the term "campaign" to describe either a campaigning group or one side of the argument, although the term was employed by many campaigners themselves. Instead, I have called each side a camp - thus the Yes camp and the No camp - and the various cohorts I have usually referred to as groups, except where this term has seemed inappropriate. The word "campaign" is thus restricted as far as possible to the dictionary definition, "an organised series of operations in the advocacy of some cause or object" (Chambers, 1979).

From what has just been said those unfamiliar with the details of the Scottish
Referendum campaign will deduce that there was no all-embracing umbrella group on
either side. Readers familiar with what happened must forgive the writer for
stating the obvious. The fact that there was no generally recognised umbrella group
on either side is nevertheless central to an understanding of the way in which the
campaign was waged and the way in which the Referendum rules were drawn up and
applied (for which see Chapter 1). The essential qualification here is "generally
recognised". Umbrellas were proffered. But some of the political actors preferred
to trust to their own raincoats and declined to come in together for warmth or protection under the self-styled umbrella groups. Their reasons will be explained
shortly. But it is immediately obvious that the absence of a recognised umbrella
group on each side makes the Scottish Referendum different from the Euro referendum of 1975.

Whether this difference was unavoidable or a luxury in which the various groups
indulged in 1979 but not in 1975 is an open question. In 1975, after all, there
had been a variety of groups who differed markedly in their rationale for supporting and opposing the Common Market.

Were the 1975 groups more selfless and disinterested, or were they pressurised into
sheltering under an umbrella by other forces and considerations? To be specific,
did Government policy and that of the broadcasting authorities make it so unat-
tractive to be outside the umbrella groups in 1975 that no substantial group stayed
outside (despite for instance the distaste of the SNP and of Plaid Cymru for the
title "National" Referendum Campaign)? And if this interpretation is valid, was
the formation of separate groups in the 1979 Referendum encouraged by the disinclination of the Government or the broadcasting authorities to refuse recognition to
splinter groups, or indeed to recognise the self-styled umbrella groups at all?

The answer is exceedingly complex but some points can be made with confidence.
Firstly, in connection with the 1975 referendum, Butler & Kitzinger (1976, p.97)
record, regarding the anti-marketeers:

> The National Referendum Campaign had to provide an even
> broader umbrella than Britain in Europe. It had to cater for
> organisations from the whole spectrum of politics, with the
> extremes as much in evidence as the centre. Many of those
> who were most active had been campaigning against the Market
> under one label or another for a dozen years and more; some
> were highly professional, but the central direction of NRC
> contained more amateurs than that of BIE.
>
> The main elements in NRC were the Common Market Safeguards
> Campaign and Get Britain Out. There was also the Anti-Common
> Market League (which had been much more important in 1962),
> the British League of Rights, the Yorkshire-based British
> Business for World Markets and, joining later after some
> discussion, the National Council of Anti-Common Market
> Associations (which was linked to Air Vice-Marshal Bennett
> and suspected of being embarrassingly right-wing). Apart
> from these, there were the three committed parties (the
> Scottish National Party, Plaid Cymru and the United Ulster
> Unionists) and the anti-Market groups within the major
> parties (the important Labour Safeguards Committee, the less
> weighty Conservatives against the Treaty of Rome, CATOR, and
> the rather nominal "Liberal 'No' to the Common Market Cam-
> paign"). The Labour ministers who in March 1975 declared
> themselves against the Market formed a somewhat separate
> group, though partly working under the same umbrella.

And, revealingly,

> It was a relief to some anxious planners that no one
> challenged the claims of these bodies to represent the two
> sides.
> (*Ibid*, p.68)

In 1978/79 the position was quite different and involved a circular argument: there were no universally accepted umbrella groups, therefore it was not worth the Government's while trying to recognise something that did not exist, and therefore in turn there was no advantage in sharing an umbrella (until it was too late, after the successful interdict preventing the IBA from putting out party political broadcasts).

A way of summarising the position, without actually explaining anything, is to say that in 1975 the received wisdom accepted the claim of two umbrella groups to recognition whereas in 1979 the received wisdom did not.

THE YES CAMP

Yes for Scotland (YFS)

One group which was disappointed at the fragmentation which occurred on the Yes side was the Yes for Scotland group (YFS). When it was originally formed it had all-party support in the sense of having reasonably prominent members of all parties in its ranks. It had a respected judge and sometime Chairman of the Royal Commission on the Constitution as its Chairman and it could also count on support from other influential quarters. Yet Yes for Scotland conspicuously failed to attract mainstream Labour or Conservative support and increasingly suffered from a necessity to demonstrate that it was more than just an SNP/SLP front organisation.

To account for the failure of Yes for Scotland to present an image as a genuinely all-party group (for it did, as has been noted, contain supporters from all parties active in Scotland) it is necessary to go back to the first cross-party Yes grouping, known at the time of its inception in March 1977 as the Alliance for a Scottish Assembly (*Scotsman*, 22.3.1977). This grouping was founded by Parliamentarians "to fight for a strong Assembly" and was led by Professor John P. Mackintosh, Labour MP for Berwick and East Lothian; Scottish Liberal Party Leader Russell Johnston, MP; former Conservative Shadow Secretary of State for Scotland[1] Alick Buchanan-Smith, MP; and James Milne, Secretary-General of the Scottish Trades Union Congress. At that stage no Scottish National Party or Scottish Labour Party (SLP) MP was publicly involved but the group, and particularly Mackintosh, had friendly relations with prominent members of both these parties. The attempt to extend this Alliance in particular to other leading Labour politicians while at the same time encompassing Nationalists and the SLP was long-drawn-out and ultimately unsuccessful.

Yes for Scotland was launched on January 26, 1978 with the specific aim of campaigning for a Yes vote in the forthcoming Referendum. Although it had an impressive list of sponsors under the nominal chairmanship of Lord Kilbrandon, the senior political members in addition to Mackintosh were Margo MacDonald, Senior Vice-Chairman of the SNP and Jim Sillars, MP, Leader of the SLP. At that stage Buchanan-Smith was named as also supporting the campaign while Johnston was reported as "apparently still considering his position" (*Scotsman*, 27.1.1978). The central

---

[1]Buchanan-Smith had resigned his front-bench position in protest at the Shadow Cabinet's change of line on an Assembly.

figure, the inspiration behind the name of the group and its convener was
Mackintosh, one of Scotland's best-known publicists and a master of the media.

One of the tragedies for Yes for Scotland was the untimely death of John
Mackintosh in the summer of 1978. It was not just that he was the chief architect
of the group but symbolically he was the only Labour MP involved. No other Labour
MP tried to fill the gap. Moreover the Conservative and Liberal MPs mentioned above
both eventually dissociated themselves from the main cross-party organisation on
the Yes side. Instead it was left to non-Parliamentarians, like Professor Nigel
Grant (Labour), Councillor Brian Meek (Conservative) and Councillor Donald Gorrie
(Liberal) to make up caretaker delegations from their respective parties.

The later attachment of Nationalist MP George Reid (a well-known television presenter), while adding to the ranks another MP, did nothing to achieve balance in
the group. For the media there is a hierarchy of quotable personalities (and MPs
have relatively high status) and so the absence of any Conservative, Labour or
Liberal MPs was a serious matter for Yes for Scotland during the actual campaign.
It is worth noting how important these omissions were, given that there did not
emerge the kind of strong grass-roots Home Rule movement composed of non-partisans
and rank-and-file party members which could have made the absence of hyper-canny
MPs insignificant.

Yet this was the dream of some YFS supporters: that the kind of Home Rule feeling
which was so spectacularly tapped and canalised by the Covenant Movement thirty
years earlier could again show itself (see MacCormick, 1955, pp. 131-135 and
passim). A year before the Referendum one visionary told the writer of his dream
of saltires fluttering from tenement windows, of people signing at tables in the
high street to support an Assembly for Scotland. It was not to be. Why? Was the
vision and organisational ability lacking? Were the Scottish people simply not in
a Covenanting mood? Or had so much come to depend upon MPs and party machines?
These questions cannot be definitively answered but at any rate a start can be made
by explaining why the missing MPs were missing.

First, the Labour case. It is not enough to say that there was only one John
Mackintosh, a man to whom back-bench rebellion was almost a way of life. Other
Labour MPs must have seen the potential publicity value for themselves, as well as
the less certain organisational value, of breaking ranks with the official Labour
line and joining Yes for Scotland. The fact that they did not join reflects two
interlinked facts. One was the decision in November 1977 of the Scottish Executive
Committee of the Labour Party to go it alone and fight a separate campaign. The
other was the legacy of dislike of the SNP which was a natural result of the Labour-
Nationalist battle which had been fought electorally in many areas.

The Conservative position was somewhat different. One potential member of YFS put
it simply: "The Yes for Scotland campaign is dominated by Jim Sillars and Margo
MacDonald" (both of whom were seen as left-wingers as well as nationalists). The
implication was clear: that no self-respecting Conservative would want to join
hands with the enemy and that any attempt to do so would simply damage the standing
within his party of the MP concerned - and he would have to live subsequently with
this reputation. There was, however, a further objection to YFS, namely that Lord
Kilbrandon in a speech in Oban (see *Evening News*, 28.10.1978) had indicated a
position too close to a Nationalist one for the taste of a Conservative. This viewpoint was also attributed to Liberal MP Russell Johnston. With hindsight it is
somewhat ironic to realise that the informal, consensual basis of decision-making
in YFS meant that, far from committing MPs of the Conservative, Labour or Liberal
Parties to unacceptable policies or tactics, the presence of additional political
heavyweights in YFS could have changed the conduct of its campaign.

Alliance for an Assembly (AFA)

Late in November 1978 two MPs who had been associated with the original cross-party
pro-devolution group in 1977 announced the formation of a second group to campaign
for a Yes vote. This revived the name Alliance for an Assembly. Buchanan-Smith
(Conservative) and Johnston (Liberal) were again joined by Milne of the STUC (who
is a Communist), but this time also by Donald Dewar, Labour MP for Garscadden, who
had returned to Parliament earlier in 1978. The three MPs each felt the need to
demonstrate broad support for devolution but were unwilling to associate themselves
publicly with the Scottish National Party. AFA might have been a serious potential
rival to YFS, but it never became that, in spite of its feat of recruiting a Labour
MP to a cross-party Yes organisation. As will be seen, AFA did not attempt to set
up any local organisation or even to play the kind of informal co-ordinating role
of which it might have been capable. The cheerfully pragmatic ("I have no hangups
about co-operating with anyone") Jimmy Milne saw it as "providing a platform for
Alick" to appeal to Conservative sympathisers for a Yes vote. It is fair to say
that the Alliance was more important to its founding MPs, as representing a
unionist-devolutionary position, than it was to the voters. When the Alliance was
launched it was of course assumed that there would be a comfortable Yes majority
on Referendum day.

The Labour Movement Yes Campaign (LMY)

If there was one party whose position should never have been in any doubt it was
the ruling Labour Party. The Scotland Act, after all, was not only a piece of
Labour legislation and the outcome of a vast amount of Parliamentary debating time
but the showpiece of the Labour Government of 1974-79. As Harry Ewing, MP put it
in a Labour Party political broadcast in September 1978 "History will record the
fact that it was Labour who gave the Scottish people a better system of government".
The only question, and it was an important one, was how the campaign for a Yes vote
in the Referendum was to be conducted. The decision to go it alone and eschew co-
operation with other parties or groups was taken by the Executive and subsequently
endorsed by the annual conference of the Scottish Council of the Party in March
1978. The Party line was communicated to constituencies in a circular sent out the
day after the launching of Yes for Scotland. The rationale behind this tactical
decision was set out clearly in the circular:

> To: Constituency Labour Parties
>
> Dear Colleague,
>
> Referendum on Devolution
>
> At its week-end Conference in Kilmarnock in November, the
> Scottish Executive of the Labour Party made a number of
> decisions regarding Party strategy on the proposed refer-
> endum on the Scotland Bill. Most of these decisions were
> views to government on the timing of the referendum, the
> timing of the first Assembly elections and so on. Others
> were concerned with Party organisation and included a
> decision to select candidates after the referendum.
>
> The main policy issue decided by the Executive, however,
> was that the Labour Party in Scotland would fight for a
> "Yes" vote on the Scotland Bill only with the Scottish TUC
> and the Co-operative Party and with no other parties or
> groups. In addition, it was decided to fight only one cam-
> paign as a Party - a united campaign for the endorsement of
> the Bill. Any groupings within the Party who seek the

opposite result will therefore be opposing Party policy and
can be given no official support or recognition.

All of these decisions will be put before Annual Scottish
Conference in Dunoon in March 1978 and the final decision
on the points raised will rest with Conference.

In the meantime, it is important for the Party and its constituent organisations to know why the decision on "no
collaboration" was taken.

First, the Labour Party is the only Party in Scotland which
believes in devolution for its own sake. Some others believe
in it because they want to make it a short-cut to separation.
Others believe in it because they see it as developing into
their desired federal constitution. Only Labour believes
that a Scottish Assembly with appreciable and yet not damaging powers, will consolidate and strengthen the United Kingdom. To share the campaign for a devolved Assembly with
those whose declared objectives are so far from our own,
would be to compromise totally our own case for devolution.

Second, the achievement of an Assembly for Scotland will
be ours and it would be wrong to allow our consistent opponents - including those who helped to destroy the last
Bill - to claim credit for this constitutional advance.

Thirdly, the main but yet still misleading arguments of
the 'No' lobby is that devolution will somehow pave the way
to a separate Scottish state. Our position is on the contrary: that it will prevent that happening. To associate
with the separatists would be to provide our opponents
with a major propaganda weapon.

The history of Labour's fight for devolution, both for
Scotland and for people in general, precedes by a century
the rise of the separatists. We have now in Parliament
reached that point at which real and desirable home-rule
is almost with us, yet within the framework of a United
Kingdom. That this was achieved by a Labour government in
power at Westminster is as much a blow for our opponents
who decry anything non Scottish, as it is an achievement
for the Labour Party in Britain as a whole. We as a Party
secured that Commitment and translated it into reality,
and it is crucial that the terms on which it is ensured are
ours and not those whose motives are completely suspect.

Rest assured that a number of 'fronts' will be established
for this campaign, some genuine, but many also designed
only to give authenticity to the S.N.P.'s desire to take
credit for Labour's achievement. The S.N.P. cannot win and
cannot be allowed to win. Their stand is for complete separation. For them, devolution and the Scotland Bill are
but a halfway house. And yet they will seek to demonstrate
that they are a party of devolution, but can only succeed
in that if we allow them.

(Helen Liddell, Scottish Secretary, 27.1.1978)

Mrs Liddell went further. At a press conference she said: "We will not be soiling
our hands by joining any umbrella Yes group. We will be fighting for devolution
only with the Scottish TUC and the Co-operative Party [a Labour subsidiary]"

(*Daily Record*, 14.11.1978). LMY thus used not only official Party campaigning material but also STUC leaflets and posters and, more notably, a striking T&GWU
broadsheet as part of its literature. The joint Labour Movement approach meant
that the unions most committed in terms of resources as well as ideology to the
Assembly were able to cross-subsidise, so that members of other, less committed
unions could take advantage of the material offered. Similarly, devolutionist
individual members of anti-devolution or neutral constituency Labour Parties could
use LMY as an outlet. As will be seen, official party backing ensured that LMY,
unlike YFS and AFA, was not desperately short of funds, even if these did not match
those of the central organisations in the No camp.

In sum, LMY can be seen as an attempt to gain the credit for a Yes victory for the
ruling party and possibly to ensure a greater amount of rank-and-file support than
might have been forthcoming for a cross-party Yes campaign. Certainly the performance of LMY was all-important for mobilising the big battalions - the party with
the largest number of supporters, and the unionised workers.

The SNP Yes campaign

The position of the Scottish National Party on the Referendum was never in much
doubt (despite some resistance by a minority within the Party). Indeed, it is
difficult to see how a party which was committed to democracy and to self-government for Scotland could have failed to support the Yes side of the argument, even
if there was a privately-expressed fear amongst some members that the establishment
of a Scottish Assembly might satisfy the electorate sufficiently to postpone the
achievement of independence indefinitely. On the other hand, to boycott the campaign or to go for a No vote would have portrayed the Party as an extremist, all-
or-nothing party. So the hardliners lost the argument quite conclusively within
the Party. A message from the Party's Chairman, President and Parliamentary Group
Leader dated December 1978 spelled out the reasons for campaigning for a Yes vote:

> The SNP is not just another political party. It embodies the
> will of the Scottish people to determine their own future
> as a free nation. As committed advocates of full self-
> government for Scotland, we share your disappointment at the
> weaknesses of the Scottish Assembly proposed by Westminster.
> We believe, nevertheless, that a resounding "Yes" vote will
> inaugurate a new era in Scottish politics. It will give
> Scotland a political voice again after 272 years of enforced
> silence - Scotland's first truly representative and demo-
> cratic voice. It will give the people of Scotland a forum
> in which to debate the future of their country - a forum in
> which SNP will be able to present its case for a self-
> governing Scotland.

The Party's position is central to an understanding of the conduct of the Referendum campaign. There were two possible courses of action the Party could follow
to mobilise support for the Act. One was to lend its official support to the
umbrella Yes for Scotland group, *tout court* (as was virtually the position of the
SLP). The danger of that course was that it might have given force to the argument
that YFS was little more than an SNP front organisation (just as, on the other side,
SSN was frequently portrayed as a Tory front organisation). The alternative was to
mount its own campaign. The calculation here was - as with LMY - that the Party
could, by producing its own 'SNP Yes' leaflets, stickers, etc, be able to say what
it as a Party had done during the campaign. As Jim Sillars of YFS put it, all the
parties who mounted their own campaigns were "fishing for post-Referendum credits".

In the event the SNP leadership opted for a compromise, consonant with the Party's decentralist ethos, whereby branches - or Constituency Associations - could opt for either strategy as the local situation dictated. A circular from the Campaign Director, Stephen Maxwell, makes this quite clear:

> ### Co-operation with other organisations and parties
>
> Use your own judgement in the light of local conditions about the degree of co-operation with "Yes" campaigners from other organisations or parties. Balance your impulse to make short-term SNP propaganda against the need to maximise the "Yes" vote. (15.12.1978)

In practice the option exercised depended on the views of the local activists, and, as will be seen in Chapter 3, the practice varied considerably and not in any very readily predictable way. It is clear that the SNP activists were the mainspring of many local YFS groups as well as of the SNP Yes campaign. But many Party members felt that the trumpet gave forth a more uncertain sound than might have been expected.

The Conservative Yes Campaign (CYC)

While the majority of Scottish Conservatives accepted the Party line of opposition to the Scotland Act the dissenting minority was not insignificant and contained some prominent members. In addition to Buchanan-Smith, already mentioned, Malcolm Rifkind, MP continued to support devolution and hence advocated a Yes vote despite the perceived defects of the Act. Other Tories were active under the umbrella of Yes for Scotland. One small group of about six pro-Assembly Conservatives on the South side of Glasgow decided, in addition to working for YFS locally, to establish a formal group called the Conservative Yes Campaign. The main figures in the creation of the CYC were a Glasgow University student, Ron Aitken, former Secretary of Cathcart Young Conservatives, and Mrs Helen Millar, a member of the Pollokshields Branch of the Party and Chairman of the Pollok Constituency Yes for Scotland committee.

The group produced posters and leaflets bearing the Conservative symbol and quoting former Leader Ted Heath in support of devolution. One factor which spurred the CYC to step up its campaign was the intervention of Lord Home. The fear was that Conservatives loyal to the Party but pro-devolution would be swayed by Home's plea for a No vote; hence the need for a specifically Conservative Yes campaign. Despite the last-minute, *ad hoc* nature of the CYC it succeeded in distributing literature in over 25 constituencies from Ayrshire to Aberdeen.

The Liberal Party

It might have been surmised that the Scottish Liberal Party, with its long history of support for devolution, would play a leading role in the Yes camp. To be sure, the Party advocacy of a Yes vote was never called in question. But the problem of deciding on tactics was not made easy by the differing attitudes of the three Scottish Liberal MPs, none of whom gave their sponsorship to the main *ad hoc* Yes group, YFS. Elder statesman Jo Grimond was understandably preoccupied with the special problems of his island constituency of Orkney & Shetland (each archipelago was to register a No vote, against his advice) and declined an invitation to join YFS. David Steel, the British Liberal Leader, issued a statement expressing concern at the "real danger that parties and movement calling for a 'Yes' vote [would] go their own way" (*Scotsman*, 27.11.1978). The following day saw the launching of AFA by his colleague Russell Johnston, MP for Inverness and Leader of the Scottish Liberal Party (*Scotsman*, 28.11.1978). On October 14, 1978 and again on

December 2, 1978 the Party's Executive discussed the problem, which was also debated by the National Council on November 5, 1978. One participant observed that

> the Party was in organised indecision on whether to back
> officially the Alliance, the Yes for Scotland or go it
> alone. The indecision was entirely on the tactical question
> of how best to salvage joint effort in the face of intran-
> sigence by the Labour Party. In the end the National Coun-
> cil approved an "enabling" motion encouraging each constitu-
> ency to play a leading part in any or none of the co-oper-
> ative ventures in their own areas according to the particu-
> lar circumstances they found.

The upshot was that Liberal activity varied very much from place to place. In the Borders, for instance, David Steel lent his name to a joint statement (in leaflet form) with the neighbouring Labour MP for Berwick & East Lothian, John Home Robertson appealing for a Yes vote. West Aberdeenshire Liberals produced a Liberal Yes car sticker, soon in demand from other constituencies, while Liberals were active in YFS, notably in Argyll, Edinburgh and Dumfriesshire. In sum, the Liberal effort varied in accordance with the perceptions of MPs and local activists.

The Communist Party

The commitment of the CPGB to a Scottish Parliament is also of long standing, and the Scottish Committee of the Party is proud of its campaigning record. Indeed one activist stated scornfully that the Labour Party was an electoral machine and did not know how to run anything other than an election campaign. The Communist Party distributed both posters and leaflets saying "Scottish Communists say vote Yes" - a further example of "fishing for post-Referendum credits", since there was hardly a substantial Communist vote to deliver. Despite its paucity of resources the Party threw itself with vigour into the Yes campaign, backing both YFS and (where poss-ible, via the unions) LMY, and made a contribution out of proportion to its size.

The Scottish Labour Party (SLP)

Another party which had a disproportionate impact on the Yes campaign was the SLP. This is not altogether surprising since it was the devolution issue which had led to the breakaway from the British Labour Party in the first place (see Drucker, 1978). With even fewer resources than the Communist Party the SLP provided key figures in YFS, ranging from Sillars in the national campaign to activists, mainly in the cities. The Party also produced its own Yes leaflet and distributed it, par-ticularly in its Ayrshire base.

THE NO CAMP

It is true that the No side of the campaign did not present such a bewildering array of groups "advocating a particular result" (as the Referendum Order 1978 coyly put it), and that this should have made the task of co-ordination easier. Nevertheless the No camp was not monolithic, and somewhat similar considerations applied as on the Yes side.

Scotland Says No (SSN)

As on the Yes side there was an *ad hoc* group which harboured ambitions of being the umbrella group on the No side. It went public on St Andrew's Day 1978 under the title of Scotland Says No, with a list of prominent citizens, including Conservative and Labour MPs and a number of leading figures in the business world, on its campaign committee.

Although SSN was first heard of in late November 1978 it was anything but a hastily formed coalition to oppose the implementation of the Scotland Act. It was in effect the public re-launching of the Scotland is British campaign group (SIB) but with three differences. In the first place, the name was changed to have both wider appeal and greater relevance to the task on hand - gaining a large enough No vote to stop devolution. Secondly, it was enlarged by the addition of 14 new members. And finally, the list appeared minus the names of a number of Labour members of SIB who were involved in the Labour Vote No campaign (LVN). Thus, the fact that just over half of the 32 members of the SSN campaign committee were members of SIB understates the continuity: the core of Scotland is British simply moved across to run Scotland Says No. Accordingly to understand the making of SSN it is necessary to look briefly at its predecessor.

Scotland is British was not the first group to be formed to oppose legislative devolution. In May 1976 a body called Keep Britain United (KBU) had been formed by Scottish Tory MP, Iain Sproat, together with Parliamentary colleagues, notably Betty Harvie Anderson and a number of other Scottish Tories. The group, however, failed to broaden its appeal beyond the Conservative Party in Scotland and it became increasingly involved in the Union Flag group which was formed late in 1976 from among English, Welsh and Scottish Conservative backbenchers and remained a merely Parliamentary party grouping (see Jordan, 1979).

Scotland is British was rather different.[2] Although it too was formed in late 1976 to fight the Scotland and Wales Bill, the brains behind it were not MPs but the London journalist Adam Fergusson (now a Conservative member of the European Parliament) and the former Labour MP for Motherwell, George Lawson, together with trade unionist Archie Birt. From the start it aimed to enlist the support not only of Conservative and Labour members of both Houses of Parliament but also of outsiders who were strongly opposed to the plans for legislative devolution to Scotland. Launched on November 23, 1976 it gained experience of campaigning which was to prove invaluable in the Referendum battle, both organisationally for SSN and in terms of liaison with LVN. The death in July 1978 of SIB Director George Lawson, while a sad blow to the group, was lessened in its impact by the part played by his widow, Margaret Lawson, and by the cohesion which SIB had already attained. Fergusson remained in London as linkman during the Parliamentary phase of the campaign and Lawson's place in Scotland was effectively taken by John Risk, President of the Glasgow Chamber of Commerce, assisted by Deirdre Hutton, who acted as Secretary to SIB from the Chamber of Commerce Office.

Given that some of the most active Labour members of SIB campaigned under the Labour Vote No banner, the question has to be answered as to why the Conservative supporters who constituted the core of Scotland Says No did not simply throw in their lot with the Conservative Party's official No campaign which had been announced formally by Francis Pym, MP at the Party's Brighton conference on October 11, 1978. The answer is that they had little confidence that the Party would mount a campaign which was sufficiently vigorous and at the same time unequivocal in its opposition to devolution to suit the veterans of Scotland is

---

[2]Iain Sproat decided to keep out of SIB since he was so prominently identified with the Conservative Party. Nevertheless he kept in close touch with SIB, and Adam Fergusson was involved in both KBU and SIB. SIB and the Union Flag group collaborated in holding a meeting at the Conservative Party conference in Blackpool in 1977.

British. So it came about that it was the Conservative Party (see below) which
supported SSN rather than *vice versa*.

The Conservative No campaign

The Conservative Party's circumspection in its opposition to the Scotland Act
derived from its desire to reconcile three objectives. In the first place it was
highly desirable to embarrass the Labour Government and the SNP through defeating
this Act, with the hope that this might lead in turn to the fall of the Government,
in circumstances providing an ideal setting for a Tory electoral comeback. But
secondly, while the scent of electoral victory was intoxicating, there were risks,
namely that a Yes victory might damage the prestige of a party which had nailed its
colours to the anti-devolution mast. Hence the instinct for caution among some Conservatives who did not desire the major loss of face a Yes landslide would have
represented. The third point was that the Party had been in favour of an elected
Assembly at the October 1974 General Election (and indeed for some time after
Mrs Thatcher had become leader continued to support the idea [Miller, 1980, p.109]),
and had suffered a traumatic split in the House of Commons vote on the Second
Reading of the Scotland and Wales Bill. In that division a majority of Scottish MPs
had rebelled against the new hard line adopted by the Shadow Cabinet and six had
offered their resignation as Opposition spokesmen (Jordan, 1979, pp.7-9, 31-32).
These rebels could claim that they represented Party orthodoxy as contained in the
manifesto on which they were elected. The problem was how to campaign for a No vote
without doing further damage to Party unity - something highly prized in the Conservative Party.

The solution adopted was to make a fine distinction between saying No to the Scotland Act and opposing the principle of devolution, which had come to acquire the
status of a sacred Highland cow. A letter from the President of the Scottish Conservative and Unionist Association to constituency chairmen spelled the strategy
out quite explicitly:

> Dear Chairman,
>
> Scottish Referendum, Thursday 1st March, 1979
>
> At the Annual Conference in Perth in May of this year it
> was, by an overwhelming majority, agreed that the Party
> would campaign vigorously for a "No" vote in the Referendum
> on the Labour Government's Scotland Act.
>
> At the meeting of the Central Council in Motherwell on 4th
> November, 1978 it was agreed that:-
>
> a) the Party would campaign for a "No" vote on the under-
> standing that some members may wish to vote "Yes".
>
> b) the Party will co-operate with a "No" umbrella organis-
> ation.
>
> c) Constituency Associations will be encouraged to establish
> "Vote No" committees.
>
> Let me make it quite clear that in campaigning for "No", the
> Party will not be campaigning against Devolution for Scot-
> land but only against the type of devolution contained in
> the Act. In the event of the "no" campaign being success-
> ful, the Party is committed to the establishment of an all-
> Party Conference to discuss better forms of Devolution. A
> booklet containing our preliminary draft of submissions to
> such a Conference has been published, along with a Refer-
> endum Campaign guide. I would ask you to study these book-

lets carefully.

Teddy Taylor, Shadow Secretary of State, announced last
week at a press conference the reason for the Party's wish
to co-operate in the Umbrella organisation and a copy of
his statement has already been sent to you.

The Umbrella organisation has now been established. It is
the "Scotland Says No Campaign", with offices at 90 West
Campbell St., Glasgow G2 6RU (tel. 041 226 4705). This
body embraces a wide cross-section of Scottish life and is
as representative of the Scottish electorate as such a body
can be. All types of campaign material will be provided by
it, free of charge, to our constituency organisations. At
present posters and car stickers are available and large
quantities of two pamphlets will be ready for distribution
in the second week in January. In addition the Party will
be producing other literature, including door-step aids.

Bearing in mind that the "no" campaign can be supported by
all who are opposed to the present Government's proposals,
no matter what their views may be on the principle of
Devolution itself, will you please use your best endeavours
to establish a "Vote No" Campaign committee within your
Constituency Association as quickly as possible, and let me
have the name and address of its Chairman. In due course the
"Scotland Says No Campaign" will form Regional Committees
with which our Constituency Campaign Committees may co-
operate. I shall send you the name and address of the leader
of your Regional Committee whenever it is formed.

Lastly, let me remind you that it is fully appreciated that
there are loyal members of the Party who hold sincere views
opposed to the "No" Campaign. They must feel free to pursue
these views during the Referendum, and we must never forget
our prime objective is to win the forthcoming General Election which may follow very quickly after March 1st.

> Yours sincerely,
> (Russell Sanderson,
> President, 11.12.1978)

In summary, the Conservative Party distributed its own leaflets and ran its own
campaign (while not denying normal facilities to MPs on the Yes side) but encouraged its activists to support the activities of SSN at the grassroots (which, as
Chapter 3 shows, they did) and gave everything but financial assistance to Scotland
Says No. This posture was virtually a mirror image of the SNP's position on the Yes
side.

The Labour Vote No campaign (LVN)

The other important group in the No camp was the Labour Vote No campaign. It originated in a meeting, held once the Referendum was clearly going to happen, of a
small group of Labour Party members centred on Tam Dalyell, uncrowned "leader of
the opposition" to the Scotland Bill (and its predecessor) in the House of Commons
(see Dalyell, 1977). The key question the group had to decide was whether or not
to become involved in an umbrella organisation. Although some of those in LVN were
SIB members, the chances are that it would have mounted a separate campaign anyway,
but any doubts about the wisdom of keeping their distance from other No groups were
dispelled by the imminence of the General Election. In those circumstances they did

not wish to be seen as "ganging up with the Tories", since, as Dalyell put it, "that would have been the death of us politically". A further consideration of equal weight was his conviction that such an alliance (in a cross-party organis- ation) would in any case have failed to maximise the No vote.

This strategy becomes clear when one considers that the target was not the public at large so much as the habitual Labour supporter - Party activist and traditional voter alike. As has been seen, Labour Movement Yes had the weight of official party approval, not to mention finance, behind it. It aimed to deliver the Labour vote for a Yes; Labour Vote No aimed to prevent it. "What we had to do" - to quote Dalyell - "was to make it clear that there was an authentic section of the Labour Party which believed that devolution would lead to separation. Our job was to get as much Labour support as possible." Hence the "audacious and successful bid to associate the Labour name with an anti-Labour policy" (Miller, 1980, p.113).

The indefatigable Dalyell, with his small group of supporters in LVN, proved as assiduous in this task as he and his fellow anti-devolutionaries in the Commons had been in opposing the Scotland and Wales Bill and the Scotland Bill.

The Student Campaign against the Devolution Act (SCADA)

There sprang up during the campaign a number of small, specialised *ad hoc* bodies on either side, most of which vanished from public view after the inaugural press conference. SCADA, however, merits special mention because of the literature it generated and in particular because its lapel stickers were distributed by SSN and Conservative Central Office to young people beyond the obvious target "constituency" of university and college students. Its campaign material was produced with the help of Scotland Says No.

The group was formed by two Conservative student activists, Brian Monteith (Chair- man of the Scottish Conservative Students) and Peter Young (Chairman of the Feder- ation of Conservative Students), who approached Teddy Taylor, MP and Tam Dalyell, MP for support and advice. Leaflets, giving Monteith's home in Edinburgh as a con- tact address, listed Labour and Conservative MPs as patrons - Dalyell as Hon. President and as Vice-Presidents Taylor, Sproat and Robin Cook. SCADA claimed to be an "all party No party campaign" and stated: "Whether for, or against, Devol- ution we believe the 'Scotland Act' is bad for the future of Scotland."

RELATIONS AMONG GROUPS

While there were prominent examples of gentlemanly behaviour across the Yes/No boundary (mainly in holding public debates, most notably the Sillars-Dalyell "travelling circus", which pulled in sizeable audiences up and down the land), it is the question of relations among the groups on the same side which principally concerns us here. It is not possible to state with precision the degree of co-oper- ation or rivalry which characterised inter-group relations on each side. There are a number of indicators of co-operation between groups. One is the formal over- lapping membership of campaigning groups, another the degree of formality involved in such interlocking arrangements (i.e. whether individuals were there in a purely personal or representative capacity). A further consideration is the status and influence the individual possesses within the "other" body. The details of com- mittee membership listed below give an indication of the extent of integration (national *versus* local; for the latter see Chapter 3), and finally the extent of purely informal contacts. The picture is therefore complex and the analysis which follows is based on an appraisal of all these factors.

The Yes camp

YFS/SNP co-operation was fairly good, extending to exchanges of press releases,
the use of the same speakers under different banners, and the interlocking of key
personnel such as Reid, MacCormick and Mrs MacDonald. YFS got on well too with the
Scottish Liberal Party, or at least with certain prominent figures in Liberal
headquarters (Donald Gorrie being the official liaison man). The leading position
of Sillars also ensured the virtual integration of the Scottish Labour Party with
YFS. The Communist effort was largely in support of YFS and, as and where appropriate, LMY. Some assistance was given also by YFS locally to the guerrillas of
the CYC. The official position of LMY was modified to the extent that details of
speaking engagements and plans for meetings were exchanged (with YFS if not directly with the SNP) so as to avoid having meetings in the same place at or about
the same time; but such contacts were quite unofficial.

Rivalries must also be recorded. The most prominent example was the attack on the
SNP, and separatism generally made by some LMY speakers, extending even to an alle-
gation that the Nationalists were merely going through the motions of campaigning
by day while nightly praying for a No victory (Dickson Mabon, MP, LMY Press Release,
23.2.1979). The accusation was returned with interest, albeit privately, by the
Nationalists.

The No camp

Although there was a certain amount of cageyness displayed in relations between
LVN and other No campaigners (Dalyell for instance tried to avoid sharing a platform with Conservatives), it is true to say that the No camp operated in much
closer harmony (if not in unison) than was the case with the Yes side. Certain key
individuals (MPs Taylor and Cook in particular) spoke under the banner of Scotland
Says No as well as in their own party campaigns (Conservative and LVN, respectively), and there was a certain overlapping of membership with all three No groups.
But arguably the most important factor of all was the close understanding which
had developed during the campaign against the two devolution Bills. Thus, Parliamentarians like Dalyell and Miss Harvie Anderson from opposite sides of the House
were in political agreement on devolution; even more significant was the previous
experience of working formally together in Scotland is British. As is shown below
virtually every member of the SIB campaign committee was to be found in either
Scotland Says No or Labour Vote No.

Nevertheless, as will be seen from the analysis below of press statements and
literature, the lines of argument diverged - from the Conservative assertion that
a No vote would not mean the end of devolution to the SSN car sticker attributed
to Andrew Herron which proclaimed: "Assembly be damned. Keep Britain united". This
divergence of views is not unlike the difference of opinion on the Yes side about
whether devolution was a step towards independence or the best way of preventing
it. The organisation of each camp gave as much scope as the parties concerned desired for expressing different reasons for advocating the same result.

ORGANISATION AND FINANCE

When it comes to internal group organisation, a basic difference is readily apparent between the official party campaigns and the *ad hoc* groups. The parties, of
course, as Bochel and Denver point out in Chapter 3, are geared for campaigning.
They have headquarters and staff, press officers, a regular system of liaison with
local activists, and at least some funds on which they can draw. *Ad hoc* groups
possess none of these advantages. The main questions to be asked of the parties

concern the degree of commitment which they displayed in pursuing their chosen
Referendum line. Bochel and Denver analyse this at local level in Chapter 3 but
assessment of the national commitment is difficult. The tables below showing the
number of leaflets, etc. produced and the amount of money spent centrally are some
guide.

Leadership

When the two main cross-party groups went public each was at pains to display the
breadth of support they enjoyed. The result was very large national committees.
Their committees and that of LVN are listed below; party affiliation is given only
when this was widely known, but those who are well-informed will doubtless be able
to identify or guess many more. The descriptions are as given officially.

TABLE 2.1   The Yes for Scotland (YFS) Committee

The Right Hon. Lord Kilbrandon - Chairman   *Jim Sillars*, MP (SLP) - Vice-Chairman
Margo MacDonald (SNP) - Vice-Chairman   *George Reid*, MP (SNP) - Vice-Chairman
Iain R. Hoy (Con.), Businessman -   *Paul Martin* (Con.), Student -
               Secretary   Asst Secretary

Prof. Sir John Brotherston,   *Prof. Donald I. MacKay*,
   Community Medicine, Edinburgh Univ.   Economics, Heriot-Watt University
Catherine M. Carmichael,   *The Very Rev. Dr James G. Matheson*,
   Sociology, Glasgow University   former Moderator Church of Scotland
Seán Connery, actor   *Councillor Brian Meek* (Con.),
Andrew Cruickshank, actor   journalist
Ronald MacDonald Douglas (nationalist)   *Arthur Montford*, broadcaster
Alastair M. Dunnett, retired journalist   *Iain Noble*, banker,
Councillor Donald Gorrie (Lib.)   Gaelic College Organiser
Prof. Nigel Grant (Lab.)   *Timothy Noble*, businessman, Glasgow
   Education, Glasgow University   *The Very Rev. Father Anthony Ross*,
Angus Grossart, banker   former Hon. RC Chaplain to Edinburgh
J.D.M. Hardie (Con.), businessman   University
Captain John Hay of Hayfield   *Graham Salmon*, lawyer
   (SNP), landowner   *The Rev. Dr Duncan Shaw*, Church of
Ludovic Kennedy (ex-Lib.),   Scotland (Moderator of Edinburgh
   writer and journalist   Presbytery), Edinburgh University
Anthony J.C. Kerr (SNP), translator   *Prof. R.S. Silver* (SNP), Glasgow Univ.
Alex H. Kitson (Lab.),   *The Very Rev. Dr R. Leonard Small*,
   Trade Union official   former Moderator Church of Scotland
Norman MacCaig, writer   *The Very Rev. Dr David Steel*,
Prof. Neil MacCormick (SNP),   former Moderator Church of Scotland
   Law, Edinburgh University   *Sir Simpson Stevenson* (Lab.), Greater
Roderick MacFarquhar, Highland Fund   Glasgow Health Board and Doctor
Farquhar MacIntosh,   *Nigel Tranter*, author
   Rector, Royal High School   *Wendy Wood* (nationalist)

TABLE 2.2   The Scotland Says No (SSN) Committee

*Lord Wilson of Langside,
    former Labour Lord Advocate
    Joint Chairman

Betty Harvie Anderson, MP (Con.)
Alex Fletcher, MP (Con.)
Peter Doig, MP (Lab.)
Dick Buchanan, MP (Lab.)
William Hannan, former MP (Lab.)
Bernard Scott (Lab.), Strathclyde
    Regional Councillor and Convener
    Finance & Industry Committee
Alex Cameron MA (Lab.),
    former Glasgow District Councillor
    and Convener Finance Committee
*Sir George Sharp (Lab.), former
    Convener Fife County Council and
    Chairman Glenrothes New Town Dev.
    Corp.
*David Edward QC, advocate
*D.B. Weir QC, advocate
James Sutherland, solicitor
George Morton, solicitor
*Douglas F. Hardie,
    former Chairman CBI (Scotland)
*C.J. Risk BL, former President
    Glasgow Chamber of Commerce
*Viscount Weir, Industry and Commerce
*Lord Polwarth TD DL, Industry and
    Commerce

*The Very Rev. Dr Andrew Herron,
    former Moderator Church of Scotland
    Joint Chairman

*Sir John Toothill CBE, Industry and
    Commerce
*Harold A. Whitson CBE, Industry and
    Commerce
David Landale, Industry and Commerce
†*Donald McGregor,
    Secretary for Scotland of UCATT
*Sir Charles Wilson,
    former Principal Glasgow University
Prof. Tom Wilson, Adam Smith Chair of
    Political Economy, Glasgow University
Prof. Sir William Ferguson Anderson,
    Geriatric Medicine, Glasgow University
Margaret Lawson, member Hamilton Health
    Council, member Hamilton Constituency
    Labour Party
*Adam Fergusson (Con.), journalist
Ronnie McNeil
*Oliver Thomson, publicist
Maurice Shinwell
*Deirdre Hutton, Asst Campaign Manager
    and Research Assistant
    (seconded from Glasgow Chamber of
    Commerce)
James Main, farmer

Hew Carruthers (Con.), Campaign Manager
Ian Grant Cumming, Press Officer

* Member of Scotland is British Campaign Committee
† Member of Labour Vote No Campaign Committee

TABLE 2.3   The Labour Vote No (LVN) Committee

*Brian Wilson, Glasgow - Chairman
Robin Cook, MP   - Vice-Chairman
*Dan Crawford, Glasgow - Vice-Chairman

Cllr Charlie Snedden, Bo'ness
Willie Boyle, Gourock
†*Donald McGregor, Glasgow
Barbara Mathie, Kilsyth
Jane Jackson, Alexandria
*David Graham, Falkirk
Duncan Milligan, Edinburgh

Tam Dalyell, MP   - Vice-Chairman
*Archie Birt, Gourock   - Secretary
Len McGuire, Cumbernauld - Treasurer

Bob Irvine, Edinburgh
Lord Taylor of Gryfe, Kilbarchan
Alan Dick, East Kilbride
Adam Ingram, East Kilbride
W.F. McKenzie, Dundee
Cllr Eric Milligan, Edinburgh
Jack McLean, Glasgow

* Member of Scotland is British Campaign Committee
† Member of Scotland Says No Campaign Committee

Two political parties also (Labour and Liberal) each set up an official committee to oversee the Referendum campaign and their composition is given below. In each case the committee concerned was a sub-committee of the Executive Committee and drawn from it; the positions on the Executive Committee held by the members are indicated in brackets.

TABLE 2.4   The Labour Party (Scottish Executive)
Devolution Working Party (LMY)

Gordon Brown	Chairman of the Sub-Committee
Janey Buchan	(Chairman)
Sam Gooding	(Vice-Chairman), T&GWU
Norman Buchan, MP	(Treasurer)
Charlotte Haddo	(Constituency Section)
George Galloway	(Constituency Section)
Gerald O'Brien	(Constituency Section)
Dickson Mabon, MP	(Co-operative Party)
James Milne	STUC
[John Henry	STUC alternate]

TABLE 2.5   The Scottish Liberal Party Devolution Sub-committee

Terry Grieve	(Chairman)
Charles Brodie	(Vice-Chairman)
Malcolm Bruce	(Vice-Chairman)
Ray Michie	(Vice-Chairman)
Fred McDermid	
David Miller	(Chief Agent)
R.L. Smith	
Jim Wallace	
*Donald Gorrie	
Russell Johnston	(Leader)

* Member of YFS Committee

It is clear that most of these committees were too large to be able to organise a campaign. In practice they met infrequently in full session and then principally to approve publications already prepared in draft. What happened instead is that in each case an informal inner executive met frequently to deal with the day-to-day business of the campaign. Membership fluctuated because of the extensive travelling undertaken by some members but the following can be listed as the core members. In most cases they were also the key decision makers, but obviously the political heavyweights of each group were capable of exercising considerable influence even when they were not present as frequently as, for instance, some of the young members of YFS. But the impression gained is of informal, cohesive working parties.

TABLE 2.6   Core members of *ad hoc* groups

TABLE 2.6A   YFS

Jim Sillars, MP (SLP)	– Vice-Chairman	Chloe Munro
Margo MacDonald (SNP)	– Vice-Chairman	Neil MacCormick (SNP)
Ian Hoy (Con.)	– Secretary	Nigel Grant (Lab.)
George Reid, MP (SNP)	– Vice-Chairman	Donald Hardie (Con.)
Paul Martin (Con.)		Alex Kitson (Lab.)
Chris Cunningham (SNP)		Farquhar MacIntosh
Lindsay Paterson (SLP)		Duncan Shaw
Chris Maclean (SNP)		

TABLE 2.6B   SSN

*Adam Fergusson (Con.)	
*John Risk	
*Andrew Herron	Joint Chairman
*Lord Wilson (then Lab.)	Joint Chairman
Hew Carruthers (Con.)	Campaign Organiser (full-time)
*Lord Weir	Vice-Chairman & Finance Convener
*Douglas Hardie	
Margaret Lawson (Lab.)	
*Deirdre Hutton	Asst Campaign Organiser (seconded)

* Member of SIB Campaign Committee

TABLE 2.6C   LVN

*Brian Wilson	-	Chairman
Tam Dalyell MP	-	Vice-Chairman
Robin Cook MP	-	Vice-Chairman
*Dan Crawford	-	Vice-Chairman
*Archie Birt	-	Secretary

* Member of SIB Campaign Committee

TABLE 2.6D   CYC

Ron Aitken
Helen Millar

It is worth noting that the day-to-day running of the official party Referendum campaigns was in practice similarly devolved upon a small number of people but, at least in theory, with the constitutional restraint of the party in question. But there was some feeling in each case that much of the work was being left to relatively junior party workers. For the record the key figures in the day-to-day campaigns (with party positions indicated in brackets) were:

TABLE 2.7   Core members of the official Party campaigns

TABLE 2.7A   SNP Yes

Stephen Maxwell	Campaign Director
	(Exec. Vice-Chairman [Publicity])
Duncan MacLaren	(Press Officer)
Steve Butler	(Industrial Officer)
*George Reid, MP	
Alan McKinney	(National Organiser)
*Margo MacDonald	(Senior Vice-Chairman)
*Neil MacCormick	(Executive Member)
*Bob Crawford	(Research Officer)

* Member of YFS Committee

TABLE 2.7B   LMY

Gordon Brown	Campaign Director
Bruce Millan, MP	
Helen Liddell	(Scottish Secretary)
John Smith, MP	
Jimmy Allison	(Scottish Organiser)
Alf Young	(Research Officer)
Harry Ewing, MP	

TABLE 2.7C   Scottish Liberal Party

Terry Grieve	(Chairman)
David Miller	(Chief Agent)
*Donald Gorrie	Councillor Lothian Region

* Member of YFS Committee

In the <u>Conservative</u> case Teddy Taylor MP, Shadow Secretary of State for Scotland, played the leading strategic role in the campaign, while the day-to-day adminis-tration of the Conservative No campaign was undertaken by one of the two Deputy Directors.

Internal communication

For parties running an official campaign, with or without the addition of a Refer-endum committee, the network already existed for contacting activists at the grass-roots and distributing campaign material. Accordingly the Referendum campaign was handled in a fashion similar to a general election, albeit with rather less urgency. For the *ad hoc* campaigning groups, however, and in particular for the major cross-party group on each side, the task of establishing a working nationwide organis-ation was far from easy. The officially co-operative attitude of the political parties involved did not solve the problem and in some cases indeed complicated it.

A comparison of the two major *ad hoc* groups reveals some fairly striking contrasts even though both faced similar problems. The claim by Yes campaigners that "they've got the money but we've got the people", although an exaggeration, contains more than a grain of truth. But it is far from clear in political campaigning that either asset is sufficient to guarantee success: organisational ability is also a vital ingredient, as are experience and enthusiasm. There is something of a paradox in that SSN appeared to some commentators (e.g. Kauppi, 1979, p.17) to have got off to an earlier start than YFS, although, as has been seen, YFS was officially launched many months earlier than SSN. One explanation is that SSN used its pre-vious experience in SIB and its business contacts to set up, within the short space of a month, about the same number of local contacts as YFS were able to list - just over 50 in each case.

An apparently minor difference between the two groups concerned their telephonic communication. To be specific, SSN had at least a fortnight's start as far as telephone queries went, since dialling Directory Enquiries for the respective phone numbers drew a blank for YFS in Edinburgh for fully two weeks during which time the SSN number in Glasgow was available to callers. This may seem a small point, but a fortnight in January 1979 was a long time out of the two months between New Year and polling day and indicates the greater degree of organisation of SSN. This argu-ably represented a significant handicap for YFS since there was a steady flow of requests from individuals for literature, stickers and information. The telephone was in fact the essential means of communication between Headquarters and the grassroots for both organisations, YFS and SSN. Both sides practised devolution to their local groups - YFS rather more than SSN.

A visit to the two headquarters in turn pointed up some very visible differences. Symbolically, SSN was staffed by experienced campaigners (including Campaign Direc-tor Carruthers, a former Conservative agent, and Mrs Hutton, seconded from Glasgow Chamber of Commerce), while YFS HQ was manned mainly by enthusiastic but less ex-perienced young people (average age under 30). SSN was housed in premises at 90 West Campbell Street in central Glasgow, leased out at a nominal rent by Coats Patons (the firm of John Risk). The much smaller YFS rooms bore the names of trade unions (Amalgamated Society of Painters and Decorators; NUFTO; ASW No.1) and were situated at 166 High Street in the historic Royal Mile of Edinburgh, between Covenant Close and Old Assembly Close and a stone's throw from the old Parliament House.

Finance

Professionalism amongst the *ad hoc* groups was linked with finance. The subject is a tricky one, not just because no accounts were subsequently published, nor because the question became a campaign issue, but because of the difficulty of arriving at a national total in cash and cash-equivalent terms. All that can be done is to reproduce the figures produced by the office bearers interviewed, giving the respective *central* budgets, i.e. leaving out of the reckoning amounts raised and spent locally. Inevitably, too, the sort of detail given on both income and expenditure varies from one group to another.

TABLE 2.8   Central expenditure

	Yes		No
YFS	£15-20,000	SSN	£100,000
SNP	£1,500 - £2,000*	Con.	£ 8,000
LMY	£36,200 (STUC £1,200)	LVN	£ 4,600
Lib.	£2,400	SCADA	?
CYC	?		
CPGB	Over £3,000		
SLP	? *		
AFA	minimal		
TOTAL	over £63,000		over £112,000

Notes: * Most expenditure was incurred by constituencies and
           branches, which produced or purchased leaflets, etc.
        ? indicates figures unavailable

TABLE 2.9   Sources of income

	Yes		No
Lib.) CPGB) SLP	Party funds	Con.	Party funds
LMY	Central Party funds; donation from STUC (£1200) and T&GWU broadsheet	SCADA	Donations (some from SSN)
		LVN	Donations (some from unions)
YFS	Donations, "none more than £1,000"; sale of membership cards (10p. each)	SSN	Donations, "none more than £5,000".
SNP	Donation of £1,000 from SNP Association in US and Canada; balance party funds.		
CYC	Donations		
AFA	Not applicable		

THE REFERENDUM EXPERIENCE

OPINION POLLS 1975–79

Fig 1   Preferred Constitutional Options.

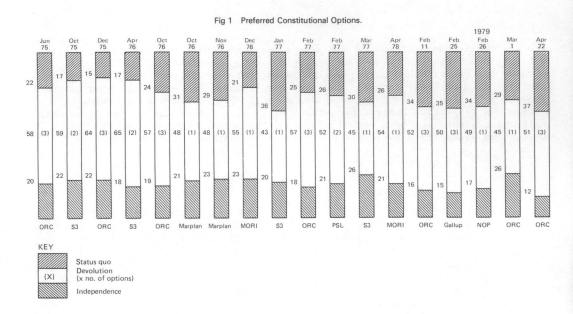

KEY

Status quo

(X) Devolution
(x no. of options)

Independence

Fig 2   Attitude Towards Government's Devolution Proposals.

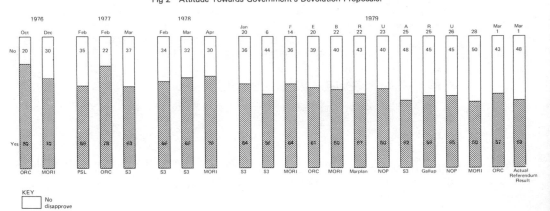

KEY

No
disapprove

Yes
approve

Source: *The Scottish Government Yearbook courtesy of Paul Harris Publishing*

TABLE 2.10 Campaign material printed (official estimates)

Organisation		Leaflets	Posters Small (window) size	Posters Large (hoarding) size	Stickers Car	Stickers Lapel
YFS	(a)	1,000,000	10,000	–	3,000+	141,000
	(b)	400,000				
AFA		–	–	–	–	–
CYC	(c)	30,000	6,000	–	–	–
LMY	(d)	450,000	?	1,000	5,000	?
	(e)	500,000	5,000 STUC	–	–	–
	(f)	750,000				
SNP	(g)	525,000	13,000	–	10,000	200,000
	(h)	175,000				
Liberals	(j)	220,000	–	–	–	–
	(k)	?				
CPGB	(l)	80,000	–	2,000	–	–
	(m)	20,000				
SLP	(n)	110,000	–	–	–	–
YES total		4,260,000+	34,000	3,000	18,000+	341,000
SSN	(p)	750,000	16,000*	800	23,000*	70,000*
	(q)	500,000				
	(r)	100,000				
	(s)	350,000				
LVN	(t)	50,000	2,000	13	–	30,000*
	(u)	5,000				
	(v)	5,000				
	(w)	2,000				
SCADA	(x)	10,000	?	–	–	16,000*
Conservatives	(y)	1,000,000	–	–	–	–
NO total		2,772,000+	18,000	813	23,000	116,000
GRAND TOTAL		7,032,000+	52,000	3,813	41,000+	457,000

Notes: ? indicates figures unavailable
        – indicates nil
        + indicates a minimum figure
        * several designs

NB Some figures appear to be overestimates; some organisations allowed local re-
    printing and estimates of these were not always available. The SNP estimated
that in addition to the above figures some 15-20 constituency newspapers (something less than 300,000 copies) appeared during the campaign.

Key to leaflets:

YFS	(a)	Vote Positively Yes
	(b)	Yes - get the facts
CYC	(c)	Vote YES for freedom!
LMY	(d)	We've fought hard
	(e)	An Assembly for Scotland (STUC)
	(f)	Yes! And so say all of us (T&GWU broadsheet)
SNP	(g)	We say YES. A voice for Scotland
	(h)	In the national interest
Lib.	(j)	Scotland needs you!
	(k)	Let Scotland Prosper (Young Liberals)
CPGB	(l)	Scottish Communists say vote Yes (single sheet)
	(m)	Scottish Communists say vote Yes (folder)
SLP	(n)	The Scottish Labour Party says YES
SSN	(p)	Know your mythology
	(q)	Have you found out ...
	(r)	Think it out for yourself
	(s)	Vote NO Today
LVN	(t)	Time to count the cost
	(u)	Devolution equals Separation
	(v)	Labour Vote NO Campaign
	(w)	Dear Tony [Benn]
SCADA	(x)	Vote NO
Con.	(y)	The right vote for Scotland

TABLE 2.11   Advertising (centrally organised)

TABLE 2.11A   Poster sites/week

		4 sheet sites	16 sheet sites
LMY		(900-1,000 sites) (a)	
SSN	(b)	2,032	1,492
LVN	(c)	26	–

TABLE 2.11B   Newspaper advertising: number of insertions

YFS	1	(d)
LMY	7	(e)
SNP	1	(f)
SSN	177	(g)
LVN	?	(h)

Notes:
(a) Poster campaign cost approx. £20,000.
(b) Dec. 1978: 122; Jan. 1979: 335; Feb. 1979: 424 sites.
(c) 13 sites each for two weeks, all in the greater Glasgow area;
     last fortnight in February 1979.
(d) In the *Daily Record*. Paid for by earmarked anonymous donation. Cost £1,000.
(e) Cost approx. £9,000.
(f) In the *Scottish Daily Express*. Paid for by earmarked donation from SNP Association of North America. Cost £1,000.
(g) National and local newspapers. Size varied from 4 cm x 2 columns to
     25 cm x 4 columns.
     NB A total of 230 was recorded (see Chapter 5) in the local press. The
         balance was presumably paid for by local groups.
(h) "One or two in the *Record* and the *Express*."

CAMPAIGNING STYLE

Elsewhere in this volume (Chapter 5 on the local press) an estimate is made of the number of public meetings held, while Chapter 3 gives figures (from the more active constituencies) of the amount of canvassing and polling day activity that went on. As these activities were essentially devolved they do not fit into this chapter except to assert that the total impact of such activities must be significant and may have been crucial in affecting turnout. Here the concern is less with the *impact* of campaigning and more with the *output* from the central organisations. In Table 2.10 are given - with an important reservation concerning press statements - the maximum estimated figures of nationally produced material; there is no doubt that not all of the material was delivered to its target. This seems to have been most true of the parties which were split in their attitude to the Scotland Act. Not included in the data are some local leaflets (mainly on the Yes side) for which no reliable figures are available. With posters and stickers of various kinds, it is likewise safe to assume that substantial numbers were never used.

A further aspect of nationally organised publicity was advertising, both in the press and on hoardings. This was one area where extreme variations occurred as between the various groups. Advertising was a vital part of the SSN campaign, very important for LMY, played a small role for LVN, and played virtually no part at all in the other central campaigns. Again the caveat must be entered that this does not take account of local initiatives such as press advertising or flyposting. Table 2.11 gives details of central expenditure on press advertising and poster sites.

Clearly the press campaigns waged by the two camps (or more accurately the groups within them) were very important, and Chapter 6 deals with press treatment of the Referendum campaign. It is not intended to duplicate this here; instead an attempt is made to analyse the output of the various groups in the form of press releases. There are difficulties with this approach (some are mentioned below), but it does provide some quantitative data on the issues which the groups thought important enough to type up as press handouts. What follows is an analysis of the press release files of the respective groups.

TABLE 2.12   Volume of press statements, Jan.-Feb. 1979

	Press releases				Press releases and press conference appearances			
Group	Total	Rank order	February only	Rank order	Total	Rank order	February	Rank order
YFS	24	5	22	5	67	2	65	2
AFA	2?	8	2?	8	4?	8	4?	8
SNP	86	1	65	1	90	1	69	1
LMY	35	3	35	2	57	3	57	3
Con. Yes	4	6	4	6	5	7	5	7
YES total	151		128		223		200	
SSN	45	2	32	3	45+	4	32+	4
LVN	2?	7	2?	7	33	5	27	5
Con.	27	4	26	4	27+	6	26+	6
NO total	74		60		105+		85+	

? indicates uncertainty about figures
+ indicates figure was exceeded by an unknown amount

The figures given are not all equally reliable but do give an indication of the relative output of the various groups - and also the comparatively greater reliance by YFS and LVN on press conference appearances. It will be noted, too, that some groups held their fire back for the later stages of the campaign to avoid "peaking" too early.

For the record, the leading spokesmen, as defined by press releases and press conference appearances, were as follows:

YFS   Sillars, MP (SLP);   Prof. N. MacCormick;   Reid, MP (SNP).

AFA   Dewar, MP (Lab.).

SNP   Reid, MP;   Maxwell;   G. Wilson, MP;   Crawford, MP;   MacCormick.

LMY   G. Brown;   Dewar, MP;   Young;   Liddell, Murray, MP (Lord Advocate).

Con. Yes   Buchanan-Smith, MP;   Rifkind, MP.

SSN   Lord Wilson;   Carruthers;   *Cook, MP (Lab.);   Herron;   Hardie;
             *Sproat, MP (Con.).

LVN   Dalyell, MP;   B. Wilson;   Cook, MP;   Cunningham, MP.

Con. No   Fletcher, MP;   Taylor, MP;   Ancram, Brittan, MP;   Monro, MP;
             Sanderson (Party President).

             * Not official member of SSN campaign committee

CAMPAIGN THEMES

For an analysis of the arguments deployed during the campaign three sources have been utilised. For the first two - slogans and leaflets - the reader is referred to the facsimiles of the most important leaflets, posters, stickers etc., reproduced elsewhere in the book. They repay careful study. It must be emphasised that for many electors these items were of the utmost importance since it can be assumed that the majority of the populace (i.e. all but those who were housebound in areas of zero campaigning activity) would have encountered at least some of the literature or slogans reproduced.

A brief summary of the themes of the leaflets is called for. On the Yes side, the arguments of the main YFS leaflets were grouped under two headings. "Vote Positively Yes" argued that it was "now or never", that Scottish self-respect demanded a Yes vote, and that the future of Scotland was at stake; it went on to give examples of areas of Scottish life where the Assembly could be expected to make an impact; and went on further to stress that there was only one devolution scheme currently on offer. The second leaflet ("The Facts") stressed that the Referendum was not about separatism but about devolution; that there was only one Assembly plan being offered; and appealed to voters to go forward for a Scottish victory.

The SNP's main leaflet urged voters to vote Yes for Scotland; to give Scotland a voice; and to set up an Assembly which would mean self-government over certain areas of Scottish life and democratic control over the bureaucracy.

The LMY's main leaflet ("We've fought hard") stressed that only the individual voter's Yes would implement the Act and would allow Scots to create the Scotland they wanted to see, ensuring Scottish, democratic control while preserving the unity of the United Kingdom. The electorate was invited to help build the future with Labour's Scottish Assembly.

On the No side, four themes were deliberately reiterated in all the SSN leaflets.

Summarised, they were that the proposed Assembly would mean more taxes; more government; more conflict (i.e. constitutional problems); but no tangible benefits for the citizen. The "Know your Mythology" leaflet set out to refute 11 arguments in favour of the Assembly, prefaced by: "The people pushing hardest for a Scottish Assembly are those who hope to profit politically or personally from it. Many see it only as a stepping stone to separation. Others have made claims for it that do not stand examination." The leaflet concluded with: "We already have devolution. Would it not be more sensible to improve what we already have without adding another tier of governmental interference to run our lives for us?"

The Conservative leaflet ("The Right Vote for Scotland") picked up many of the same themes: more taxes, no economic benefits, and a weaker constitutional position, but was at some pains to stress that a No vote was not a vote against devolution (only against the Scotland Act 1978), and that a No majority would not mean the end of devolution.

The main LVN leaflet stressed the objections to the Assembly of cost, constitutional friction and irrelevance to economic problems. It answered arguments about the 40 per cent rule, appealed to Labour voters not to be swayed by Party loyalty or the No line-up, and argued that there was an alternative: real change through strong Labour government on a United Kingdom basis.

Many of these themes were reflected also in the press releases of the various campaigning groups. Table 2.13 lists the themes of the respective press campaigns.

Before leaving the subject of the press campaign, it should be stressed how important advertising was for SSN (and to a lesser extent LMY). The main advertisements for these two groups are reproduced elsewhere in this book. For those who had no direct contact with any campaign literature or campaigners, these advertisements and the reporting of the media (see Chapters 5, 6 and 7) presented the arguments on which they were expected to base their decision on how to vote on March 1.

CONCLUSION: AN ASYMMETRICAL CAMPAIGN[3]

In concluding this chapter, some observations are prompted by the striking differences visible between the two camps and among the various groups on each side as regards the volume and nature of activity, the arguments deployed, and the progress of the campaign. These differences were facilitated by the absence of common factors such as effective umbrella groups, broadcasts on each side, leaflets to all electors etc. - themes alluded to in Chapter 1 and recurring in Chapter 11.

Briefly, however, and at the risk of oversimplification if not caricature, the two sides each suffered from certain problems or handicaps, but each equally possessed certain undoubted advantages. The existence or deployment of these factors arguably accounted for the narrow Yes majority.

Commencing the analysis at the start of the campaign, the strengths and weaknesses of the two sides can be summarised as follows. The Yes side had the apparent advantage of appealing to patriotism, and the title of the main non-party campaigning group, Yes for Scotland, was as powerful a slogan as its symbol, a white St Andrew's cross on blue with the word Yes. The historically reasserted desire of the Scottish people for some form of Home Rule was not in doubt: to date there has

---

[3] For assessments of the campaign see Ascherson, 1980; Bain, 1980; Balsom and McAllister, 1979; Buton-Tesson, 1980; Drucker and Brown, 1980, Ch.10; Hache, 1980; Kauppi, 1979; Miller, 1980; Perman, 1979.

TABLE 2.13   Campaign themes in press releases

TABLE 2.13A   The Yes camp

Theme	Priority accorded by			
	All	YFS	SNP	LMY
New opportunity, democracy, improved system of government	1	4=	2	2
Opportunity for various sectors/sectional interests	2	1	1	4=
Attack on other side	3	4=	4	3
"This Assembly or no Assembly"	4	3	5=	5=
Economic benefits	5=	–	5=	4=
40 per cent rule (and electoral register)	5=	–	3	–
Challenge, vote positively	5=	4=	5=	–
Middle way, strengthen UK, diversity	8	–	–	1
Progress of campaign	9=	2	9=	–
Control bureaucracy	9=	–	9=	–
More Scottish control, influence	11	–	8	–
United front	–	4=	–	–
Attack on Nationalists, separatism	–	–	–	5=

TABLE 2.13B   The No camp

Theme	Priority accorded by			
	All	SSN	Con	LVN [(a)]
Irrelevance (especially to economic problems), would lead to irresponsible government	1	2	2=	1
More government	2	–	1	–
Danger of friction, break-up of UK	3=	1	–	5=
Alternatives to Scotland Act	4	–	2=	–
Progress of campaign	5=	–	–	–
Financing the Assembly (more taxes)	5=	3	–	–
"Save Labour's Skin" aim of Referendum	7	–	4	–
Abstention not equal to voting No	8	–	–	4
Vote solely on Scotland Act	9=	5	–	–
Cost of Assembly	9=	4	–	–
Geographical areas urged to vote No	9=	–	–	–
Broadcasting issue	9=	–	–	2=
"Fanatical" supporters of other side	9=	–	5=	–
Less Scottish influence in London	9=	–	5=	–
Labour activists against devolution	–	–	–	2=
Financing the campaign	–	–	–	5=

Notes: – indicates low priority or no reference
         = indicates an equal number of mentions
      (a) based on press reports as no press releases available

never been a majority in any opinion poll against devolution. Devolution was the policy of all the political parties save one (and even the Conservative opposition was, strictly speaking, restricted to opposing the Scotland Act 1978 rather than the principle of devolution). It was also the policy of the established Church, the Scottish Trades Union Congress and most of the unions, not to mention the Govern-

ment of the day, and it was supported by important sections of the press. (For an
account of the attitudes of various interest groups, see Hache, 1980, pp.43-54.)
The No side definitely started off as the underdog, especially as it seemed likely
that there would be more local activist support for the Yes side.

One key factor which gave heart to the No side was the 40 per cent rule which made
the outcome of the Referendum something other than a foregone conclusion and therefore to make a fight of it was worthwhile. The *hostilité des investisseurs et du
patronat* to devolution (Hache, 1980, p.44) meant that Scotland Says No could count
on the fairly solid support of industry and commerce (see Risk, 1977). The No side
in general had, in addition to this backing plus that of the Conservative Party and
most Regional (if not District) councillors, the support of prominent dissidents
within the bodies which were officially Yes. The No side also brought an impressive
professionalism to the campaign. This was in part due to having no real financial
problems (SSN succeeded in raising just over its target of £100,000); it was in
part the fruits of the experience of Scotland is British; and it was in part the
result of the professional experience of some of the key figures involved and their
ability to work in harmony. Thus the main themes of the No campaigners, despite
the existence of three separate No groups, came across to the public as a concerted
campaign. The campaign themes (clearly foreshadowed three years previously [see
Thatcher, 1976]) were: more government and bureaucracy, more cost, and the danger
of friction between Edinburgh and London, possibly leading to the break-up of the
UK. It is clear that these points made an impact on the voters (see Kauppi, 1979,
p. 34).

The No side had some balancing disadvantages, however. One was the doubt about the
number of troops it could count on at the local level (hence the concentration on
advertising). Another was the imbalance in planned Party political broadcasts (3:1),
while the pro-devolution stance of the established Church and of the trades unions
was a source of worry. Last but not least there was the need to establish the No
side's patriotic credentials, to demonstrate that respectable and respected Scots
could with a clear conscience give a thumbs-down to the call to say Yes for Scotland.

Various weaknesses on the Yes side were apparent even before the campaign got under
way. One weakness was the complacency prevalent among some Yes supporters, which
derived from the knowledge, confirmed in poll after poll, that there was solid
majority support for devolution. This complacency was fuelled by a mistaken belief
that the No side would not campaign hard, and certainly not on the doorsteps. The
rationale for this dangerously mistaken view was that the No side could not hope
to win but could hope only that an apathetic electorate (helped by a low-key campaign) would not turn out in sufficient numbers to overcome the 40 per cent hurdle.
Logically, therefore, it was argued, the No side would try to keep interest to a
minimum for fear of awakening the sleeping Yes giant (it was recognised that devolution, while theoretically popular with the voters, suffered from low saliency as
an issue).

Such complacency (certainly not universal in the Yes camp: YFS leaders were well
aware of the problems facing them) made the second handicap more understandable,
namely the very visible divisions on the Yes side, divisions which were more
serious than those on the No side. Whereas the various No groups acted in harmony,
the Yes campaign was punctuated by some discordant notes. On the Yes side there was
a greater concentration on group and above all on party identities, as well as explicit statements of differing viewpoints on the consequences of devolution. This
had the net effect of reducing the effectiveness not only of YFS but of the whole
Yes campaign. But if the result was going to be - in the words of the chant of
Scottish fans on the terracing at Hampden - "easy", then it seemed unnecessary to
go overboard in sacrificing money or long-established habits. The antagonism

between Labour activists and Nationalists was but the most acute form of this *cordon sanitaire* approach.

Other weaknesses were uneven. Thus, LMY had cash and they, like the SNP and Liberals, had a well-practised organisation. But YFS was struggling all the time to raise cash and was short of experienced professionals at the centre ("I don't know what we'd have done without the band of keen young people manning the office", as a leader of YFS put it).

A weakness of a different sort was the Scotland Act 1978, which was not quite the same ship as the Scotland Bill originally launched by the Government. Yet, despite the holes shot in it by the House of Lords and their back-bench Commons allies, it was the vessel which the Yes camp had to defend as the only ship in which the new Scotland could set sail.

It is tempting with hindsight to depict the campaign as an unrelieved series of set-backs for the Yes side. But this would be an incomplete picture. The Yes camp, particularly Yes for Scotland, could take comfort from the sight of Yes window posters, lapel badges and car stickers heavily outnumbering those of the No side, and from the knowledge that they were ahead in the distribution of leaflets. Resentment of the 40 per cent rule was a further early bonus, even if it wore thinner as time went on.

If that was the good news for the Yes camp, the progress of the campaign was punctuated by a series of blows of varying severity. The most important were: the intervention on February 14 of Conservative elder statesman and one-time devolutionist Lord Home to urge doubters who still believed in devolution to "vote No for a better Bill"; the successful LVN initiative in the courts issuing in Lord Ross's judgement which put an end to Party political broadcasting (and, because there was no agreement on the Yes side on a fall-back position, an end to any broadcasts by the campaigners); the resolution moved by Andrew Herron of SSN at a Commission of Assembly meeting to halt the reading out from Church of Scotland pulpits of a call to vote Yes (which gave the impression that the Church of Scotland had moved into neutral gear[4]); and, last but by no means least, the slide of the Yes vote in the opinion polls. The Yes camp began to wonder rather belatedly whether they were on a slippery slope to defeat but clung to the belief that it would be "all right on the night".

Morale on the No side, not surprisingly, was on a rising curve. Apart from a minor flurry about the last-minute guerrilla tactics of CYC, their main worry was that the prolonged discussion of the 40 per cent rule might persuade their supporters to stay at home rather than to vote No. But generally they were confident that their campaign had correctly gauged the mood of the Scottish people, especially the "don't know"s.

Optimism was certainly not a term one would use to describe the mood of Scotland in January and February 1979. A bitter winter (and the weather was mentioned by several Yes campaigners as a factor handicapping the campaign in the country), exacerbated by strikes which were rarely out of the headlines (see Chapters 6 and 7) and which had a direct impact on most electors, added up to a depressed and sometimes bitter mood. The Labour Government hit a patch of unpopularity which meant that the LMY campaign for *Labour's* Assembly, and the prominence given to Prime Minister Callaghan

---

[4]Which was not the case, but it was the popular impression which was important. The Church of Scotland monthly *Life & Work*'s February 1979 issue gave the same impression.

in the main LMY poster, were, in retrospect, unfortunate. As the SNP was also unpopular at the time[5], devolution was struggling to get through on its own merits
rather than as the policy of parties which could "deliver" a vote. (The other side
of the coin was, of course, the hardening of the Tory No vote, allied to the recovery of Conservative support from its previous depths. Liberal supporters
divided fairly evenly, with a small majority against the Scotland Act: see Kauppi,
1979, p.16). Scepticism about the ability of governments and politicians to solve
basic problems was widespread and the mood of the doubters[6] was receptive to the
No message.

So, to return to the nautical metaphor, the deck of the devolution ship was visibly
tilting. As polling day approached, the question was whether and by how much HMS
Scotland Act would remain afloat.

RETROSPECT

Long after the campaign was over I put the question to campaigners from various
groups: "If you had it all to do again would you do anything differently?" There
were some on the Yes side who felt that there was merit in running separate party
campaigns, with the aim of simultaneously tapping party loyalty and mobilising
party machines in a straightforward way as at a general election. But the predominant view was in favour of a concerted campaign. One senior LMY campaigner said:
"We would have to look very closely at the possibility of an umbrella group", and
other respondents were even more emphatically in favour of having a single pro-
devolution umbrella group.

The No side, perhaps not surprisingly given that they got the result they wanted,
were confident that they had done all the right things. Although a leading LVN
campaigner expressed a desire to get away from the 40 per cent rule and all the
complications it produced, the general feeling was that if it proved necessary
the No campaigners would do it all again in much the same way.

REFERENCES

Ascherson, N. (1980). After devolution. *Bulletin of Scottish Politics*, 1, 1.
     (Autumn 1980).
Bain, D. (1980). Doing it ourselves. *Bulletin of Scottish Politics*, 1, 1. (Autumn
     1980).
Balsom, D. and I. McAllister (1979). The Scottish and Welsh devolution referenda
     of 1979: constitutional change and popular choice. *Parliamentary Affairs*, 32.
     (Autumn 1979).
Butler, D.E. and U. Kitzinger (1976). *The 1975 Referendum*. Macmillan, London.
Buton-Tesson, A.M. (1980). The SNP 1974-1980. Unpublished Master's thesis,
     University of Poitiers.
Chambers Twentieth Century Dictionary (1979). Chambers, Edinburgh.
Dalyell, T. (1977). *Devolution: the end of Britain?* Jonathan Cape, London.

---

[5]The row over the expulsion of a little-known, former prospective candidate
 dragged on, with attendant press publicity, for months.

[6]For example, the establishment of Radio Scotland, which rapidly achieved widespread unpopularity, owing to certain early policy decisions, was held up by No
 campaigners as a foretaste of the disasters likely to follow devolution in other
 areas of public life. This question dominated correspondence columns of the
 quality newspapers for some weeks.

Drucker, H.M. (1978). *Breakaway, the Scottish Labour Party*. E.U.S.P.B., Edinburgh. [n.d.]

Drucker, H.M. and G. Brown (1980). *The Politics of Nationalism and Devolution*. Longman, London.

Hache, J.-D. (1980). Les Causes de l'Echec de la Dévolution écossaise. Unpublished thesis for Diploma in Applied Studies, Ecole des Hautes Etudes en Sciences sociales, Paris.

Jordan, G. (1979). The committee stage of the Scotland and Wales Bill. *Waverley Papers*, Scottish Government Studies, Occasional Paper 1. Univ. of Edinburgh.

Kauppi, M.V. (1979). The 1979 Scottish referendum results: explanations, rationalizations and protestations. Paper read at the sixth annual meeting of the Rocky Mountain Conference on British Studies, October 1979. Colorado Springs, Colorado.

MacCormick, J.M. (1955). *Flag in the Wind*. Gollancz, London.

Miller, W. (1980). The Scottish dimension. In D.E. Butler and D. Kavanagh (Eds), *The British General Election of 1979*. Macmillan, London.

Perman, R. (1979). The devolution referendum campaign of 1979. In H.M. Drucker and N. Drucker (Eds), *The Scottish Government Yearbook 1980*. Paul Harris, Edinburgh.

Risk, C.J. (1977). Devolution: the commercial community's fears. In H.M. Drucker and M.G. Clarke (Eds), *The Scottish Government Yearbook 1978*. Paul Harris, Edinburgh [n.d.]

Thatcher, M. (1976). We shall defend the unity of our kingdom. *Conservative Monthly News*, February 1976.

CHAPTER 3

LOCAL CAMPAIGNING

John Bochel   and   David Denver

Local campaigns by political parties are a familiar and fairly well-documented aspect of British elections. Parties are organised on the basis of electoral units
and a significant part of their routine inter-election activity is concerned with
the maintenance and tuning of an election "machine". During the campaign period
party workers at local level perform a variety of tasks designed to mobilise maximum support. Amongst these activities are canvassing, distributing literature,
addressing envelopes (for the free postal delivery of election addresses), regis-
tering postal voters, arranging public meetings, providing transport to the polls,
knocking-up supporters on election day and so on. Activities such as these are an
integral part of British elections and, although there is some debate about the
precise electoral impact of local campaigning, no one would deny that without it
elections would be even more lifeless and bland than some critics allege they now
are. We also suspect that the complete absence of local campaigning would result in
lower levels of awareness of, and participation in, elections than are currently
recorded. Despite the "nationalisation" of election campaigns, encouraged by,
amongst other things, media concentration upon national personalities and issues,
it seems to us that at local level some interest can be generated and marginal
voters roused from their apathy.

Unlike elections, however, referendums in Britain are a novel and infrequent experience for party organisations and voters alike. In an election the party machine
is operated by a core of experienced workers who can organise an election with
their eyes shut, as it were, since there is a formula, a set of procedures and a
"kit of tools" with which most are familiar. But a referendum presents an unfamiliar situation, aspects of which may create problems as far as local campaigning by
parties is concerned.

First of all, it is to be expected that in a referendum campaign organisations other
than political parties will be involved - *ad hoc* groups, groups with a long-standing
commitment on the issue in question and groups of people not normally involved in
political activity. This clearly complicates the campaign scene with parties having
to determine their relationship with such groups. Secondly, parties may not be
united on the position they should take on the referendum question. Referendums
may, indeed, be held precisely because parties are not united on some issue, as
was the case in both British referendums to date. But even if a party at national
level is more or less united and gives a clear lead to its local branches, there is
no guarantee that local parties will be united or accept the orders of party headquarters. This is in marked contrast to elections where there is rarely any doubt
about the unity of local party organisations in fighting a campaign. Thirdly,

43

referendums also differ from elections in that they are unlikely to arouse party passions to the same extent. In an election the enemy is clear - all other parties; however in a referendum erstwhile enemies may suddenly appear as allies. Also referendums do not result in the election of a government, with all that that implies over a wide range of issues, but are held to decide a single issue which may or may not be considered to be of central importance by party workers. Whereas in an election old and powerful loyalties can be called upon to arouse and inspire the faithful this is less true of referendums. Finally, referendums, unlike elections, do not have candidates at local level to provide a focus for a campaign. Candidates can attract the loyalty of party workers but in a referendum there is no visible and immediate pay-off for party workers in the sense of getting a candidate elected.

For these reasons, then, local campaigns in a referendum are likely to be organised and run somewhat differently from election campaigns. It is worthwhile considering in a general way how they might be organised in order to provide a framework within which local campaigning in the Scottish Referendum can be described and analysed.

In a referendum it seems likely that there will be three main sets of actors as far as campaigning is concerned. Firstly, there will be the political parties with permanent national headquarters and a network of local organisations experienced in running campaigns. Secondly, there will be *ad hoc* groups formed specifically to campaign on one side or the other in a referendum. These groups may consist of people from a number of parties or from none. Thirdly, there will be pre-existing groups such as trade unions, business organisations, churches and so on which may take up a position on the issue in question and seek to mobilise their own members and others. There will, of course, in addition be a variety of individuals with strong commitment but no particular attachments at the outset and it seems likely that these will join with like-minded others in an appropriate *ad hoc* group.

In the case of each of the three major actors the initiative in organising local campaigns may be taken nationally or locally. We can describe different forms of campaign organisation in terms of a simple six-cell matrix as follows:

	Parties	*Ad hoc* groups	Existing groups
National initiative	A	C	E
Local initiative/ discretion	B	D	F

Each cell represents a different way in which local campaign activity might be organised and undertaken. Cell A approximates the situation which occurs in elections. The parties dutifully carry out instructions, receiving organisational support and encouragement from headquarters. If national party instructions are ambiguous or non-committal, or if instructions are ignored by local parties, then cell B best describes the situation. *Ad hoc* groups at national level (cell C) will generally seek to get the support of parties so that the latter's electoral machines will be mobilised in the campaign and they will also try to set up local branches of their group in order to plan and co-ordinate local campaign activity. The initiative may, however, be taken at local level (cell D) if a group of like-minded people from different parties or none get together and set themselves up as an umbrella group to run a local campaign. Existing groups, either local or national, may decide (cells E and F) to mount campaigns of their own but more commonly they might be expected to associate themselves with an umbrella group.

Using this framework we can now describe what happened as far as local campaigning is concerned in the Scottish Referendum. All four main parties did give a fairly clear lead to their local associations. Constituency Labour Parties were asked to campaign for a Yes vote - the official Labour campaign being called "Labour Movement Yes" - but to avoid co-operation with any other parties or groups. Local Conservative Associations were asked to throw their weight on the No side and to co-operate fully with the Scotland Says No organisation. Liberal Associations were encouraged to support Yes umbrella groups and SNP branches were asked to mount campaigns either on their own or in co-operation with others via the Yes for Scotland group. But in most cases opting out of or dissent from national party recommendations seems to have been tolerated.

There were also national *ad hoc* groups seeking to promote local campaigns. Scotland Says No and Yes for Scotland were the most important of these and both set up local groups. The strategy of the unofficial Labour Vote No group was slightly different in that their main aims were to provide a focus for dissident Labour people and to dissuade Constituency Labour Parties from throwing their full weight behind the Yes campaign.

Existing groups such as the Scottish TUC and the CBI in Scotland did take up positions but generally they asked their members to involve themselves in the campaigns of the *ad hoc* groups.

Despite the instructions, advice, encouragement and requests for support emanating from these bodies at national level, however, there were good grounds for thinking before the event that campaign activity at local level would be rather less than intense. The Labour Party, by far the largest party in Scotland in terms of popular support and the party with the most extensive (though not necessarily most efficient) electoral machine, was divided on the issue of devolution. In a sense devolution had been forced on an unwilling Labour Party in Scotland. Many activists regarded it as a sop to Nationalist sentiment and, having fought the SNP at local level for 12 years or more, many Labour people must have found it disconcerting, to say the least, to be asked to campaign on the same side as their erstwhile opponents. Moreover, the evidence of by-elections, opinion polls and local elections suggested that SNP support was in decline so that it was arguable that the Nationalists had already been "dished" and that there was now no pressing need to pursue the devolution policy.

Other parties too were divided or indecisive in their approaches to devolution, as other contributions show. Many Conservatives favoured devolution but saw the Scotland Act as a poor vehicle for it. Many in the SNP could not make up their minds whether to accept the half (or less) loaf of devolution or to insist on the whole loaf of independence. Although the Liberals are generally credited with a consistent commitment to devolution, they too, as later data show, seem to have had some doubts about full-hearted campaigning.

In addition all the parties had, or anticipated, other calls on their resources in Referendum year. Even during the Referendum campaign some were in the process of selecting candidates for scheduled European elections in June (which was also a new experience for them). A general election too had to take place some time in 1979. The slim financial and manpower resources of most local parties were sorely pressed by these demands.

More generally, devolution was not an issue which aroused very much excitement, despite the space given to it in the press and the time devoted to it in Parliament. Although polls regularly found large majorities favouring devolution they also found that it was an issue of low priority for voters, lagging behind bread-and-butter issues such as prices and unemployment. The polls may, however, have given rise to a certain amount of complacency on the Yes side. At the start of the campaign they were pointing to a comfortable Yes majority.

Two major problems faced attempts to set up effective *ad hoc* umbrella groups at local level. The first was the difficulty of getting people from different parties to work together. This was particularly the case on the Yes side where Labour was determined to keep other parties at arm's length and some local SNP associations explicitly campaigned for a Yes vote on the grounds that this was a first step to complete independence for Scotland. The second problem was that, although umbrella groups might attract to political activity people who would not normally partici-pate in campaigns, such people would be "amateurs" when it came to organising a campaign, lacking the expertise and experience of regular party workers.

What then actually happened on the ground in the way of campaign activity during the Scottish Referendum? In order to avoid answering this question in a purely im-pressionistic way - though impressionistic accounts can convey the flavour of local campaigning vividly and with insight - we seek to describe local Referendum cam-paigning on the basis of responses to questionnaires which we sent to constituency organisations of the four major parties and to those local branches of umbrella groups which we were able to identify. Questionnaires were returned by 142 local parties (31 Conservative, 43 Labour, 34 Liberal and 34 SNP) and by 47 groups (27 YFS and 20 SSN). Most of the parties concerned were constituency associations, but three were "city parties" covering more than one constituency. Two of the groups which responded covered more than one constituency, 25 covered a single con-stituency, two part of a constituency, 15 a town or village and three a single ward. To supplement the data from this survey we also have reports from 36 individ-uals, ordinary electors, living in towns and villages throughout Scotland whom we asked to note campaign activity in their localities. (We do not know how represen-tative the parties and groups which responded were, so our data should be read as relating only to those. The only check we have on representativeness is a *Scotsman* survey reported on January 16, 1979. Neal Ascherson contacted 67 of the 71 Con-stituency Labour Parties. He found that about 64 per cent of them had decided or were about to decide to campaign for a Yes vote with three giving ambiguous replies. Ascherson also reported that 30 per cent of CLPs had replied that they were not setting up a committee to work for a Yes vote. These proportions are close to our own. We should have preferred to have interviewed respondents but resources did not enable us to do so. We regard our data as indicative rather than definitive.)

Considering first the political parties, Table 3.1 shows what local parties de-cided to do in the Referendum campaign.

TABLE 3.1   Decisions by Constituency Parties

	Con. %	Lab. %	Lib. %	SNP %
To campaign for Yes	0	67	68	97
To campaign for No	74	0	0	0
To do nothing	26	33	32	3
	(N=31)	(N=43)	(N=34)	(N=34)

There is evidence here of considerable local initiative by parties in that, while no constituency party did the opposite of what was recommended by their national organisations, substantial minorities of Conservative, Labour and Liberal organis-ations decided not to campaign. (The single SNP association which is shown as doing nothing did not opt out of the campaign but decided to leave campaigning to its constituent branches.)

The immediate question which arises is why so many local parties decided not to go along with the official line. More than 80 per cent of the inactive Labour Parties gave as their reason the fact that the CLP was divided on the devolution issue. The others were either indifferent or had MPs who were opposed to devolution. Of the inactive Liberal Parties more than half claimed that they did not have the resources for a campaign or that they wished to conserve resources for the general election. Rather surprisingly, three Liberal Associations claimed to be divided on the devolution issue, while another was indifferent. The eight inactive Conservative Associations gave a variety of reasons for not participating in the campaign. In two cases the active members of the Association were said to be in favour of the Assembly; one other Association was said to be split; one had a pro-devolution MP; one wanted to conserve resources and three were either completely indifferent or did not care enough about the issue to want to campaign.

It should not be assumed, however, that party people were totally inactive in the Referendum campaign in the areas in which constituency associations decided not to take part. In half of the inactive Conservative Constituency Associations some individual branches helped the No campaign, while in three CLPs and two Liberal Associations some branches of the party were reported to have helped the Yes side. Moreover, when the secretaries of the non-campaigning parties were asked whether individual members of their parties were active in the campaign the answers, summarised in Table 3.2, show that a high proportion had individuals involved on one side or another.

TABLE 3.2   Activity of Individuals in Non-Active Parties

	Con. %	Lab. %	Lib. %
Some helped Yes	–	27	60
Some helped No	50	9	–
People active on both sides	38	46	–
No one active	–	9	30
Don't know	13	9	10
	(N=8)	(N=11)	(N=10)

The most striking feature of this table is the extent to which Labour people were divided by the devolution issue and this is confirmed by other data. We have already seen that the most common reason for local Labour Parties refusing to campaign was the fact that they were divided on the matter. But even among those CLPs which did campaign, only 21 per cent reported that this decision was unanimous compared with 91 per cent of Conservative Associations, 94 per cent of SNP branches and 67 per cent of Liberal Associations. Moreover, 45 per cent of CLPs which campaigned for a Yes vote said that some of their members worked on the opposite side, whereas this was the case in only 18 per cent of Conservative Parties, nine per cent of Liberal Parties and in no SNP organisation. The extent of the division in the Labour Party can be further illustrated by the case of one CLP (which did not reply to our questionnaire) where, according to our information, the executive decided by 12 votes to 11 to campaign for Yes, whereupon the chairman resigned and was active in the No campaign!

Of the four major parties, then, only local SNP Associations seem to have (with one exception) unequivocally followed the official line. Conservatives and Liberals seem to have been less than enthusiastic while local Labour Parties were very hesitant and divided about what to do in the Referendum campaign. Nevertheless, as

our contribution on the local press shows, in the areas in which most local newspapers circulate, Labour held more than a quarter of the advertised meetings on
the Yes side and obtained a quarter of the press coverage. It should be remembered,
however, that few local weekly papers circulate in Scotland's most densely populated centres, the big cities. And in any case the holding of public meetings does
not imply an active doorstep campaign.

As we noted above, we received replies to our questionnaire from 47 local *ad hoc*
umbrella groups. These groups were formed specifically to campaign at local level
in the Referendum and most of them came into existence only a short time before
Referendum day. Sixty-three per cent of the Yes groups and 80 per cent of the No
groups were formed two months or less before Referendum day.

The initiative in setting up the groups seems to have come largely at local level.
Sixty-six per cent of the groups resulted from local initiative while in 15 per
cent the prime mover was the national headquarters of an umbrella group. The remainder resulted from a combination of local and national initiative. In this respect there is little difference between the Yes and No sides. They did differ,
however, in respect of the particular people who took the initiative at local level.
On the Yes side in 13 cases out of 27 it was SNP people alone who took the initiative, in three cases it was the SNP members plus individuals not attached to any
party and in one case SNP activists plus people from other parties. In only one
case did the initiative come entirely from unattached people. Similarly on the No
side unattached people took the initiative in only one case, all other examples of
local initiative (11 out of 20 groups) being due to Conservatives. In both cases
the role and significance of local political parties is striking.

More details of the extent of party involvement in the groups are given in
Table 3.3, which shows the proportion stating that the parties listed were involved
in their group as organisations or through individual members.

TABLE 3.3   Party Involvement in Groups

	YES	NO
	%	%
Conservatives	15	70
Labour	22	25
Liberals	41	–
SNP	85	–
Communists	11	–
SLP	22	–
Any party	93	89

Only the SNP was involved in more than half of local Yes groups - and it played a
part in the great majority of such groups - while most No groups had some local
Conservative involvement.

The same sort of pattern is evidenced in Table 3.4, which summarises the answers
given by our respondents when asked to estimate the proportions of their active
campaign workers who were members of the different parties. Clearly Yes groups
were dominated by SNP members and No groups by Conservatives while in both cases
the Referendum appears to have brought relatively small numbers of people into
political activity. Moreover the actual number of people actively involved in the
campaign under the aegis of these groups was relatively small. Overall, it seems
that relatively few people were involved in group activity. Half of the No groups
and 59 per cent of the Yes groups had fewer than 20 campaign workers.

TABLE 3.4   Party Affiliation of Group Members

Mean percentage who were:	YES %	NO %
Conservatives	4	74
Labour	2	8
Liberals	6	2
SNP	65	-
Communists	1	-
SLP	4	-
Not usually active	7	12

One final piece of evidence showing the extent to which party people dominated the *ad hoc* groups is the fact that most of our respondents, who were secretaries, chairmen or organisers of the groups, were themselves party activists. Of the 27 Yes group respondents, 20 were active in the SNP, two in the SLP and one each in the Liberal and Conservative Parties. Only one respondent was not normally active in a party. Sixteen of our No group respondents were active Conservatives, one was a Labour activist and three were not in any party.

Relationships between the political parties and umbrella groups were very fluid and varied from area to area. One reason for this is that the groups themselves tended not to be very formally organised. Only 36 per cent of all groups were formally constituted with a chairman, secretary and so on, the rest being run informally; fewer than half (40 per cent) had a committee to run the campaign. The Yes groups tended to be somewhat more formally organised than the No groups, but the difference was not great. Another problem is that in some areas political parties simply adopted an umbrella group's name (Conservatives becoming Scotland Says No and the SNP operating under the Yes for Scotland banner) so that, while a few people from other parties did become involved, in these cases group campaigns and party campaigns were difficult to distinguish.

An exception to this, however, is the Labour Party. When asked which campaign their constituency organisation was attached to, all active CLPs said the official Labour Movement Yes campaign and only three CLPs in our survey said that they had co-operated in any way with an umbrella group. In the case of the other major parties the situation was more complex. Of Conservative Associations 22 per cent said that they were part of the Conservative Party campaign, 39 per cent reported being part of Scotland Says No and 39 per cent claimed to be part of both. Similarly, 28 per cent of SNP organisations said they were part of the SNP campaign, 22 per cent were part of Yes for Scotland and 44 per cent saw themselves as involved in both (the remainder said they simply ran their own local campaign). Liberal Associations were less uniform in their campaign affiliation - some saying they simply ran a Liberal campaign (30 per cent), others claiming to be part of Yes for Scotland (25 per cent) and one seeing itself as belonging to the Alliance for an Assembly. The rest mentioned some combination of these three. Large majorities of these three parties reported co-operating with local umbrella groups - 78 per cent of Conservative Associations with Scotland Says No, 70 per cent of SNP Associations with Yes for Scotland and 65 per cent of Liberal Associations with either Yes for Scotland or the Alliance for an Assembly.

From the point of view of the groups, local co-operation with political parties was clearly of importance - we have already seen the part that party people played in setting up and running group campaigns. In addition, when asked directly, 88 per cent of our Yes group respondents and 70 per cent of No group respondents rated local party help and co-operation as "very" or "quite" important for their campaigns.

What form did this co-operation take? One form is did *not* usually take was financial. In our survey only two local parties (one Liberal and one SNP) reported receiving small sums from umbrella groups and only one CLP, three SNP and 10 Liberal Associations said that they had donated money to groups (the Liberals possibly having little else to offer).

More commonly, parties simply provided manpower and experience, usually operating as campaign units while seeing themselves as part of an umbrella group and sometimes having representatives upon the local Yes or No committee. None the less, in their relations with local groups, local parties did find themselves co-operating, however loosely, with one another. Table 3.5 shows the percentages of local parties which reported co-operation through an umbrella group with other local parties listed on the left-hand side of the table.

TABLE 3.5   Inter-party Co-operation

	Con. %	Lib. %	SNP %
Worked with no other party	61	13	17
with Conservatives	–	13	30
with Labour	33	0	43
with Liberals	17	–	65
with SNP	0	50	–
with SLP	0	6	13
with Communists	0	13	35
	(N=18)	(N=16)	(N=23)

The clearest case of co-operation is between the SNP and Liberals – perhaps the two parties most firmly committed to devolution.

The relationships we have discussed so far are horizontal relationships - between local parties and local campaign groups. There is another dimension to consider - vertical relationships between local units and the headquarters of parties and of groups.

The headquarters of the Conservative, Labour and Scottish National Parties appear to have serviced the campaigns of their local parties in the normal way. Large majorities of party campaigners reported being offered literature, posters, badges, speakers' notes and so on. All of this was at a much lower level in the case of the Liberal party. The near indivisibility of the Conservative and Scotland Says No campaigns is illustrated by the fact that many local Conservative Associations received the same sort of help from the headquarters of the umbrella group. To a lesser extent the same was true of the SNP and Yes for Scotland. The intimacy of the link between these parties and groups is emphasised by the fact that local groups appear to have used both party and group headquarters about equally in order to service their campaigns. It is worth noting, however, that the groups had a financial connection with their headquarters which was entirely absent in the case of parties. Twenty per cent of Yes groups and 25 per cent of No groups claimed that they had donated money to headquarters, while eight per cent of Yes groups and 59 per cent of No groups reported receiving money from the national headquarters of their groups.

A summary of these horizontal and vertical relationships is given in Table 3.6

which shows the percentages of local campaign units which thought that the organisations listed on the left-hand side of the table were "very" or "quite" important for their campaign.

TABLE 3.6 Horizontal and Vertical Relationships

	Con.	Lab.	Lib.	SNP	Yes groups	No groups
	%	%	%	%	%	%
Party headquarters	61	67	21	41	59	36
Group headquarters	48	3	8	25	63	79
Local groups	35	3	50	28	-	-
Local parties	-	-	-	-	88	70

Clearly, Labour's local campaigns were dependent to a considerable extent upon the initiative and assistance of party headquarters. The Conservatives and the SNP on the other hand were, in addition, involved with umbrella groups at national and local level, while the Liberals were mostly content to be part of a local group. The figures also show that local groups, especially on the Yes side, were dependent to a considerable extent upon help from political parties both locally and nationally and this usually meant the SNP. Comparing the Conservatives with other parties and the Yeses with the Noes, it would seem that the headquarters of Scotland Says No played a more vigorous role in organising local campaigns than did its Yes counterpart.

We turn now to the local campaigns themselves. How effectively were they organised and what actually happened on the ground? Running an effective campaign requires good organisation, some money, and effort and enthusiasm on the part of campaign workers. By these criteria the local party campaigns in the Referendum were not very effective. Table 3.7 shows the proportions of campaign units which had a single person in charge of the campaign, central committee rooms (typically for the whole constituency) and local committee rooms - all of which would be expected in a general election.

TABLE 3.7 Campaign Organisation

	Con.	Lab.	Lib.	SNP	Yes groups	No groups
	%	%	%	%	%	%
Organiser/Agent in charge	23	13	33	56	48	75
Central committee rooms	35	53	13	61	52	40
Local committee rooms	22	20	0	38	27	15
	(N=23)	(N=29)	(N=23)	(N=33)	(N=27)	(N=20)

As can be seen, the campaigns seem to have been organisationally weak. It is difficult to conceive of any sort of campaign being run without central committee rooms, which was common, and the rarity of local committee rooms suggests that campaign organisation was relatively flimsy.

Finance is an important part of any election campaign. Money is needed in order to pay for propaganda in the form of leaflets, posters and the like, to hire rooms for meetings, pay speakers' expenses and so on. According to our survey, however, the amounts of money expended by the parties on the Referendum campaign could fairly be described as derisory. On average active CLPs spent about £85 on the campaign, Conservative Associations £37 and Liberal Associations £30. Only SNP organisations with an average expenditure of about £250 seem to have invested their funds in a campaign effort. These figures compare very poorly with the amounts spent in general elections. Expenditure by groups was a little more generous. The mean expenditure for Yes groups was £180 (with just over half of them spending less than £150) while No groups averaged £90 (85 per cent spending less than £150).

Overall it is clear that locally the Yes side in the Referendum expended more money than their opponents - whether they spent wisely is, of course, an open question. But our data refer only to expenditure by local parties and groups. On both the Yes and No sides most of the literature, posters, stickers and so on were provided free by party or group headquarters (and for the Yes side alone by unions). Nearly all the extensive press advertising by the No side was also paid for by headquarters - as were, no doubt, the expenses of speakers.

To some extent the activities of the Referendum campaign followed closely the routine activities associated with normal election campaigns but on a reduced scale. Table 3.8 shows the percentages of active parties and groups which reported undertaking the activities listed.

TABLE 3.8 Campaign Activities

	Con.	Lab.	Lib.	SNP	Yes groups	No groups
	%	%	%	%	%	%
Organising postal votes	44	13	17	46	33	40
Canvassing	0	20	25	61	63	20
Knocking-up	26	27	29	82	85	25
Transport to polls	70	33	50	85	85	55
Distributing literature	96	90	79	97	96	100
Fly-posting	17	20	30	64	67	30
Holding meetings	57	60	63	79	82	90
Loudspeaker car	39	60	33	94	89	65
Motorcades	4	7	0	33	33	0
Press releases/adverts	3	10	21	9	7	10
	(N=23)	(N=30)	(N=23)	(N=33)	(N=27)	(N=20)

Two general features stand out from these data. First of all, the SNP and *ad hoc* groups appear to have had a higher level of campaign activity than the other parties. Secondly, the most arduous but most effective campaigning techniques - organising postal votes, canvassing and knocking-up - were not pursued to the extent that would be expected in an election.

Given the fuss about the inaccuracy of the register and about the 40 per cent rule, it is surprising that the Yes side did not put more effort into the postal vote. Even those organisations which did canvass did not do so very vigorously or widely. Labour parties canvassed only their own supporters; only one Conservative Association, one Liberal Association, five SNP branches, five Yes groups and one No group attempted a full canvass. And when we look at the proportions of campaigning organisations which canvassed and kept records for knocking-up on polling day, the figures are Conservative five per cent, Labour 11 per cent, Liberal 13 per cent, SNP 50 per cent, Yes groups 41 per cent and No groups nil. Other evidence suggests that even these modest claims may be somewhat exaggerated.

Public meetings were held by most local campaigning organisations. According to
their own reports the groups and parties covered by this survey organised 564
public meetings between them. The SNP led with 142 meetings, Yes groups held 119
and No groups 110. Trailing behind these somewhat, Labour organised 87 meetings,
the Liberals 57 and the Conservatives 49. These figures do not tally with those
we discovered from our studies of the local press. On the whole our respondents
claimed that their organisations held more meetings than we were able to trace.
There are three reasons for this. Firstly, local weekly newspapers do not circulate widely in large cities and some of our responses included these. Secondly,
some meetings were held that were not advertised or reported in the press. Thirdly,
some respondents may have over-reported activities by their parties and groups.
Main speakers at these meetings were most commonly MPs (especially at Labour, Conservative, Yes and No meetings); prospective Parliamentary candidates (especially
at SNP and Yes group meetings); local councillors and representatives of the
umbrella groups. Attendance at meetings was very variable, according to our campaign "monitors". Several reported an attendance around 30 and a few suggested
that 50-60 people attended. As in election campaigns, however, many of those who
attended meetings seem to have been committed supporters in any case. Other reports suggest thinly attended meetings. At Inverurie, for example, our monitor
noted only 13 people at an SNP-organised meeting "including the speaker (prospective SNP candidate), a supporting SNP speaker and his wife, the SNP chairman and
myself. Of the remaining eight, seven seemed to be connected with the local SNP
branch and the remaining person was English."

The distribution of literature was the commonest campaign activity reported in our
survey. During the Referendum campaign it would appear that Scotland was awash
with leaflets, broadsheets, lapel stickers and so on. According to their own reports, local parties distributed a total of about two million leaflets or broadsheets, 37,000 posters, 160,000 lapel stickers and 15,000 car stickers. The umbrella groups reported that they disposed of about 980,000 leaflets, 45,000 posters, 94,000 lapel badges and 23,000 car stickers and these figures are based only
on responses that we received; see chapter 2 for national figures). This kind of
campaign activity is, of course, relatively easy to undertake and probably rather
ineffective. Voters get used to leaflets being pushed through their letter-boxes
or pressed into their hands in the street and seem likely to pay relatively little
attention to them.

With the exception of literature distribution, then, it seems to us that local
parties (and it should be borne in mind that we are discussing here only those
parties that actually did mount a campaign) and groups did not have very well organised, extensive or effective campaigns. If the reports of our campaign monitors
are typical then local campaigning does not appear to have made much of an impression upon the electorate at large. Of the 36 monitors who noted campaign activity, 78 per cent reported receiving leaflets and 56 per cent noticed advertisements
for public meetings. No other campaign activity was noticed by more than half of
them. Forty-two per cent noticed at least one poster on a hoarding, 33 per cent
noticed car stickers, 28 per cent noticed window posters, 25 per cent noticed
open-air leafleting, 25 per cent also saw cars taking voters to the polls, 22 per
cent saw lapel stickers and 17 per cent saw campaign workers outside polling stations. Only one person (in Dingwall) was canvassed and no one saw a motorcade.
When it is remembered that our informants were on the lookout for campaign activity, these figures do not suggest that the parties and groups made any great impact
on the public at local level.

The overriding impression given both by our survey and by monitors' reports is of
lacklustre, unexciting and barely visible local campaigns. Of the parties involved,
only the SNP appears to have made a serious campaign effort. The following extracts
from monitors' reports illustrate what we mean.

"A very low-key campaign. No campaign did not exist. Only the SNP mounted any kind of campaign. Little interest or enthusiasm appeared to be generated." (Thurso)

"Not much voting; no activity; no cars to polls; no literature; really pathetic." (Berwickshire)

"The Referendum was clearly not marked by intense activity in this part of West-Central Scotland." (Bishopton)

"Political activity during the Referendum campaign was significantly absent. No major drive for votes was mounted by the Yes or No campaign or by any of the major parties." (Inverurie)

"The Referendum campaign was very low-key in marked contrast to the General Election which, whilst not frenzied, was moderately active." (Drymen)

"SNP was the only party which actually campaigned for a Yes vote. The Tories used the campaign as a stick to beat David Steel with; Labour didn't participate." (Hawick)

"It is the quietest political campaign which I have witnessed locally." (Gourock)

"The whole thing was very low-key. Most effort came from the SNP but even they seemed to be cooling off." (Fort William)

"Referendum day itself seemed characterised by widespread inertia and numbing apathy. One SNP Yes board was the only visual stimulation to be seen." (Peebles)

"A very low-key campaign - certainly less activity than in the recent by-election, let alone general elections." (Haddington)

"There were no campaign meetings, no canvasses; I enclose the only leaflet which came through the door. Altogether a very low-key campaign." (Eastwood)

It is clear, that the political parties did not put a great deal of effort into campaigning in the Referendum. We asked our party respondents to estimate the overall campaign effort of their parties as compared with general and local elections. The responses are shown in Table 3.9.

TABLE 3.9   Campaign Effort of Active Parties

	Con. %	Lab. %	Lib. %	SNP %
As in general election	0	0	4	13
More than local, less than general election	23	27	25	56
As in local election	9	10	13	22
Less than local election	46	37	17	6
Very little effort	23	27	42	3
	(N=22)	(N=30)	(N=24)	(N=32)

The relative lack of effort on the part of constituency parties was in large part a consequence of a lack of enthusiasm among party workers. We asked our respondents to estimate the enthusiasm of their workers in the Referendum campaign. As Table 3.10 shows, party workers were not very enthusiastic, especially in the Labour Party. Indeed, two-thirds of Labour Parties described their workers as "not very" or "not at all" enthusiastic.

Not surprisingly *ad hoc* group members showed more enthusiasm but even in these cases the figures for "very enthusiastic" are rather lower than one might expect.

TABLE 3.10 Enthusiasm of Party Workers

	Con. %	Lab. %	Lib. %	SNP %	Yes groups %	No groups %
Very enthusiastic	17	7	8	24	41	50
Quite enthusiastic	52	27	46	64	56	50
Not very enthusiastic	30	57	46	9	0	0
Not at all enthusiastic	0	10	0	3	0	0
	(N=22)	(N=30)	(N=24)	(N=32)	(n=27)	(N=20)

Clearly then, the factors we discussed above - an impending General Election, division in the Labour Party, the lack of a traditional enemy and the generally low
priority accorded the issue by local party workers, resulted in low enthusiasm and
relatively weak campaign efforts at local level. Whether more vigorous local campaigning would have made any difference to the Referendum result is doubtful. What
does seem clear is that in the circumstances of the Scottish Referendum vigorous
and effective local campaigning was not a genuine possibility. When grassroots
party workers are half-hearted, hesitant, apathetic or hostile to the official
party line, then party headquarters can do little about it. And in the absence of
full commitment by the parties' electoral machines local campaigns are bound to be
muted.

CHAPTER 4

THE CAMPAIGNS IN THE CITIES

The previous chapter sought to provide an overview of how local campaigning was organised and carried out in the Referendum. The quantitative approach adopted there inevitably limited the extent to which it was possible to convey the "feel" of local campaigning - the organisations and personalities involved, the arguments used, the reactions of local people and so on. In order to capture something of this we invited colleagues based in the four Scottish cities - Aberdeen, Dundee, Glasgow and Edinburgh - to write descriptive and impressionistic accounts of the Referendum campaign as they saw it. We made no attempt to standardise these pieces so that what we have here are five distinctly personal accounts of local campaigns. Taken together, we think they provide valuable insights into how Referendum campaigning operated and the impact it had at local level on the urban populace which accounts for 24 of Scotland's 71 Parliamentary constituencies.

I.   ABERDEEN AND THE GRAMPIAN REGION

Michael Dyer

Introduction

The electors of the Grampian Region rejected the Scotland Act by a majority of 6500. Perhaps more noteworthy than this, however, was the fact that in recording the lowest turnout on the mainland (57.9 per cent), the Region not only produced the eighth lowest Yes (27.9 per cent) amongst the 12 declaring authorities, but also the tenth lowest No (29.8 per cent) as a proportion of the total electorate. The Grampian Region was actually less No than the Central Region which scored the highest Yes! In producing the least decisive result of all in a generally confusing national decision the Region was reflecting its peripheral position in both the United Kingdom and Scotland. As we shall see, the apparent indecision of the electorate was evident also in the conflicting and confusing attitudes of the traditional mobilisers of public opinion - the local parties, Members of Parliament, Parliamentary candidates and the media.

On the face of it the Grampian Region might have been expected to produce a firm, positive vote for devolution. For more than 20 years the rural parts had been showing increasing dissatisfaction with Westminster government. In the early sixties the Liberals carried West Aberdeenshire, while in the early seventies Nationalists dislodged Unionist MPs from Moray & Nairn, Banffshire and East Aberdeenshire. In

October 1974, Russell Fairgrieve held West Aberdeenshire for Conservative with
barely a third of the votes, and his colleague, Alick Buchanan-Smith, counted himself fortunate to hold North Angus & Mearns against the SNP. In Aberdeen, the
threat of nationalism constrained the Labour MP in the North constituency, an
opponent of decentralisation, to make the proposed Scottish Assembly the most prominent item in his October election address. Even in South Aberdeen, a Conservative
seat marginally held from Labour, there was a substantial third-party vote.

It could not, however, be assumed that an apparent No to the United Kingdom was
the same as a Yes for Scotland. Peripheral discontent need not necessarily imply a
rejection of the centre, particularly, as in the Grampian case, when the centre
provides high levels of financial assistance. The defeat of the three Conservative
MPs could have been due more to failure to represent constituency interests than
to any fundamental opposition to the system. Furthermore, there is very little
similarity between the rural, small-town North-east, where even in October 1974
the Conservatives polled most votes, and the industrial West, dominated by Glasgow,
trade unions and the Labour Party. Thus, ironically, the spirit of Unionism, which
had been at a discount in 1974 for its failure to promote and defend regional interests, in 1979 emerged as the champion of local identity against the threat from
Scotland.

The Parties and the Campaign

Although there was a close relationship between the parties and the various campaigns, the degree of association was less than perfect. On the Conservative side,
while most activists were against devolution (and even more against the Scotland
Act), a significant minority in the rural Associations favoured the principle -
which, together with the need to outmanoeuvre the SNP, dictated a cautious public
stance. Within Labour ranks strong, probably majority, antipathy was tempered
by loyalty to national party policy. Such complications had important consequences
for the organisation and effectiveness of the respective campaigns and mavericks
amongst the MPs ensured that Labour and Conservative voters received contradictory
advice from their leaders. Within the SNP there was tension between the Home Rulers
and the fundamentalists but both groups supported the Act, if with varying enthusiasm.

The Conservatives and Scotland Says No. Conservative MPs and prospective candidates best exemplified the differences of opinion within the party and the state
of confusion which had descended on the subject of devolution following the change
in national leadership.

Buchanan-Smith, the party's senior Parliamentarian in the Region, demonstrated
that his party was no longer exclusively Unionist. Having strongly endorsed the
Declaration of Perth, and having served in Heath's Scottish Office, he had emerged
as a leading Tory federalist. His view of the need "for political control of the
administration within Scotland" as "the first vital step towards federalism" led
him to resign his post as Shadow Secretary of State for Scotland, to vote for the
second reading of the Scotland Bill and to abstain on the guillotine motion in
November 1977. During the Referendum campaign his heretical views were well publicised in the Aberdeen *Press and Journal* and *Evening Express*, and he held meetings
on his own account in North Angus & Mearns to urge a Yes vote.

Buchanan-Smith's somewhat Whiggish support contrasted sharply with the populist
opposition of Iain Sproat, Member for South Aberdeen, author of numerous amendments to the Bill and unequivocally hostile to the Act. "Devolution", he informed
an Aberdeen audience, "meant more government, more civil servants, red tape and
interference ... and powers taken away from Aberdeen and centralised in Edinburgh",

but even worse, "a Socialist-dominated Scotland ... whose leaders include Mick McGahey ∫the Communist miners' leader⌉, Jimmy Reid ∫ex-Communist co-organiser of the Govan Shipbuilders'sit-in⌉, and Alex Kitson ∫boss of the Scottish Transport Workers, who had favourably compared the advances of the Soviet working class with those of Britain⌉." However, Sproat alone of all the local Conservative MPs and prospective candidates campaigned actively for a No vote, so that his position was hardly less idiosyncratic than that of his Yes neighbour.

The regiment of "fearties" was led from behind by Fairgrieve, Chairman of the Scottish Conservative Party, and sometime federalist, who abstained on the Scot-land Bill's second reading and voted against the guillotine. He took no part in the campaign and only on the eve of poll when it was clear that public opinion was drifting towards a No did he declare that the Act was no more than a move by Labour to ditch the Nationalists and "had as little to do with devolution as Socialism has to do with prosperity". Prospective candidates took a similar line. Alex Pollock in Moray & Nairn pronounced the proposal "a bad Act"; it was "the correct form of devolution" that was needed. In Banffshire David Myles told a Craigellachie whist drive that although a No he wanted an "all-party conference". Perhaps the most reticent of all was Albert McQuarrie, facing the largest SNP majority, in East Aberdeenshire, who contributed virtually nothing to the debate. His one intervention was to move a vote of thanks at a No meeting addressed by Bob Boothby in Aberdeen, but this had more to do with his general election ambi-tions than with the Referendum.

Conservative councillors played little part in the campaign, although Regional Councillors Kelty and Sorrie expressed opposition through the local press. The most notable local government critic, predictably, was Sandy Mutch, leader of the party group on, and Convener of, Grampian Regional Council. He complained that £7M of rate support grant had already been switched from the North-east to the West and that he "held out no hope of a Strathclyde-dominated Assembly altering the trend".

The local Associations outside Aberdeen eschewed alliance with the No campaign, preferring to stay neutral or pursue a purely Conservative or obfuscatory course. This was exemplified by a letter from the Chairman of the Moray & Nairn Associ-ation to the local press. Denying that his party had adopted a neutral stance, he stated "we did not feel that some of the views being expressed by the umbrella 'Scotland Says No campaign' accorded with our views ... many of our members are not opposed to devolution" (but the Act), so "we have decided to distribute leaflets which give the Conservative point of view". In East Aberdeenshire there seems to have been a strong lobby within the local Association for a Yes vote, which forced the executive to deny the rumour and call for a No. North Angus & Mearns was neu-tralised out of deference to its devolutionary MP; so was West Aberdeenshire, by the vacillating ways of its MP and a number of leading activists. Consequent on the absence of effective party organisation in the Aberdeen North constituency, Scotland Says No was heavily dependent on the resources of Aberdeen South Con-servative Association and its crusading MP.

In early January 1979, some 20 persons attended an open non-party meeting in Aber-deen organised by leading members of the Chamber of Commerce to legitimise the local Scotland Says No organisation. Mrs Reid, wife of South Aberdeen's full-time Conservative agent, was elected director of the campaign. There was no committee, indicating the lack of any need to federate a variety of political interests and a desire not to publicise the narrow base of the organisation. Fergus Watt, former Chief Executive of Aberdeen District Council, offered his services on a "strict non-party basis", and was a tireless secretary in the somewhat luxurious head-quarters hired for the duration. Contacts were made by Mrs Reid with sympathisers outside the city (a hundred names were claimed) who were undoubtedly Conservatives, although there was a natural reluctance to reveal this. Failure to incorporate Labour Noes within Aberdeen was an obvious deficiency, and reflected the depth of social and political prejudice dividing the parties as well as the subordination of the issue to other political considerations. The task of the campaign was to ensure that Conservatives in the shires were given a more decisive lead than their local Associations could give, and to show Labour supporters that they could vote No with a good conscience.

Although the Noes held few meetings, those that they did organise were well attended, partly because they were well-publicised and partly because they took the form of confrontations between leading Yeses and Noes. About 70 people attended a meeting, chaired by Sandy Lyall of the Chamber of Commerce, to hear Tam Dalyell debate with Sandy Stronach, perennial SNP candidate in South Aberdeen. At Keith, another, organised with the assistance of Independent District Councillor Leonard Mann, under the chairmanship of the Chairman of Banffshire's NFU, brought Iain Sproat and Brian Wilson of the Labour Vote No campaign, in opposition to Hamish Watt, the local SNP Member of Parliament, and Steve Rodan, prospective Liberal candidate for Moray & Nairn, before an audience of 300. A similar occasion in Elgin, addressed by MPs Sproat and Dalyell on one side, and Rodan and Donald Barr, prospective SNP candidate for Inverness on the other, again proved popular. It appears from observation and a variety of witnesses that the Noes tended to get the better of the arguments. These meetings, which sought to indicate No sentiment within the Labour ranks, were supplemented by a more explicitly Conservative crusade by Sproat who took the cause to Huntly (West Aberdeenshire), where he addressed an audience of 50, and Stonehaven in the heart of Buchanan-Smith territory. It was he, too, who put fire into the Boothby meeting already mentioned – a barely concealed Conservative occasion.

The Noes were quite successful in organising the distribution of literature. Most households in the North-east received at least one communication but there was little evidence of the house-to-house canvass promised by Mrs Reid early in the proceedings. Advertising in the press and on poster sites (done nationally rather than locally) was moderately extensive. They clearly spent more than the Yeses but not inordinately so. The Noes also kept a close watch on correspondence in the local press so that national figures such as Dalyell, Lord Wilson of Langside, Brian Wilson and George Cunningham, MP, replied promptly to criticisms made in the most minor columns.

On polling day the limitations of the campaign were clearly evident. Outside Aberdeen a tour round the Region revealed a car parked outside the polling station at Macduff bearing the slogan "Vote No Thank You" as the solitary pressure placed on voters as they arrived to vote. In Aberdeen there were a number of cars at work in South Aberdeen during the evening, but, as Mrs Reid noted, this was in contrast to general elections when workers would have taken the whole day off work. In any event there were no canvass cards with which to locate No voters. What the Noes were relying on was the strength of No sentiment amongst the old and cosmopolitan professional classes to produce a high enough turnout to offset weakness elsewhere. They were so rewarded.

Labour and the Labour Movement Yes campaign. There was little indication of enthusiasm within Labour ranks for either the proposed Assembly or even the principle of devolution, but few were prepared to go as far as Bob Hughes, who, having supported the Bill in the Commons, associated himself with the Labour Vote No campaign. Nevertheless, he probably spoke for many party workers when he declared in the local press, in a piece piquantly placed alongside a Yes article by Buchanan-Smith, "I cannot claim to have had a consistent attitude to devolution over the years. I have been torn between my loyalty to the Labour Party and Government and my own analysis of the situation". He claimed that he "never accepted the proposition that conceding devolution would stem the tide of the SNP" but felt that the Assembly would prove "divisive" and that in order to tackle Scotland's economic and social problems "we need to have the support of our English colleagues and to retain their class solidarity".

Hughes's opposition typified the intransigence of the old working class oligarchy, consisting principally of his colleagues on the former Aberdeen Town Council and their friends in Aberdeen North who wanted no truck with any scheme designed to placate the Nationalists. A number of them had become part of a Labour rump on the Regional Council and must have realised that it was only through the reorganisation of local government by a Scottish Assembly that they could hope for the Tory Region to be abolished or its powers reduced (and thereby Labour values restored to the local administration of education and the social services). Despite this, they remained opposed to the proposed Assembly. Although this group was under pressure from younger members, including District Councillor Norman Bonney (an English sociology lecturer in his thirties and prospective candidate for East Aberdeenshire) to support the Act, the Constituency Party merely decided not to campaign for a No. With the Chairman and Secretary both firm anti-devolutionists this ensured that the Labour Yes effort in Aberdeen North, the only Labour seat in the Region, was effectively crippled.

Support for the Act was stronger in South Aberdeen where it was thought that the Nationalists had denied the Party victory in 1974 and the General Management Committee decided to campaign for a Yes. Aberdeen District Council, following a whipped vote within the controlling Labour group, also called for a positive vote. Significantly, the leaders of the group were predominantly young, English university lecturers of recent arrival, residing in Aberdeen South, which contrasted with the traditional Aberdonian working class establishment in Aberdeen North.

Somewhat tangential to the Labour Party stood the Aberdeen Trades Council, which had long ceased to be an arbiter in working class politics beyond providing a platform for non-Labour Party forces within the working-class movement (traditionally Communists, but more recently Nationalists and members of the Scottish Labour Party as well). Industrially it was more important, however. Predictably, the Trades Council endorsed a Yes and provided the link between the trade unions and the Labour Party for the conduct of the local Labour Movement Yes campaign.

Despite having a regional remit the *ad hoc* committee charged with running the Labour-STUC campaign found that the collapse of the Party outside Aberdeen served to confine their activities to the city. The Chairman, David Clyne, appropriately straddled both sides of the movement as an AUEW delegate to the Trades Council, Chairman of Grampian Regional Labour Party, and Secretary to Aberdeen District Labour Party. He was assisted by Regional Councillor Bob Middleton, a post office engineer, 1974 candidate in South Aberdeen, member of the Scottish Party's Executive Committee and a latter-day convert to the devolutionist cause. The District Council leader, John Sewell, an English academic in his thirties, gave moral support, and he was joined by Iain Elrick of the University Labour Club, Mrs Panko, a technical college lecturer from suburban West Aberdeenshire, and Regional Councillor Eric Hendrie, a draughtsman and strong devolutionist from North Aberdeen. The Trades Council delegation was headed by executive member Jimmy Allardice, an SLP member, Maggie Havergal, a NALGO Hospital Administrator who had been associated with the SNP, and three others possessing a similar nationalist left-wing bias. Although there were conflicts of interest between the Labour and non-Labour members in that both sides hoped to gain from a Yes vote amongst the same clientèle, Labour influence proved dominant, and was able to override SLP objections to a leaflet entitled "Vote for Labour's Scottish Assembly".

The appeal of this campaign, emphasising the need for greater control over the

Scottish administration and a weakening of centralising tendencies, was the most sophisticated because it was neither nationalist nor Unionist, and democratic rather than socialist. "Socialism", said Clyne in the press, "half-way through this century got a wee bit paternalistic and less democratic and you got this idea that everything had to be done through Westminster. Now the emphasis by people like me within the Labour movement is that we are democratic socialists. We are democrats first ... you've got to view the Scotland Bill as an extension of democracy ... Once the rest of the UK see this happening ... you'll have a series of Assemblies taking this kind of work over from Westminster." But was this appeal, similar to Buchanan-Smith's, understood, let alone shared, by the working class electorate to whom it was directed?

The centre piece of the Labour-STUC campaign was a meeting in Aberdeen attended by some hundred persons under the slogan "United We Stand". On the platform, presided over by Clyne, were MPs Michael Foot, Bruce Millan and Dick Mabon, plus Jimmy Milne of the STUC and behind them sat the local Yes committee and Helen Liddell. Absent, however, from this show of solidarity was the whole of the District Labour group, who refused to postpone their caucus meeting, and half-way down the hall sat a rejectionist front of Labour Regional Councillors with their cronies, which added a certain irony to Milne's opening remarks that "rarely are the Trade Union Movement and Labour Party in agreement", as they were deemed to be on that occasion. The burden of the arguments presented was that the Labour movement had always been devolutionary, with Michael Foot commending federalism in the USA as an expression of democracy, and Bruce Millan stating there was a need for more political control over the Scottish Office. Missing from the pantheon of Labour Home Rulers invoked before the audience was Ramsay MacDonald, who had, after all, been Secretary of the London Home Rule Association and was a native of the North-east.

More prosaically, the committee decided to distribute 5,000 to 10,000 STUC leaflets in workplaces, and a Labour leaflet to households. This task, however, proved difficult to implement as there was a great gulf between institutional support and individual commitment. Clyne claimed that the trade union effort hardly existed outside his own AUEW, and that the T&GWU and GMWU, despite being the unions which had forced devolution on to a reluctant Labour Party in Scotland, did nothing locally. He was also bitter that South Aberdeen, whose part-time agent was a No, contrary to their resolution to "campaign", failed to mobilise their electoral machine for the Referendum. Consequently, given the position in Aberdeen North, leafleting was mostly confined to some working-class parts of South Aberdeen. The shortage of workers was such that on polling day there were fewer helpers than in a recently held District Council by-election where the winning Labour candidate had secured fewer than 450 votes. The Labour Movement Yes campaign was in truth a paper tiger.

The SNP, the Yes for Scotland campaign and others. It was the SNP rather than the Labour Party which was committed to campaign for a Yes and, despite fundamentalist distaste for devolution, the more moderate Home Rule bias of Hamish Watt, MP for Banffshire and his daughter Maureen (standing in North Aberdeen) became the public position, because for them all a No would constitute a bitter psychological blow in election year.

There was a tendency for the SNP to eschew the umbrella Yes campaign for, as with the city Labour Party, it had little desire to give others credit for the Act. Consequently, in West Aberdeenshire for example, Dr Hulbert (prospective SNP candidate) addressed more than half a dozen meetings supported solely by Nationalist speakers, including Regional Councillor Coull of Peterhead, and advertised as partisan occasions in the press. Again, in East Aberdeenshire, where the party described the Assembly as "an important step in the right direction", Douglas Henderson's meetings were held under the sign of the thistle, as they were in Kincardineshire.

Even in Moray & Nairn, where there was co-operation with the umbrella Yeses, Mrs Ewing,MP,also spoke under exclusively Nationalist auspices; and in Aberdeen the concluding highlight of the non-Labour campaign was a rally organised by the SNP addressed by Henderson and Colin Bell, a journalist standing for the party in the forthcoming EEC elections. Consequently, the case for devolution presented in the rural areas was predominantly the Nationalist one: that the Assembly was a step on the road to independence.

Despite limited funds the SNP communicated with most of the rural voters. Enthusiasm for the campaign and commitment were, however, somewhat restricted amongst Nationalists and their supporters. The number of meetings held was substantially below that of general elections and attendances were small, while concentration on the iniquities of the 40 per cent rule and errors in the register suggested a lack of confidence in the result. The almost total absence of party activity on polling day was relieved only in Huntly where the owner of "Black Donald's Craft Shop" ferried SNP members to the polls. Even in Peterhead, the centre of Grampian nationalism, the only evidence of SNP activity was a couple of Yes posters outside one of the stations.

The Liberals made a minor contribution in that their candidate in West Aberdeenshire addressed the odd meeting calling for a Yes, and his constituency party placed advertisements in the local press. Beyond that, they were strongly associated with the Moray umbrella Yes and marginally so in Aberdeen. Communist participation was virtually non-existent, although they had a couple of posters prominently displayed in Peterhead and Bucksburn declaring: "Scottish Communists Say Vote Yes", which would seem to have clinched Sproat's arguments. The SLP concentrated their meagre resources on Yes For Scotland.

Yes For Scotland appears to have been established principally through SLP contacts in Elgin and Aberdeen, for the secretary and organiser of the North campaign, respectively Elgin schoolmaster Danus Skene, former member of Labour's Scottish Executive and Chairman of the Aberdeen District campaign, and lecturer Bob Tait, exoffice holder in Aberdeen North SNP, were both SLPers. Significantly, the activities of the umbrella Yes were confined to Moray and Aberdeen North.

The Yes campaign in Moray was characterised by considerable co-operation between members of the non-Conservative parties, although Labour was officially neutral. At a meeting chaired by Skene and addressed by Lord Kilbrandon and Winifred Ewing were Dr Scobie (Labour) and Steven Rodan (Liberal), prospective Parliamentary candidates in the constituency. Bi-partisanship was also in evidence when Skene shared a platform with the Nationalist, Donald Barr, and at another gathering the Liberals and SLP supplied the speakers. After the campaign, the chairman of the Moray Liberals was to describe the Nationalists on the committee as "a pleasure to work with". Although their resources were small and their meetings sometimes poorly attended, their speeches were well-reported in the press and they themselves were not slow to issue press releases and write letters to ensure their case was heard. They were not, however, particularly visible on polling day.

The Aberdeen contingent, formally headed by its president, Professor Robin Barbour, Moderator-designate of the Church of Scotland, included, in addition to Tait, District Councillor Forbes McCallum, 1974 Liberal opponent to Hughes; a Young Conservative, Brian Davidson; Regional Councillor Hendrie and Jimmy Allardice, who provided informal links with the LMY committee; George Rodger, part-time agent of South Aberdeen SNP and Maureen Watt, the real driving force behind the group who sought to embarrass Hughes through this campaign as part of her run-up to the General Election. A major problem for this group was finance, as it was expected to find funds not only for its own effort but for the national campaign as well. Responsibilities were divided between the various parties, which meant that the Liberals concentrated on their own local government wards and the SNP elsewhere.

So slender were campaign funds that YFS activities were semi-clandestine. Its meetings, for example, were not advertised (and hence not reported) in the press. Instead notices were pushed through several hundred doors in the vicinity of each venue, all of which were in North Aberdeen. Attendances were chronically bad - 10, seven, six, six and 10, respectively (including the speakers, chairman, and this observer) - and consisted almost exclusively of SNP members. Miss Watt was the ubiquitous main speaker with occasional support from McCallum, Hendrie and Tait. Her appeal, which was Home Rule in character, tended to stress the social benefits which would derive from the Assembly, and that it would operate on the basis of non-partisan consensus:"what was best for the people of Scotland", rejecting the adversarial politics of Westminster. She also foresaw further devolution within Scotland itself. By far the most interesting speech of the whole campaign, however, came from Councillor Hendrie, because it indicated that nationalism was by no means a prerogative of the SNP. Having commended the Church of Scotland and the superior qualities of the Scottish educational system, he continued: "I care about our Scottish heritage being increasingly Anglicised ... Give us in Scotland a new pride and sense of purpose ... they (the critics) speak of a slippery slope to separation - 'Separation' has always irritated me! Why don't they say independence? ... We had our traitors in 1707. We have their counterparts today - Cunningham must be one; Dalyell - they are the modern Quislings".

On polling day YFS did some trawling in council housing estates but with such limited means it was unable to make a great impact. Very little was attempted in Aberdeen South where the local SNP leadership was little enamoured of devolution. It was, of course, the activists within YFS who were most depressed by the result which was probably a mortal blow to what was left of the SLP.

The Media

The regional and local media in the absence of official campaign appeals on television played a creditable part in communicating the varying viewpoints. In Aberdeen the *Press and Journal* and the *Evening Express* provided wide coverage. Editorially, however, they gave no strong lead, although in the end the *P&J*, whose official policy was pro-devolution but anti-separation, curiously came out for a weak No. Grampian Television operated in a more minor key, but on the eve of poll there was a long programme "Scotland: the vital decision", during which Northern MPs Johnston, Wilson, Fairgrieve, Hughes and Ewing, together with Alan Devereux of the Scottish CBI,discussed the issues.

Of particular importance in the rural North-east is the local press. It helps to sustain the role of local community and political leaders, and during the Referen dum campaign their columns carried extensive correspondence, reports of major meetings, advertisements from the warring factions and in some cases forthright leading articles.

Editorial policy was particularly evident in the *Buchan Observer* (Peterhead), whose Unionist sympathies were unambiguous. "Just as Paddy's troubles stem mainly from the partition of Ireland", opined its editor to a strongly Protestant readership, "are we now in the first throes of divisiveness in Scotland - a breeding ground for irreconcilables on a national scale?" The paper further quoted with some relish a speech of Henderson's indicating that "the present proposals for devolution should be regarded as phase one in a scheme for the transfer of powers to Edinburgh". More graphically, the *Observer* twice published a *Scotsman* map showing two Assemblymen standing by Peterhead and serried ranks near Glasgow, while it described the method of finance as "a bottomless purse, a girnal with the lid off". The paper also gave prominence to Boothby's No. Similarly, the *Fraserburgh Herald*, referring to nationalism as "the cancerous growth eating away the body politic", suggested, "we may live to regret the Scotland Act of 1978".

By contrast, the *Banffshire Journal* (Banff) in endorsing the Act made an overtly
nationalist case for it: "This newspaper sincerely believes in the basic right of
a nation, large or small, to have a measure of self-government should the people
of such a nation desire it ... We look forward to the opportunity for a Scots
Assembly being the first step on the path of Scotland taking her rightful place as
a self-governing nation." In West Aberdeenshire, the *Inverurie and District Advertiser*, together with her East Aberdeenshire sisters, the *Ellon and District Advertiser* and the *Turriff and District Advertiser*, called for a Yes but on the basis of
a Home Rule appeal when, under the slogan "Half a Loaf Better than None", the editor
wrote: "We fully support the idea of a directly elected Scottish Assembly sitting
in Edinburgh dealing with purely domestic affairs".

Other papers eschewed firm advice. The *Northern Scot* (Elgin) carried a leader
which an independent observer might have felt was biased to the Noes, but a subsequent letter from a Morayshire Liberal evidently did not think so - "As one of the
Liberals closely associated with the Yes campaign, I should like to pay tribute to
you for your very fair and impartial coverage". Similarly the *Banffshire Journal*
(Keith) devoted much space to the debate without committing itself decisively.
Somewhat cursory attention to the campaign was paid by the *Forres, Elgin and Nairn
Gazette* and by the *Banffshire Advertiser* in Nationalist Buckie. Least attention of
all, however, was paid by the *Mearns Leader* (Stonehaven) and the *Kincardineshire
Observer* (Laurencekirk), whose charting of the campaign was confined to the adver-
tising of meetings and the odd letter.

Conclusion

The seven constituencies wholly or in part within the Grampian Region, with the
very recent exception of South Aberdeen, have never been noted for high levels of
participation in either local or national elections, and, to the extent that any
area can have a collective persona, it could be said that its voters know what they
are against without knowing what they are for. Thus, for example, while the Conservatives now hold six Parliamentary seats, it is with only 39.4 per cent of the
poll. The reluctance of the party machines to commit their resources to the Referendum battle and the disinclination of activists to associate themselves with the
formal campaigns, indicated not only divisions within the parties, uncertainty as
to the likely result and its consequences, but also the genuine indecision of the
public at large. As with the EEC referendum, which produced the same turnout, the
economic advantages and disadvantages of saying Yes or No were more difficult to
determine in this peripheral area than in central Scotland.

To the extent that a decision was made, the result in the context of 1979 was a
triumph for the *cartel des nons*, and especially for the Conservatives. Iain Sproat
and his colleagues could justly claim party credit for having secured a No majority
and for breaking SNP morale on the eve of a critical General Election. In Aberdeen
North, Hughes was to crush Maureen Watt into third place, increasing his vote and
majority substantially, while the SLP challenge to his centralising values failed
to materialise; and by contrast the devolutionary Labour Party in the South was to
see Sproat's slender majority doubled.

On the other hand, the Yeses could claim with some justification that not all the
Noes were against devolution, particularly as Fairgrieve and prospective Conservative candidates drew a distinction between the principle (which they favoured) and
the Act (which they opposed). Furthermore, Buchanan-Smith not only increased his
general election vote by more than 50 per cent, but the improvement in his share
of the poll (+13.9 per cent) was more than twice that of any other Conservative in

the Region except McQuarrie (+7.3 per cent) in East Aberdeenshire. It is difficult to believe that this was entirely unrelated to his devolutionary stance.

The decisive element in the Referendum result was undoubtedly the attitude of the Labour voters in Aberdeen, for, had they sided with the SNP, Liberals and less numerous Conservative Yeses, there would have been a positive conclusion. But, coming at a time when the credibility of the government and the unions was at its lowest ebb, and with the local MP against the Assembly, there was little to induce Labour Noes to stand by the national policy of their Party. Nevertheless, on the most reasonable assumptions, it appears that the Labour vote was biased against rejection. As in Scotland as a whole, Labour was exposed on its unionist as well as nationalist flank and failed to propound the unique advantages of an Assembly.

Looking to the future, the assumption that devolution is dead could well prove premature. The Referendum in the Grampian Region, as in Scotland as a whole, is not an isolated event but one of a series in two decades of profound political change, and, whatever its influence on future developments may be, one doubts whether it is the final verdict on Scottish nationalism and peripheral discontent.

II. DUNDEE

John Berridge and Mona Clark

The city's two parliamentary constituencies (Dundee East and Dundee West) each have approximately 65,000 electors and show roughly the same socio-economic patterns – patches of solidly owner-occupied areas scattered over the constituencies and large council housing estates on their Northern fringes. In addition, Dundee East includes an area virtually all middle and upper-middle-class owner-occupiers, who still see themselves as a separate unit with a community identity, though the area was long ago absorbed into the city. It is this area, Broughty Ferry, with its large amount of recently built private housing full of younger electors who tend to be floating voters, which provided the Nationalists with the support enabling them to hold the seat. Gordon Wilson won Dundee East for the SNP from Labour in February 1974 and has held it since, the SNP share of the vote averaging around 42 per cent. In the West constituency, Labour have held the seat since it was created in 1950. The Liberal Party, which has fought intermittently in general election campaigns, has achieved in both constituencies, although on different occasions, almost five per cent of the vote.

Initially, therefore, one would assume that, on the basis of the normal electoral support for the three parties fighting for a Yes vote, the 40 per cent requirement would have been fulfilled. However, the SNP vote in Dundee was an unknown quantity. Conservative Party canvasses had shown many Conservative voters defecting to the SNP for tactical reasons, seeing no prospect of a Conservative victory. This was particularly evident in Dundee East, where the Conservative share of the vote had fallen from 42 per cent in 1970 to just under 17 per cent in October 1974. How these Tory defectors would vote in the Referendum was an open question, since, when it came to the crunch, they seemed to be strongly pro-union and anti-Assembly.

There was also some doubt about the Labour vote: despite the Party's strong public commitment, basic, deeply-held centralist philosophies were likely to conflict with party loyalties on polling day. And the SNP recognised with some trepidation that a percentage of committed SNP supporters might vote No, fearing that the Act was likely to create a "historic compromise" which could defeat their ultimate aim. All three parties therefore found their traditional electoral machines shackled - they could identify their normal supporters easily enough, but could not in this instance be sure they were getting out the votes they wanted. These factors were not restricted to Dundee but might well have had greater significance in a Region with three of the 11 seats which the SNP had at that time.

The SNP Campaign

The SNP ran two separate constituency campaigns because of their organisational structure. The branch is the basic unit, with the constituencies exercising a general co-ordinative but not controlling role which becomes more definite during a national campaign. The practice is to use branch manpower as a "flying squad" to cover those areas of the constituency where there are no branches - Dundee West, for instance, has only three branches.

One would have expected SNP activists to be the most dedicated and enthusiastic in the Referendum. But the deep division which was evident in sections of the Party was a powerful factor in Dundee: one activist said that he was quite unable to "arouse the faithful" to work because of it. It was common ground within the SNP that the Scotland Act itself was atrocious, but, whilst some held that it was so bad it was not worth fighting for, others maintained that, bad as it was, it was the first step. There were other complications - resentment at having to "pull Callaghan's chestnuts out of the fire" (reflecting opinion in the Party that the Labour Government had no real commitment to devolution and was using it only as a device for survival), and some slight anxiety that, if the Act worked, it might make the SNP's job more difficult. So, though it was decided to work as hard as possible for a Yes vote, the enthusiasm of the workers was not as high as it might have been. In particular, they were reluctant to canvass: asking people to vote for an Act which the canvassers despised stuck in their throats. The result was that, whilst the SNP probably canvassed to a greater extent than the other parties, they did not do very much, both constituencies concentrating on leafleting, street speaking and the use of loudspeaker vans.

For these purposes they had a bigger workforce than any other party or group, especially in Dundee West. The East Chairman said that they had not nearly as many workers as in a general election, due perhaps to the reluctance of dissident Conservatives in Broughty Ferry to help. The West, however, reckoned on a leafleting force of over 200 - far above anyone else, except possibly the Labour Party, which had the trade unions to call on, and they were not all that enthusiastic.

Consequently the SNP were relatively successful in their leaflet coverage; certainly we found no evidence that their quite modest claim of one leaflet per household - 33,000 in the West and 38,000 in the East - was unsubstantiated. Such canvassing as they carried out suggested Yes majorities, even in Tory areas, though there the "don't knows" were higher in number.

Both constituencies were responsible for their own finance, with no subventions or free material from national headquarters. In the West, the SNP constituency organisation held back the January edition of its regular broadsheet *Focus*, turned it into a Referendum special and distributed it to every household. No other leaflets were distributed to houses, though Jim Fairlie (the prospective Parliamentary candidate) did a good deal of street-corner speaking with a loudspeaker van whilst helpers distributed leaflets to passing citizenry. There were few formal public meetings, though Fairlie spoke at a meeting organised by the Yes for Scotland group, not otherwise active in Dundee. The West made no attempt at a "general election" organisation on the day - no school gates manned, no throwaways or placards at polling stations, no cars picking up voters.

Apart from the cars, the same comment about SNP polling day activity was true in Dundee East. They had plenty of cars on the day though they had fewer requests for lifts than in a general election. One placard was placed at each polling station but the gates were not manned. During the run-up they also had delivered leaflets to every house and Gordon Wilson had been active with a loudspeaker van and in street meetings. For financial reasons they did not run a big poster campaign, although they advertised on the buses and fairly intensively in the local press. They particularly resented the Dundee *Courier*'s refusal, possibly as a result of No group representations, to include in a large advertisement paid for and signed by some 130 people of all political persuasions, the phrase "Remember, if you don't vote, it's counted as a 'NO' ". But they did have another advertisement accepted which one would have expected to be challenged under the *Courier*'s interpretation of what is "propaganda" and therefore not allowable under "Public Notices". That advert stated categorically: "The Assembly will do away with the Regions", a prescience other parties dared not share.

SNP observers at the count were emphatic that Dundee City had recorded a pronounced majority Yes vote, an impression shared by observers from the other side. The West Chairman claimed that in ballot boxes from some of the estates the Yes vote had been as high as 80 per cent, and even in the Tory areas there was a majority. Senior activists maintain that subsequent inquiries suggested it was the country areas, especially Perth & East Perthshire, that had voted the other way. The SNP

attributed the "anti" vote to anxiety about costs, more bureaucracy and "an extra
tier of government" (the themes constantly reiterated by the No camp). At many
meetings in the campaign we heard these "facts" asserted time after time, though
never substantiated, and they undoubtedly had a major effect.

The Labour Campaign

The City Labour Party felt no need to take a formal decision to campaign for a Yes
vote: "It was never in question that we would fight on the national party line".
From the start some members of the Party were opposed, would remain opposed, and
might even work for the No campaign - Peter Doig, the Labour MP for Dundee West,
was an uncompromising opponent of devolution - but no pressure apart from strong
moral disapproval was put upon them. The campaign was launched in Dundee in December 1978 when Gordon Brown, Chairman of the Labour Movement Yes Campaign for Scotland, attended the first meeting of the Dundee campaign committee - a sub-committee
of Labour's Executive Committee led by George Galloway, the energetic full-time
Secretary/Organiser of the City Party. At this meeting Brown outlined the way the
Scottish Council of the Labour Party saw the campaign being conducted and what help
would be available.

In the main, constituencies were expected to raise their own funds and to provide
their own material. The linking theme, the slogan "*Labour*'s Scottish Assembly", was
to appear on all campaign literature. Apart from the important strategic benefits
to the Labour Party which could develop from the devolution programme and which the
government did not intend to share with any other party, Labour organisers were
frightened that SNP support for the Yes campaign was scaring off people who were
normally Labour supporters. It was therefore vital to remind voters continually
that this was *Labour*'s Assembly and was not to be confused with anything the SNP
had in mind. The second basic decision followed from this: it was decided to campaign alone and to have nothing to do with the SNP, whose informal approaches suggesting a joint programme were instantly rejected. Less curtly, but no less definitely, the Liberals' approach was also turned down and a formal offer of help from
the Communist Party was also refused, though it was pointed out that Communist
Party members who were trade unionists could help, if they wished, as individuals
through their union.

Detailed tactics were planned at this meeting. Canvassing, difficult anyway with
the possibility of bad weather and without a candidate as a focal point, was to be
concentrated on old-age pensioners, a group which the Party felt might have been
more worried than others by anti-Assembly propaganda. Meetings were to be held in
schools (each immediately preceded by £25 worth of local press advertising and the
distribution of 500 leaflets in the area), at factory gates and shopping centres,
and there would be one major meeting addressed by a national figure. Finally, the
Labour Vote No campaign was to be attacked vigorously.

The Labour campaign stayed within these basic guidelines, with the exception of the
last, abandoned because it took time which could be more profitably used elsewhere
and because the Labour Vote No movement in Dundee was minimal. It might have been
ignored altogether but for the big No meeting which they organised at the start of
the campaign, though the matter was personalised for many Labour activists by the
fact that the man running the Labour Vote No campaign, William McKenzie, when a
Labour candidate in the District Council elections, had declared himself strongly
in favour of devolution in his manifesto, but subsequently as a Parliamentary candidate had persuaded his General Management Committee not to support devolution.

The "bread and butter" tactic was to be leaflet distribution. Dundee Labour Party
had designed and printed 70,000 copies of their own Yes leaflet and they had 25,000
copies of the LMY leaflet and 15,000 T&GWU broadsheets, both free. To this was added

(when they heard that Tony Benn, MP, was coming) 15,000 leaflets printed and distributed especially for his meeting.

The city was treated as a whole as far as the Labour campaign was concerned, the result of which was that most of the meetings, at schools and factory gates, were held, as it happened, in Dundee West. This could be interpreted as a concentration on the Labour seat because the SNP could be relied on to campaign vigorously in Gordon Wilson's constituency but it does not seem to have been a deliberate strategy. The factory gate meetings in any case were addressed to a work force drawn from all over the city, as were the audiences at the two larger meetings. One of these was a bonus; since Andy Bevan, the Youth Organiser of the Labour Party, was in the area, he was asked to do a meeting supported by the Parliamentary candidates, local councillors, the Labour Party Research Officer Joe Handy and Vic Selway, who was a T&GWU National Executive member and a bus worker in Dundee. But the high spot of the campaign was the meeting addressed by Tony Benn.

Galloway had gone after Benn from the start, after the decision to hold one major meeting round a national figure. When he agreed to come the news was received with delight by the Party and regarded as something of a *coup*. They planned the day - February 27 - carefully to get the most out of Benn's visit. The meeting - with prospective Parliamentary candidates Ernie Ross and Jimmy Reid supporting - was attended by 800, according to Labour's estimate, and Benn went on to open Whitfield Labour Club in Dundee East where he spoke to another 250.

The Conservative Involvement

In contrast to Labour and the SNP, the Conservative Associations, as Associations, were not major actors in the campaign. The minutes of the two Executive Committees imply that the East "opted out" and the West "opted in"; what actually happened was much the same in both constituencies.

The Secretary of Dundee West Executive minuted on January 24, 1979: "Mr Ian Stevenson suggested we threw our lot in with the 'No' campaign which Mrs Barbara Vaughan is to organise". That was precisely what happened; the Association did nothing, but some members were very active in the No campaign.

The minute also throws some light on the driving force behind the West Conservative effort: Ian Stevenson, their prospective Parliamentary candidate and a shrewd and experienced political campaigner, was well aware that any electoral-type activity in which the West workers could be persuaded to engage was potentially very valuable in reinforcing his image and oiling the electoral machine.

In Dundee East the situation was more complicated. At an Executive Meeting on December 1 (before the option of inviting members to work for umbrella groups was available) the Chairman made it clear that the Executive could commit the Association either way if someone else would do the organising. Despite pressure from Conservative Central Office in Edinburgh, neither he nor the Secretary was prepared to do so, or indeed to work for either side; both were strong devolutionists who had worked on Tory Party committees on devolution but both had a hearty dislike of this Act.

However, though the Executive was mostly anti-Assembly, no one was prepared or able to find the time or effort to run a campaign. By the next Executive Meeting the "umbrella" groups were under way and members were invited to contact Mrs Vaughan (the SSN organiser) or, in the absence of any approach from the Alliance for an Assembly, advised to contact Alick Buchanan-Smith, MP for North Angus & Mearns, who was known to be active in that group.

No attempt was made by the Yes groups to enlist help from either Association and, as far as is known, no one worked for them. Some East activists volunteered or were recruited to help the No group, however. The end result was much the same for both Conservative Associations - neither ran a campaign of their own but a number of activists from both East and West worked under the No umbrella.

Few Conservatives in Dundee entered the fray with crusading zeal and neither East nor West Association had a paid agent, upon whom Central Office pressure could have put a stronger obligation. Those in business or commerce or who were Regional or District councillors tended to be more emphatic in their opposition to the Assembly and more determined in their work. One factor helped both Labour and Conservatives to persuade people to work - they were on opposite sides and any doubts activists in either party may have had about their party line on the Assembly were easily repressed as they fell into the familiar task of fighting the old enemy.

The Liberal Campaign

The Liberal Party's participation in the campaign was very modest, though a determined initial effort was made in Dundee East by Charles Brodie, the prospective Parliamentary candidate and Vice-Chairman of the Party in Scotland. Recognising the financial and organisational strains which three election-type campaigns in three months would put upon the Liberals' slender resources in Dundee, Brodie wrote to Gordon Wilson and Jimmy Reid, suggesting the three parties shared a platform. Wilson replied regretting previous commitments prevented him from sharing speaking engagements, but suggesting a joint advertisement. No reply was received from Jimmy Reid or his agent, and Galloway, after checking with Glasgow, stated that the Labour Party had decided to decline the suggestion. The idea was therefore abandoned, though a joint advertisement appeared the day before polling day.

Brodie found difficulty mobilising Liberal activists. The existence of the umbrella organisations led to a vague assumption that they would do the work. But some Liberal activists felt that they should add something to the effort since they considered themselves, with some justification, as the party with the longest-standing commitment to devolution.

Concentrating on Broughty Ferry, where it was felt the chief Liberal support lay, they distributed about 10,000 leaflets (free from the Alliance for an Assembly and Liberal Central Office). On the day, they managed to keep some polling station gates manned and gave lifts to the polls to anyone willing to go, as it appeared to be in the interests of the Yes campaigners to get as many people as possible to the polls. This was the extent of the Liberal campaign; they had no canvass, no meetings, no visiting speakers, no loudspeaker van and no posters. Virtually all the Liberal activity was in Dundee East, which had a Liberal Parliamentary candidate who was clearly the key figure in the activity and had been geared up for an election since October 1978. The West had no candidate, was not intending to contest the General Election and had lost some of its leading personalities for reasons unconnected with politics. Brodie felt after the event that the Yes campaign had failed to secure sufficient votes because people had voted against an unpopular and discredited government whose motives for holding the Referendum were suspect, and because the contest had increasingly been seen, unlike the 1975 referendum on EEC membership, as a party political contest between the two major parties.

The Communist Party

The Communist Party organisation in Dundee is openly pragmatic; where there are enough members a locality or factory branch is formed - an East End branch, a Camperdown branch, etc. The branches together form a Dundee Area with an Area

Executive and Committee and the Areas together constitute a District - in this case Scotland. Ironically, the only Party which dares to call Scotland a "District" claims a long-standing commitment to devolution, going back to a pamphlet issued in 1935. In line with this the Scottish District Committee decided to campaign for a Yes vote and, by joining up with other parties similarly inclined, to form a "broad front". In Dundee this strategy was frustrated at an early stage, as both the Labour Party and the SNP refused to co-operate. According to the Communists' Area Secretary this presented a major problem, since many party members in Dundee were also members of the Labour Party (sic) and would be more likely mobilised through that Party. An attempt to circumvent the difficulty by using shop stewards who were members of the Communist Party met with little success - "We detected little enthusiasm amongst the shop stewards". The Communist effort in the Referendum was therefore limited. Their two public meetings, despite valiant efforts to drum up an audience, failed to attract the public and in one case, with an audience of four, to draw even the faithful who loyally provided 20 members at the other meeting. Nevertheless, the Party claimed to have distributed 20,000 leaflets supplied by the Scottish Committee, mainly in Dundee West.

Scotland Says No

Of the "umbrella" groups fighting the campaign, only one made any impression in Dundee - the Scotland Says No group. It was organised locally by a Conservative activist from South Angus, Mrs Barbara Vaughan, a lecturer in Economics at the College of Technology in Dundee. She had written to the campaign headquarters in Glasgow offering to drop leaflets in areas of the city which she judged, as they were Conservative strongholds, should produce No votes because of party loyalty.

Within a few days of her offer Mrs Vaughan found herself regarded as the "organiser" of the all-party No campaign in Dundee. Although she received a list from Glasgow of proffered assistance, which included local people who had responded to press advertisements for help, in the event the nucleus of the Dundee group consisted of approximately six real activists, including Ian Stevenson, the Conservative Parliamentary candidate for Dundee West, and another ten or so helpers, mainly from Dundee West Conservative Association. The Conservative candidate for Dundee East, Brian Townsend, although speaking at two meetings organised by SSN, was hardly involved, partly because of business commitments and partly because his own Executive was not as a body taking part in either campaign.

The Labour Vote No group made no move to contact Mrs Vaughan and she decided not to pursue their participation. However, Peter Doig, Labour MP for Dundee West, was prepared to speak on the SSN platform, as was James Gourlay, a lecturer from Kingsway Technical College. Although a staunch Labour supporter he had left the City Labour Party some years previously and had stood as a "Christian Democratic Labour" candidate against official Labour in the February 1974 General Election. Other "notables" on the local No committee were the ex-Principal of Dundee University, Professor James Drever and District Councillor, Miss Elizabeth Turley, who sat as an Independent but in fact had strong known Labour sympathies.

The SSN in Dundee was given virtually a clear field by the Glasgow headquarters as to how it ran the campaign and what money it spent. Any bills incurred were sent to Glasgow. As the national campaign was being organised by a retired Conservative constituency agent, the considerable degree of freedom to decide where and how resources should be allocated is probably explained by Mrs Vaughan's and Ian Stevenson's "legitimacy" within the Conservative Party and therefore obvious respectability in the eyes of the leading organisers.

All printed material was supplied from Glasgow, but the local group had a free rein in press advertising and in organising meetings. Within a short time complete press advertising for Tayside was left to the Dundee group, since the neighbouring Conservative Associations of South Angus, North Angus & Mearns, Dundee East and Perth & East Perthshire had decided to opt out of the official Tory campaign or to keep a low profile. (In North Angus & Mearns the sitting Conservative MP, Alick Buchanan-Smith, was a leading member of AFA.)

Advertising was put out through the *Courier and Advertiser* because it was considered to have the biggest circulation of any paper in the Region. The group were fortunate in having the unequivocal support of the city press but, since they felt their greatest impact would be achieved by emphasising their a-political role, they decided to run a distinctive a-political press campaign, aiming to get every day in the *Courier* an advertisement, letter, statement or report of a meeting. For example, the group released a survey undertaken during the last week of the campaign. It was published on Monday, February 26, to get publicity after a weekend in which no other activity took place. (The survey, which purported to have a sample size of 552, revealed that 48 per cent of Dundonians would vote No.)

Five public meetings were organised. No canvassing was undertaken, despite press reports suggesting there had been: there was just not the workforce available. Four leaflets were distributed - two SSN leaflets, put out in various parts of the city normally voting Conservative where support might exist, one leaflet written personally by Peter Doig, put out in the Labour stronghold of Menzieshill housing scheme, and another leaflet specifically written from the Conservative Party point of view, put out in Conservative-held wards. Conservative Regional and District Councillors were asked to distribute these, although it was admitted there was no way of establishing whether this was done in every case. However, the group estimated that 65 per cent of the city had had at least one No leaflet drop, a surprisingly high percentage considering the paucity of help.

SSN had their headquarters in an empty shop in the town centre. It was manned, theoretically, from 10 a.m. to 9 p.m. every day by at least one activist. Its real value was seen to be its role in advertising the group's presence and emphasising the all-party approach. It also proved to be useful for the dissemination of information. Inquiries at the shop reinforced evidence from public meetings that there was a great deal of confusion and lack of understanding about the Scotland Act. Having a telephone number through which people could establish contact also proved valuable, particularly on voting day, when a car transport scheme was operated.

In the final analysis, the value of the work done by the Scotland Says No campaign appeared to be that they were observed to be actually fighting on the ground, and were seen to be active in an area which had a popular sitting SNP MP in Gordon Wilson. This was considered to have drawn out No voters who might otherwise have stayed at home. The group had also strongly and persistently publicly refuted the "no vote is a No vote" assertion. At the outset of the campaign they had complained to the *Courier* that an SNP advertisement making this assertion was propaganda and a deliberate misrepresentation of the facts. The *Courier* was asked to publish an official statement from the group in answer to the SNP; not only did they do so but also made the SNP retract the assertion from a later advert.

There is no doubt that SSN was genuinely willing to adopt a cross-party approach, although in fact the personnel were overwhelmingly Conservative. The group was therefore able to capitalise not only on the anti-SNP feelings amongst Conservative supporters, but, because of its apparent all-party stance, to bring out Labour No votes. It also received help from two admitted SNP supporters, as well as a few Liberals working incognito. Those who discussed their reasons for supporting the No campaign were generally worried by the apparent cost and level of bureaucracy which the proposed Assembly might produce. But the group also felt they had tapped a definite "gut reaction" to the SNP's activities and their commitment to the Assembly as a "stepping stone" to independence. An anti-SNP and anti-separatist vote, rather than an anti-Assembly vote, was perceived. A Labour District Councillor during the count commented to one of the No activists that it was astonishing how many No votes had come out of Whitfield, the city's biggest council housing scheme with a strong SNP ward membership, a voting pattern shared between SNP and Labour, and a ward in which the Conservative Party had managed to win only 24 per cent of the vote at the last Regional election.

Public Meetings

With a few exceptions the response to public meetings during the Referendum seemed to conform to the pattern prevalent in recent elections - the speaker, the chairman, a handful of the party faithful and one or two members of the public. Indeed, the response to the first meeting of the campaign, on January 4, initiated by Tam Dalyell as one of a series throughout Scotland, in the Marryat Hall (capacity 400) suggested that this would be true of even the major meetings: Dalyell (for the Noes) and Jim Sillars (for the Yeses) attracted only six people, one of whom was George Cunningham, MP. The next meeting, to launch the Scotland Says No campaign, which was organised on behalf of the campaign by Douglas Hardie, former Chairman of the CBI in Scotland, attracted over 50 people - but a lot of effort had been put into that and over 1500 invitations had been sent out. The emphasis in this meeting, also in January, was heavily on business and commercial dislike of the Assembly - "83 per cent of Scottish industry is opposed to the Scotland Act" - and this opposition was continually stressed. It was alleged, inter alia, that 60 per cent of the companies operating in Scotland would get out if Scotland became independent and that a reduced but substantial percentage would do so if the Act came into force. The audience added other fears which were to recur and influence the campaign. A Regional Councillor was fearful that the Assembly would reorganise local government yet again and various people were worried about cost and too many levels of government. Two well-behaved SNP supporters provided some opposition but the meeting was fairly successful in its purpose as about 30 people offered to help in the campaign.

A subsequent SSN meeting in the University on Sunday, February 18, with Dundee organiser Mrs Vaughan in the chair and a moderately distinguished line-up of speakers: Alex Fletcher, MP, Conservative spokesman on Scottish affairs, Peter Doig, Labour MP for Dundee West, ex-Principal Drever of the University and Douglas Hardie - attracted an audience of around 90. From conversation afterwards it was evident that this included a number of people who were undecided and had genuinely come to hear the case, some of whom went out of their way to tell us afterwards they were now committed No supporters because of the behaviour of a few nationalists at the meeting who continually heckled the speakers until the hecklers eventually attracted a spontaneous and irritated chorus of "shut up". (Questioned subsequently, the SNP disowned them vigorously and convincingly.)

Alex Fletcher paraded the usual bogeymen - the growth of the bureaucracy, increased costs, left-wing desire for an Assembly - whilst ex-Principal Drever briefly but elegantly argued that the Scottish nation had a short history, a diverse ancestry and itself held most of the responsibility for Scottish problems. Peter Doig put perhaps the only original practical argument against the Assembly heard throughout the campaign: it would lead to the break-up of *Scotland*. "In seventeen years in Parliament", he said, "I have never known a vote which was a Scotland *v*. England vote, but in Scotland it is Strathclyde *versus* the rest. ... The British Parliament is not a cause for disunity, but there is every likelihood the Scottish Parliament would be."

There were a number of run-of-the-mill school-hall public meetings in the course of the campaign. The early ones attracted a few genuinely wanting to hear the arguments for or against the Assembly, but in the main they attracted small audiences and little press coverage. The next big meeting - indeed the only *big* meeting - was the Labour Party "Tony Benn" meeting, a label which hides the fact that other well-known names (Jimmy Reid and Mick McGahey) were also billed to appear. The Labour Party estimated an audience of 800, although an independent observer thought it was rather less. But by any standards, it was a large meeting. The content had notice-ably little to do with devolution. The "warm-up" speakers attacked the Tories, the SNP, capitalism, the Duke of Argyll (in the process of selling Iona) and the EEC; Benn conducted a classic socialist analysis of where power really lay, condemned attacks on the trade unions, advocated the abolition of the House of Lords and of patronage and urged the development of open government which latter, he said, the Assembly would help to ensure. The complaint that devolution did not figure greatly in the proceedings, apart from Jimmy Reid's speech, has considerable justification; but the audience lapped it up and it was perceived to be of more value in raising Labour morale and sending the activists cheerfully out to battle than any logic on the merits of the Assembly.

The corresponding SNP meeting was held on the eve of poll, February 28, attracting an audience of around 170 to hear Jim Fairlie and Gordon Wilson. Fairlie was some-what emotive about "Scotland's oil", but spoke specifically on the subject of de-volution, trying to deal with the "scare" stories one by one. He was well received by an audience which, like the Labour meeting, was largely composed of supporters, spiced this time with a small group of Young Conservatives.

Gordon Wilson, less emotionally, went through some of the objections which needed more serious consideration, made some predictable assertions and ended by urging the audience to "give your support to your own country". But the most interesting thing about the meeting was the questioning which followed. The sterile sloganising and the setting up of opposition "Aunt Sallies" for the platform to knock down, which so often characterises political meetings, were almost completely absent. How would the Assembly affect the position of SNP MPs who had used the Commons to good effect? How could one prevent Strathclyde domination of the Assembly? Could West-minster overrule the Assembly if the latter banned nuclear waste disposal in Scot-land? There were about 20 questions of this sort, most of them getting rational answers and often giving rise to a discussion.

If the meeting had exhibited less "tub-thumping" than others in the campaign, it closed at least on a strongly Scottish note that was not without its emotional overtones - with a folk group playing "On to Liberty" and "Flower of Scotland". But gone was the fierce, fervent nationalistic singing that one remembered from the 1974 elections. The Nationalists sat and took it calmly, admittedly singing but in the sort of polite whisper that the English reserve for hymns. Even when the group struck up "Scots Wha Hae" and the audience rose for the "national anthem", the Young Conservatives, who remained seated, attracted no more than a passing glance. This was both emotionally and chronologically an older audience - the angry young Nats appeared to have grown up, though, to judge by their work in the campaign, they had lost little of their determination.

Other Participants

The influence of a greater degree of autonomy for Scotland upon business and com-mercial interests had obvious implications for employers on one hand and employees on the other. In this connection, two interested by-standers in the wings found themselves drawn onto the stage during the campaign, albeit in minor roles. These were local "power centres" both of whom for different but related reasons could not fail to be interested in the outcome of the Referendum - Dundee Rotary Club and Dundee Trades Council.

Dundee Rotary Club asked Tam Dalyell, MP, to speak at their weekly lunch meeting on February 8. Several members on hearing this complained furiously about the invitation, objecting on the grounds that "Rotary was non-political". After arguing, astonishingly, that the Referendum was not a political issue, the club gave way to pressure to have a speaker representing the Yes side as the least which could be done to balance the situation. As a result, Alick Buchanan-Smith, representing the Alliance for an Assembly spoke a fortnight later, on February 22.

Ironically, Dalyell's speech, despite the audience reportedly being on his side, was received less well than Buchanan-Smith's. Dalyell's flamboyant style did not appeal to these pillars of the local establishment. On the other hand, Buchanan-Smith's calmer approach and the patience with which he dealt with a largely hostile audience and "loaded" questions was considered by several Rotarians to have won over some converts to the Yes cause.

The other "power centre", the Dundee Trades Council, called a big meeting of local shop stewards at the beginning of February. This was ostensibly to discuss wages policy in local industry. There was a turnout of shop stewards, approximately 200, from all the larger industries in the town and the meeting was addressed by full-time union officials. After the formal agenda was completed a directive went out to the stewards to go back to the shop floor and tell the workers to vote Yes and it was very clearly spelt out that the message had to go over that to "vote No was to vote for the Tories". Thus, the appeal to traditional class attitudes, loyalty to the party and to the working classes was invoked, to supersede any intellectual argument about the Scotland Act itself or the proposed Assembly, its functions and powers. Despite this, evidence from several sources suggests that the directive was largely ignored. Many of the shop stewards recognised that those on the shop floor who were SNP did not require to be directed to vote Yes along class lines, and many others appeared to show a great deal of apathy about the whole affair, reflecting the pattern at all socio-economic levels.

The Role of the Press

It is part of local mythology that D.C. Thomson, publishers of Dundee's daily and evening newspapers, the *Courier and Advertiser* and the *Evening Telegraph*, produce an interpretation of current affairs which one would label as "to the right of right". They are under attack regularly from the left - and the centre - for the stance they take on political and social issues. In fact, recently the Thomson press have been shifting their focus slightly towards the centre of the right-wing spectrum - for example, once strongly anti-EEC, they are now more pragmatic, arguing that, as Britain is in, we must therefore work to gain the greatest advantage.

However, as the Referendum was bound up - certainly towards the latter part of the campaign - with straight party politics, one would anticipate that the stance taken by the local press would have fallen into the familiar right-wing pattern. With this in mind, we took a "straw poll" of 100 Dundee voters, asking them what role they saw the press play.

Nine replied that they had the impression the press was on the side of the Yes campaign, 45 on the side of the No campaign and 28 saw the press as neutral. The remainder received no impression at all. These results, although not pretending to come from a statistically respectable sample, are interesting in the light of subsequent findings, as the public perception of the press's attitude was not borne out on analysis. Of the letters printed in the *Courier* 39 were pro-Assembly, 33 anti-Assembly and five neutral - 107 column inches on the Yes side and 102 column inches on the No side. The *Telegraph* was even less of a "flag-flyer". In the period under examination it printed only five letters on the Referendum, of which three were "for" and two (both written by the same person) were "agin".

Meetings were also reported with apparent neutrality in coverage. Tam Dalyell's talk to Rotary received 15 column inches (although he did also get a picture) and Alick Buchanan-Smith's, 13. Tony Benn's meeting got 11 column inches and the major Scotland Says No meeting, 10.

We cannot of course evaluate any possible covert bias. Balance was certainly shown in the letters published but we have no way of establishing what the breakdown was in terms of letters actually received, or how those printed may have been sub-edited. However, editorial comments did show the expected bias - in both papers, anti-Assembly. But the arguments were not pressed as fiercely or as continuously as they were in the national press. The *Courier* had four editorials arguing for a No vote and the *Telegraph* had three, both making the same points and on the same themes as readers' letters. Content analysis of editorials and letters showed the key issues to be, on the No side, the costs, extra bureaucracy and over-government, and the "slippery slope" theme. On the Yes side, emotional rather than pragmatic arguments were presented - the right of a nation to have control over its own affairs, an anti-English line and the belief that, given an Assembly, all Scotland's problems would be solved.

In conclusion, whilst editorial comment was certainly not neutral, news coverage was balanced in line with professed Thomson policy - bi-partisan, but with a decided leaning towards the conservative, if not Conservative, side. We can only hypothesise about the possible influence of the Thomson press on the Referendum result, but it is probably fair to say that it would have been, if anything, to harden the vote for the *status quo*. The circulation success of the right wing *Courier* in a mainly left-wing electorate is due more to its very extensive coverage of local news and its small ads than its reflection of political attitudes in the city.

Conclusion

This is inevitably and largely a descriptive analysis of the Referendum campaign in Dundee. Limitations on space prevent us spending time on the formulation and testing of hypotheses. At the back of our minds, however, was the obvious comparison with the earlier referendum. Points arising from that comparison are worth making, in particular concerning the role of the SNP. In both campaigns, though for different reasons, they fought on their own and on both occasions we think they had incidental though perhaps substantial effects on the outcome. In the EEC referendum their isolation from the umbrella groups was from choice. They had good reason to try and establish that there was a distinctive Scottish opinion on the EEC which was different from that of England. Had they become involved in the umbrella group, it is quite possible that the attitude of other parties towards the No group would have been different - both major parties in Dundee regarded them with hostility, Labour because the SNP had ousted them from a seat which they had held since its creation and the Conservatives because the SNP had taken many of their voters and pushed them into a humiliating third place. In consequence many Labour and Conservative activists and supporters who wanted to work for the No group would almost certainly have had second thoughts had they had to do so alongside the SNP. We had some evidence, too, that voting behaviour was not unaffected by the same factor, since electors who had, for different reasons, defected from the Labour and Conservative ranks in the General Election were now reluctant to give the SNP a further boost. In this Referendum, however, the boot was on the other foot. It was Labour who, for reasons similar to those which had led the SNP to "go it alone" on the first occasion, wanted to fight on their own, so that SNP attempts to co-operate were brusquely rejected, while Conservatives who had doubts or who were marginally inclined to support the Yes camp were certainly affected by the fact that Labour was the leading and enthusiastic campaigner for the Yes side in Dundee.

We think therefore, that the result in Tayside (a low turnout and a No majority) unanticipated by many people because of the SNP activity in the Region, reinforced our impression that traditional party loyalties more strongly influenced the voting behaviour than the virtues or vices of the Scotland Act itself.

III.   GLASGOW AND STRATHCLYDE

Peter Fotheringham

The Electoral Background

Voting behaviour in the Referendum was influenced by three principal forces: attitudes towards devolution and the Scotland Act; partisanship; and the impact of the
rival campaigns. The result may have been strongly influenced by changes in the
electorate's collective attitude, independent of partisanship, towards devolution.
Alternatively, the narrowness of the Yes majority may reflect the distribution of
partisanship in March 1979. The result may also reflect differences in the relative
effectiveness of the various campaigns. These three forces are interdependent, the
most problematic relationship being that between the distribution of partisanship
and opinions concerning the Scotland Act at the time of the Referendum. However,
the association of individual parties with a pro- or anti-devolution attitude
suggests that an understanding of the result in Glasgow and the West of Scotland
necessitates an analysis of the electoral background as well as of the campaign
itself.

Two attributes of the Strathclyde Region ensured that it would be of special interest when the Referendum votes were counted - its huge size and its spectacularly
strong allegiance to the Labour Party in Parliamentary and local elections since
1959.

At the time of the Referendum, the Region embraced 33 complete constituencies (including 13 in Glasgow), 94 per cent of the Argyll electorate and 26 per cent of the
West Stirlingshire electorate. More significantly, 46.7 per cent of the Scottish
electorate lived in Strathclyde. If there were to be strong regional variations in
Referendum voting, the result could be determined in Strathclyde.

Given Labour's electoral strength in the Region and the fact that the Scotland Act
was a product of a Labour Government, a substantial Yes majority might have been
anticipated. Both before and immediately after the Referendum, Labour dominated
electoral offices in Strathclyde. In the October 1974 General Election, Strathclyde
returned 27 Labour MPs to Westminster, five Conservatives and two Nationalists. The
Conservatives won only two of Glasgow's 13 constituencies. In the General Election
of May 1979, Labour won 29 seats and the Conservatives five, of which only one was
in Glasgow.

Labour domination is also evident in local government. In the 1977 District Council
elections, before the downturn in SNP support, Labour won 138 of the 406 seats in
Strathclyde. In the 1980 District elections, 14 months after the Referendum, Labour
won 267 seats. Labour representation on Glasgow District Council increased from 42
per cent of the 72 seats in 1977 to 81 per cent in 1980. That Labour's recovery of
support took place *before* the Referendum is indicated by the 1978 Regional elections
when Strathclyde returned 72 Labour councillors, 25 Conservatives, two Liberals,
two SNP and one other.

Considering votes rather than seats, Table 4.1 indicates party strength in Glasgow
between 1974 and 1980. There are two points of interest. Firstly, it is clear that
Labour rather than the Conservatives benefited from the decline in SNP support
after the 1977 District elections. Secondly, Labour and the SNP together won 69.4
per cent of the vote in Glasgow, almost 50 per cent of the registered electorate,
in the May 1979 General Election only two months after the Referendum; in Strathclyde as a whole Labour and the SNP won two-thirds of the vote.

On the assumption of a positive relationship between party support in March 1979

TABLE 4.1   Percentage Shares of Votes by Party in Glasgow, 1974-1980

	Turnout %	Lab. %	Con. %	SNP %	Lib. %	Other %
October 1974	68.7	49	20.2	26.2	4.2	0.3
May 1977	50.1	35.1	28.7	32.7	1.9	1.7
May 1979	70.7	58	25.8	11.4	4.0	0.6
May 1980	42.6	54.7	21.9	15.9	5.8	1.6

and attitudes towards the Scotland Act, the electoral history of Strathclyde prior
to the Referendum suggested that its voters would come close to giving the Yes side
the required 40 per cent share of the adjusted electorate. The results of the
General Election in Strathclyde a mere two months after the Referendum makes one
wonder why they did not do so.

TABLE 4.2   Strathclyde Voting in 1978-1979

	May 1978 Regional	March 1979 Referendum	May 1979 General Election
Electorate	1,765,635	1,750,299	1,807,680
Votes	795,712	1,105,118	1,367,531
Turnout	46.2%	63.2%	76.7%
Con. votes	242,721 (30%)		375,767 (27.5%)
No votes		508,599 (46%)	
Yes votes		596,519 (54%)	
Lab. votes	348,053 (43%)		661,487 (48.4%)
SNP votes	182,878 (22.6%)		240,493 (17.6%)
Lib. votes	14,219 (1.8%)		86,501 (6.3%)

Table 4.2 summarises Strathclyde voting in the 1978 Regional elections, the Referendum and the 1979 General Election. The outstanding feature lies in a comparison
of the Referendum No vote and the Conservative vote two months later: the No vote
exceeded the 1979 Conservative vote by an astounding 132,832 despite the lower
turnout in the Referendum (262,413 fewer voters than in the 1979 General Election).
Conversely, the Labour vote in May 1979 exceeded the Yes vote by 64,968, while
Liberal and SNP candidates obtained 326,994 votes. The pro-devolution parties thus
exceeded in May 1979 the Yes total by 391,962 votes.

The comparison of the Conservative vote in May 1979 with the Referendum No vote
suggests strongly that many "non-Conservatives" voted No in March. Conservative support in the West was similar in May 1978 and May 1979 so that the success of the No
campaign in the Referendum can hardly be said to have worked to the advantage of
the Conservative Party in the General Election. The decline in SNP support was par-
alleled by an increase in Labour and Liberal support. Consequently, the increase
in Conservative support indicated by opinion polls in Scotland as a whole in the
run-up to the Referendum seems to have come *from* a movement against devolution as
opposed to an increase in Conservative support leading *to* increasing opposition to
the Scotland Act.

It is impossible to work out for Strathclyde the relative proportions of Labour,
SNP, Liberal and other partisans within the Yes vote but, if we assume conserva-
tively that 120,000 SNP voters and 50,000 Liberal partisans voted Yes in March,
then the Yes vote could not have included more than 427,000 Labour supporters. On

this assumption, the Labour Party got out at least 230,000 more voters in their attempt to keep Mrs Thatcher *out* of office than was achieved two months earlier in the attempt to keep Mr Callaghan *in* office by securing the implementation of the Scotland Act.

The Yes margin over the Noes was higher in Strathclyde than in Scotland as a whole, but it was low in relation to combined Labour and SNP election strength in 1978 and 1979. Analysing the development of the campaign in Glasgow may provide evidence to account for this.

The Campaign in Glasgow

Any significant relationship which may have developed between the nature of the Referendum campaign in Glasgow and Strathclyde and the Region's verdict on March 1 can be seen as depending upon the various signals which the voters received from the rival Yes and No forces. Two principal channels for communicating opinions to the uncommitted and instructions to faithful partisans can be distinguished. First, Strathclyde electors were exposed to a media campaign waged mainly at a national rather than a Regional level through the press, TV and radio. Secondly, there was a series of grassroots campaigns organised at constituency level by the political parties and the inter-party groups.

The media campaign, be it in a referendum or a general election, may persuade some voters to adopt or to change to a particular viewpoint; it may confirm for partisans what their party position is; and it may be a factor in determining turnout. The special significance of turnout in the devolution Referendum, because of the 40 per cent requirement, focuses attention on the local campaigns. "Getting out the vote" is the principal aim of local campaigning and it requires the participation of a considerable number of committed supporters. The principal features of local campaigning in Glasgow will be described below, following an analysis of the campaign as it was reported to readers of the principal Glasgow newspapers, the *Glasgow Herald* and the *Evening Times*.

The *Glasgow Herald* proclaims itself to be "Scotland's Newspaper". It is therefore not surprising to find that it devoted most of its Referendum coverage to describing and analysing the national campaign rather than the local campaigns in the Strathclyde Region.

The *Herald*'s in-depth coverage of the Referendum campaign began on January 23 with a significant article by William Clark, "The sides line up for the battle of Scotland", comprising a description of the major participants in the "battle" and an analysis of the state of the parties in relation to the campaign. Both the organisational description and the analysis of party attitudes pointed out the Labour Party's divisions on the devolution issue. Attention was also directed to the "softly, softly" approach of the Conservative Party which had "discreetly decided not to have their own campaign" though Conservative leaflets attacking the Scotland Act would be distributed. The only mention of Conservative dissidents came in the description of the Alliance for an Assembly group which would give Alick Buchanan-Smith, MP, the opportunity "to articulate the Tory dissidents' viewpoint". Clark's analysis of the parties was revealing. He apprised readers of the *Glasgow Herald*, more than a month in advance of polling day, of problems in Labour's Yes efforts: "Labour's head seems perfectly in control yet its feet, at constituency level, seem leaden". Seven Constituency Labour Parties, including East Dunbartonshire and Govan in Strathclyde, were reported to be resisting the call from headquarters to participate in the Labour Movement Yes campaign. Brian Wilson, Chairman of the Labour Vote No campaign, was quoted as claiming "great support in many CLPs". Clark's analysis of the condition of the parties at this early stage of the Referendum contest now seems to possess a prophetic ring.

West of Scotland Conservatives would not find many references to support for a Yes vote on the part of Conservative office holders within the Region, while Cathcart MP, Teddy Taylor, was the most prominent of the Conservatives in opposition to the Scotland Act. Only late in the campaign, on February 27, were the names of any Conservative councillors supporting the Scotland Act mentioned in the *Herald*. Strathclyde Regional Councillor John Mair, Glasgow District Councillor Christine Campbell and Kyle & Carrick District Councillor Struan Stevenson were among the pro-Scotland Act Conservatives who had "assembled" in Edinburgh the previous day with Buchanan-Smith and Malcolm Rifkind to "urge a Yes vote". ("Assembled" may appear an exaggeration as only four local government Tories were listed.)

The Labour Movement Yes campaign received a publicity boost from the Prime Minister's visit to Glasgow on Monday, February 12, 16 days before polling. Yet the occasion was ambiguous in that devolution was not seen to be the sole significant issue in Scottish politics and the aloof character of Labour's campaign became evident. Callaghan may have addressed a "packed house" in the McLellan Galleries, but this was an all-ticket rally organised by the Labour Movement Yes campaign and attended almost exclusively by the Labour Party faithful, thus making clear Labour's determination to go it alone at the expense of an all-party Yes campaign.

Callaghan's speech to the party faithful did not set Glasgow's heather alight. The speech was described as "unexceptional" (*The Observer*, 18.2.1979) and "plodding" (*Glasgow Herald*, 13.2.1979). His themes were summed up as "it's now or never" and "it's up to you". Callaghan calculated that failure to register a positive verdict would mean the end of devolution for the foreseeable future. He also emphasised that the Labour Government had "kept faith" with Scotland; now it was up to Scotland and in particular up to his Labour Party audience to "pick up the banner and carry it forward".

It seems clear, though, that Callaghan's audience, so far as it symbolised the Labour Party in Scotland, did not pick up the "banner" with sufficient enthusiasm, perhaps because of a greater concern with other issues. Indeed, Callaghan's arrival at the McLellan Galleries was marked by demonstrations by NUPE members, then in dispute over pay as a consequence of the Government's incomes policy which had provoked the notorious "winter of discontent". Consequently, Callaghan's visit, although unmatched by a counter-visit from Margaret Thatcher, was not an unqualified success.

The main "local" issue to receive the attention of the Glasgow papers related to the future of the Regions should the Scottish Assembly be established. There appeared to be divisions in the Yes camp. The *Glasgow Herald* printed a centre page article on February 19 which analysed the implications for the Regions of success for the Yes forces, two of which, the Liberals and the SNP, were said to be hostile to the Regions, especially Strathclyde. It is difficult to estimate whether this question had much influence on voting in Strathclyde. The significance of the Regions issue lies in the possible opposition to the Assembly by supporters of the Regions and Strathclyde in particular. This point was picked up by the *Evening Times* on February 27 in a front-page report with the headline: "STUC's Shock Devo Attack". Alex Kitson was said to have accused Labour politicians of sabotaging the Yes campaign, claiming that "many MPs and councillors were either openly opposing the Assembly or taking a passive and neutral attitude which had the same result". The offending politicians were said to be motivated by "petty and vested interests" which could be "jeopardised" by a Scottish Assembly. This report was unusual in that it named Dick Buchanan, Labour MP for Springburn, and D. Crawford, a UCATT official, as Labour supporters of the No persuasion.

On polling day itself the *Herald*'s support for a Yes verdict was indicated in a front-page editorial which nevertheless devoted as much space to the shortcomings of the Scotland Act as to the attractions of an Assembly.

The press reporting of the campaign in Strathclyde was more significant in its description of the problems facing the Yes camp than for any influence it may have had on voting. The result in Strathclyde, which was not altogether surprising in the light of the Yes camp's difficulties, probably reflected the impact of the various Yes and No groups' campaigns at the grass roots.

Grassroots Campaigning in Glasgow

The 40 per cent requirement placed an unusual emphasis on the need for a high turnout on the part of Yes supporters, especially as many of them were Labour voters who have a lower tendency to vote than Conservatives. In a referendum, as opposed to a general election, the impact of the campaign depends upon co-operation between parties in addition to the individual efforts of rival political parties. The account of campaigning which follows is based on interviews with participants in the Glasgow campaign and on replies to the Survey of Constituency Parties.

The principal conclusion to be drawn from the Labour Party's campaign at constituency level is that the split reported in the media was just as evident at the grass roots. The Labour Movement Yes campaign was decentralised, i.e. it depended upon the initiative of individual Constituency Labour Parties (CLPs), which had been asked at the end of 1978 by Keir Hardie House to set up campaign committees. Although deficiencies in local party campaigning were moderated by the activities of Trade Unions and by some co-operation between parties in the Yes for Scotland campaign, the Labour Movement Yes campaign was more uneven in its impact than the Scotland Says No campaign.

Interviews with members of the Maryhill CLP revealed that the General Management Committee was hostile to devolution and decided to do nothing in response to promptings from Party headquarters in Glasgow. One all-party meeting was held in the constituency, chaired by the constituency's Labour MP, Jim Craigen. Speakers on the No side included a neighbouring Labour MP, Dick Buchanan of Springburn, and a Glasgow District Tory Councillor, Ian Lawson. Yes speakers included local SNP candidates and the Labour Party's Research Officer, Alf Young.

In contrast, the Kelvingrove and Hillhead CLPs were active in the Yes campaign. The Kelvingrove MP, Neil Carmichael, spoke in both constituencies (Hillhead has a Conservative MP). Kelvingrove CLP devoted the February 1979 issue of its *Kelvingrove Chronicle* to devolution, making its view crystal clear with a front page headline proclaiming "YES! FOR A STRONGER SCOTLAND".

The uneven character of the Labour Movement Yes campaign was reflected in replies from Glasgow to the Scottish Referendum Study's Survey of Constituency Parties. Three CLPs, including Maryhill, decided to do nothing; interviews indicate that the Garscadden CLP, despite Labour MP Donald Dewar's prominent position in the Yes campaign, was also inactive, although individual Party members did participate on both sides of the campaign even where their CLP adopted a "neutralist" public stance. The consequences of such a stance benefited the No camp to the extent that inactivity lowered turnout.

The replies of the four CLPs which reported a decision to campaign for a Yes vote appear highly significant in indicating the extremely low priority accorded to the devolution issue. The level of activity was estimated to be as low as in a local election, if not lower. The nature of activity which did take place was also significant. In particular, there seems to have been little canvassing; of the seven CLPs replying to the survey, only two reported canvassing as one of their campaign activities. Distributing literature was the main activity, though meetings were held in some constituencies. Finance available at local level appears to have been extremely low. The four CLPs which campaigned for a Yes vote confined their efforts to the official Labour campaign. Interviews indicated that Labour and Conservative participation in the inter-party Yes for Scotland campaign was limited to individuals, who were especially few in number in the case of Conservatives.

Ironically, Conservative replies to the survey did not indicate a much higher level of activity or enthusiasm. The Conservative Party in Pollok decided not to campaign for a No vote because of internal divisions. One of the few Tory office-holders known to be a Yes supporter, Councillor John Mair, represents a Strathclyde Region seat within Pollok constituency. Another Tory publicly identified as a Yes supporter, Mrs Helen Millar, lives in Pollok. Nevertheless, No campaign literature was widely distributed in Pollok.

An interesting view of the Conservative Party's efforts was presented by an activist in the Hillhead constituency who believed that there was little enthusiasm about the devolution issue among Conservatives because of a belief that the Yes camp would win. Nevertheless, the Hillhead Conservative Association did establish a Political Action Committee to co-ordinate activity, though this was considerably less intense than in a general election. A meeting addressed by the local Conservative MP, T.G.D. Galbraith, was poorly attended. It is difficult to resist the conclusion that in Glasgow the Labour and Conservative Parties waged their campaigns in the media and through the letter-box.

The limitations upon a study of this kind imposed by the nature of the counting areas are particularly evident in a constituency such as Hillhead, where the level of activity was high. The Hillhead Conservative Association and the Hillhead SNP both produced special Referendum news-sheets, as did Labour in neighbouring Kelvingrove. Hillhead CLP appears as one of the more enthusiastic CLPs in favour of a Yes vote, and the Yes for Scotland campaign was particularly active in the constituency.

Conservative voters in Hillhead could have been left in no doubt about the Party's opposition to the Scotland Act if they read the devolution issue of *Hillhead Conservative News*, which should have reached 40,000 voters. Mrs Thatcher's case for a No vote was presented on the first page. Nevertheless, the Conservative Party's low profile was indicated by the devotion of two of the four pages to local issues.

The Conservative news-sheet was matched on the Yes side by a four page Referendum issue of *Saltire*, published by the Hillhead Constituency Association of the SNP and distributed to 20,000 households. Its significance is analysed below in a description of the Yes for Scotland campaign in Glasgow.

The Conservative and Labour Parties in Glasgow treated the Referendum campaign in the same way as they fight elections: they regarded each other and the smaller parties largely as rivals. This conclusion requires some qualification due to the activities of the Labour Vote No campaign, the low profile adopted by the Conservative Party and the compensating activities of the business community in the Scotland Says No campaign, and the crossing of the party line-up on the part of individuals. The Conservative camp had little alternative to relying on its own resources because it was the major force opposed to devolution, but the Labour Party's concentration on its own campaign reflected a combination of a lukewarm attitude towards devolution and hostility to the SNP.

The behaviour of the other parties provides a marked contrast. The SNP, the Liberals and the Communist Party were prepared to forsake doctrinal differences in the short term to co-operate in the Yes for Scotland campaign. Indeed, replies to the Survey of Constituency Parties indicate that SNP members had difficulty in distinguishing between "the official SNP campaign" and the Yes for Scotland campaign. Replies from Liberal and SNP constituency organisations all indicated participation in the Yes for Scotland campaign and the Liberals also indicated support for the Alliance for an Assembly.

Inter-party co-operation on the Yes side offered one way of attaining the 40 per cent target. It is therefore necessary to evaluate the nature of the Yes for Scotland campaign in Glasgow, where an organising committee was set up in December 1978. The Committee's office-bearers were representative of the minor parties although the 15-strong membership included a Conservative and SNP members. The Committee elected an SLP Chairman and a Communist Secretary. The nature of party involvement in Yes for Scotland is illustrated by the Glasgow Committee's letter of invitation to participate in its major demonstration in Glasgow on February 24. The Committee claimed "the support of the Liberal Party, the Scottish National Party, Communist Party, Scottish Labour Party" and, in contrast, merely "members of the Tory and Labour Party ...". Yes for Scotland was most active in Hillhead, Govan and Pollok. The Committee attempted to raise funds by organising a Burns Supper, a highly successful Disco in a Glasgow nightspot, a less successful Folk Night and street stalls in Hillhead and Govan.

There were two significant aspects of the Yes for Scotland campaign in Glasgow. The SNP clearly decided to channel its efforts through this "all-party" campaign: indeed, the SNP in Craigton went further by organising a "Craigton Says Yes" campaign in an effort to develop local community support. Secondly, the Yes for Scotland campaign enabled enthusiasts from the minor parties, such as the Liberals, the SLP and the Communists, to pool their limited resources.

The SNP involvement in the inter-party Yes for Scotland effort is clearly stated in a special edition of the Hillhead SNP newspaper *Saltire*. The front page featured photographs of Alick Buchanan-Smith, Ludovic Kennedy, Russell Johnston and Jimmy Milne along with the SNP Chairman William Wolfe and local SNP candidate, Gordon Borthwick. Support for a Yes vote was expressed in quotations from or in articles by a wide range of personalities including Ted Heath, Catholic Bishop Devine of Glasgow, former Church of Scotland Moderator David Steel, Lord Kilbrandon, a T&GWU member Jim Sillars, a Glasgow Tory (Helen J. Millar of Pollok Conservative Association) and the former chairman of Hillhead Liberal Association.

It is impossible to gauge the impact of a political news-sheet such as *Saltire*. Yet the contributions, despite their impressive all-party character, are notable in the common belief that the defects of the Scotland Act would have to be remedied once the Assembly had begun its operations. Perhaps an impression of less than whole-hearted conviction was communicated to readers.

SNP replies to the Constituency Survey indicate a higher level of activity and enthusiasm than Labour and Conservative replies. Yet even in the case of the SNP, activity was estimated to be less intense than in a general election, despite the importance of getting a high turnout. Even the SNP, the party with (arguably) most to gain from a positive outcome, was unable to match its efforts in earlier general elections.

Conclusions

Despite the efforts of the Yes for Scotland campaign in Glasgow it appears that the co-operation *between the parties* was extremely limited although *individuals* from all the parties did participate in the Yes campaign's activities. On the face of it, the Yes effort would have benefited from co-operation between the parties in favour of the Scotland Act, particularly Labour and the SNP, *and* from a strong canvassing operation by the parties, either jointly or individually, to get out the vote. The at arms length attitudes of SNP and Labour Party organisations should not have mattered if the Parties had worked independently but enthusiastically to get out the Yes vote. Indeed, individual party effort was probably more essential than inter-party co-operation. Labour voters, whatever their attitude towards devolution, were more likely to heed a Labour Party exhortation to vote Yes than an alliance movement's promptings.

Evidence from Glasgow suggests that the efforts of the two major Yes parties simply did not approach their performance in Parliamentary elections. This was particularly crucial in the case of the Labour Party, the dominant party in Glasgow and Strathclyde and the major force in the Yes camp at a time when support for the SNP appeared to have fallen to about half the level attained in the 1974 October General Election. In Glasgow, Labour was divided on the Referendum issue. It seems plausible to argue that the No voters who could not have been Conservative partisans included many Labour supporters.

IV.   EDINBURGH'S SILENCE

Roger Mullin

Perhaps Edinburgh's terrible inability to speak out,
Edinburgh's silence with regard to all it should be saying,
Is but the hush that precedes the thunder,
The liberating detonation so oppressively imminent now?

                                        Hugh MacDiarmid
                    Talking with Five Thousand People in Edinburgh

There were not quite five thousand campaign organisations in Edinburgh, but more
than enough to make contact with all of the city's voters, raise all the issues,
air every ideological idiosyncrasy and knock on every door ... or so it seemed on
paper: Labour Vote No, Yes for Scotland, Labour Movement Yes, Conservative No campaign, the Alliance for an Assembly, Scottish Labour Party Yes, Communist Party Yes,
Scotland Says No, SNP Yes, Liberal Yes and so on. Each claimed active support and
all operated in Scotland's capital city. Add to this the fact that the SNP and the
Liberal and Conservative Parties had their national headquarters in Edinburgh, as
did the Yes for Scotland organisation, and the formal organisational network seemed
impressive. But where the media were obliged to generate "balance", this vast array
of organisations appeared intent on generating sleep.

Yet, Edinburgh seemed to offer the prospect of intense campaigning during the Referendum period for reasons other than purely organisational ones. Here was Scotland's capital, centre of Scotland's distinctive legal system, symbolic home of
Scotland's established church, base for Scotland's civil service headquarters at
New St Andrew's House, theatre for a great international festival, ancient seat of
learning - but minus that political head of most capitals, a legislature. The regaining of something of its former political status seemed within reach. The new
Scottish Assembly was to sit in the converted Royal High School building over-
looking Edinburgh's life from high on Calton Hill.

The prospect of an Assembly brought with it all sorts of plans and promises which
seemed to hold out the possibility of Edinburgh's generating a political life which
would bring everything from an expansion in professional and administrative jobs
to a new focus on Scotland's political life. The University of Edinburgh would have
become a centre for research into Scotland's changing political scene. TV and radio
companies were planning extensions to their Edinburgh bases. Scottish political
journalism was about to receive real stimulus and challenge. Even before the Assembly seemed imminent, the mere possibility had played its part in attracting back
to Scotland and Edinburgh such significant political journalists as Neal Ascherson.
It seemed that Edinburgh was to become much more than a focus for cultural life.
Politically, it was suggested that the electoral and economic muscle of Glasgow
and the West of Scotland could be matched by the influence which inevitably accrues
to the legislative centre and forum for political conflict.

For these and many other reasons it was thought that Edinburgh would more than any
centre in Scotland derive immediate benefit and stimulus from the establishment of
a Scottish Assembly. Edinburgh had, therefore, almost special interests in the
Referendum. What with the great number of campaigning organisations operating in
the city, it would have been not unreasonable to expect the capital to be particularly alive to campaign issues and particularly suited to intense campaigning.

If such was the promise, it was a promise unfulfilled. Rather than a place of political life and high drama, Edinburgh too often gave the impression of being a political ghost town. As Ian Grant Cumming, the public relations agent of Scotland Says

No, put it when asked about campaign activity in Edinburgh: "I was never aware of
all that much activity in Edinburgh. Most of our meetings and activity seemed to
take place in Glasgow". Press releases were issued of course, leafleting did take
place, meetings were held and even some canvassing took place, but in the main, as
key activists readily admitted in the survey reported in chapter 3, the intensity
of campaigning rarely reached local government proportions and often fell well below even that level. Of the 13 replies received from Edinburgh (see chapter 3),
nine estimated their efforts to be less than during a local government election.
Only one reply, from Edinburgh North SNP, estimated their activity to be similar
to general election proportions. TV, radio and newspaper coverage was more intensive, approaching general election levels, and there can be little doubt that this
tended to obscure the rather half-hearted efforts of the grass roots campaigners.
Why did the political machines rarely move out of first gear? What was the effect
of so many organisations attempting to run independent campaigns in Edinburgh?
Such questions can only be answered within the context of the particular and often
unique interests which were born of the Referendum itself.

The Party Scene

All the political parties knew that soon after the Referendum they would face EEC
elections, a general election sometime before November 1979 and possibly Scottish
Assembly elections during the autumn of 1979. Together with the Referendum, this
made four major nation-wide elections between February and November, 16 weeks or
thereabouts of door-knocking, many more weeks of planning and fund raising. Nine
or ten months of non-stop activity was inevitably going to drain human and financial resources. Bearing this in mind makes the low level of commitment in terms of
man hours of campaigning and finance more understandable. Most significantly, such
competing demands were more than matched by severe political constraints which were
particularly acute in Edinburgh. The combination of organisational, financial and
political pressures on the parties was to prove too great a burden to carry in the
context of campaigning expectations during the Referendum. No party seemed to treat
the Referendum with the priority which might have been expected.

The Labour Party was, as Christopher Harvie makes clear (in the piece following
this), deeply divided. In Robin Cook, MP for Edinburgh Central, they had one of the
most active No campaigners in the country. As a result, and despite his Constituency Labour Party's having declared itself in favour of the Scotland Act, it decided to do nothing as a CLP during the Referendum campaign. While individuals were
active, as an organisation it had effectively made itself impotent. In other constituencies - Edinburgh Pentlands and Edinburgh North - CLPs decided against launching campaigns in order to maintain unity in organisations severely split over
the issue of devolution. In any case, the Labour Party was understandably most concerned about the coming General Election. Industrial unrest throughout the country
appeared to be severely threatening the Labour government's chances of re-election.
And being oriented towards the establishment of power in a British context through
political conflict in essentially a two party fight, devolution was to many not
merely a distraction from the essential fight but one which raised the status of
minor parties, potentially further loosening the two party system which had for
some years seemed in decline.

If the Labour Party was aware of the need to play down the divisions in the party
with a view to the forthcoming General Election, this was more than matched by the
traditional drive for power of the Conservative Party. The leadership of Margaret
Thatcher together with Teddy Taylor's effective leadership in Scotland had driven
the Tories in the late 1970's well away from the devolutionary path once trodden by
Edward Heath. The traditional British nationalism of the Tories and their belief
in the unitary state once more asserted itself. Even if Tom Nairn's view be accepted that this "was no longer even faintly recognisable as the ideology of a great

state, confident in its future. It was more like the philosophy of a society on the
run, already aware of its own decomposition", it nevertheless confined the issue of
devolution for Scotland within a conception of what was of central political interest: regaining governmental control of the unitary British state. If Mrs Thatcher
is accused of reviving pre-Keynesian economic doctrines, she should also be credited with aiding the emergence of a new embattled form of British nationalism. But
a few Conservative MPs like Malcolm Rifkind, the articulate and ambitious MP for
Edinburgh Pentlands, continued to sail the devolutionary ship against the tide. His
influence in Edinburgh is difficult to assess, but he did have significant support
for devolution within Edinburgh's Tory ranks. Brian Meek, leading Tory Regional
Councillor, headed a small band of pro-devolution councillors. The Conservatives
were not so solidly behind the No campaign as might have been expected - although
Tory Yes supporters were undoubtedly fewer and of much less influence than Labour
No supporters. Rifkind's own Constituency Association decided not to campaign as
an organisation during the Referendum, one leading figure in the constituency informing me that "interested members were free to follow their own line of thought".
Perhaps of most interest in this out-of-step Constituency Association was the way
in which it proved a classic example of an organisation which suppressed the potential activism of members, thus preventing the public split becoming too severe to
allow an easy regrouping for the coming General Election. In response to questioning it was stated by one leading official that the membership of the Association
was "very enthusiastic (about the Referendum) ... but completely divided". In spite
of this enthusiasm the net result was activity estimated by the same official at
"less effort than a local election". Certainly some branches within the constituency supported the No campaign, with individuals contributing to both sides. But
the Tory tradition of being less accommodating towards its rebels than the Labour
Party, seems to have made Tory Yes supporters in general more circumspect in their
activism than Labour Noes.

If the Labour and Conservative Parties had traditional British political interests
which reduced the comparative status of the Referendum, it might have been thought
that Liberal activism would not be so restrained. Here after all was the party with
a long history of devotion to the cause of Home Rule, a party led by a Scot, David
Steel, and a party with no reason to accommodate the traditional two-party view of
British politics so much identified with Labour and Conservative. Yet even in
Edinburgh the Liberal effort was not particularly intense. Donald Gorrie, Edinburgh's leading Liberal and Regional Councillor,did work as hard as could be expected, and some Liberal branches and individuals put in considerable work. But at
least three factors served to dampen the general level of Liberal activity -
besides the understandable shortages of manpower and resources. Firstly, and like
all the parties, since the Scotland Act did not exactly meet the traditional
demands of the Liberals, the opportunity for dissent was ever-present. In Edinburgh, some Liberal organisations were divided and decided not to campaign - Edinburgh Leith being a specific example where according to one local official there
was neither an overall constituency-led campaign, nor any effort by any local
branch nor by one individual local Liberal to campaign during the Referendum
period. Secondly, there was a lack of realistic leadership from Scottish Liberal
headquarters. It would have seemed that co-operation with Yes for Scotland, which
had an active organisation in Edinburgh, would have held most attraction for
Liberals, given their limited resources and some internal dissent. And for a party
seemingly keen on the idea of coalition or multi-party government, the dislike of
inter-party co-operation which seemed to affect both Labour and Conservative activists was hardly likely to apply to the same extent. It proved a problem, therefore, when the leading Scottish Liberal Russell Johnston,MP threw in his lot not
with Yes for Scotland but with the hastily concocted Alliance group. This could
hardly have helped Yes for Scotland's legitimacy in the eyes of potential Liberal
activists, and with the Alliance in reality having no organisation at all in Edinburgh (and by the time it was announced, no realistic chance of setting up one in
time to campaign effectively), the temptation to do nothing was too readily avail-

able. Finally, the type of leadership offered by David Steel at the British level
seemed more than ever to be settling Liberals within a strongly British and West-
minster-oriented political nexus. When he won the leadership contest against John
Pardoe, it was a victory against the anti-system radicals within the Liberal Party.
Steel was leading Liberal opinion along a path which he hoped would gain status and
influence for the Liberal Party by Liberal involvement in government via the establishment of what he termed a "People's Parliament". In essence the Steel strategy
depended upon co-operation with one or other of the main two parties in a "hung"
parliament. Not surprisingly then, the looming General Election was of dominating
concern for the Liberals too. Liberal politics which had often been characterised
by principled campaigning on specific issues (as during the EEC referendum) were now
moving towards a tactical concern for gathering some governmental power through a
power-sharing Westminster. Like Labour and Conservatives then, the likelihood of a
general election soon after the Referendum reduced the relative standing of the
Referendum in Liberal Party eyes.

Perhaps most surprising was the comparatively low key campaigning of the SNP (albeit more active than the other major parties). It was none the less fascinating
that the party held responsible, rightly or wrongly, for bringing the issue of
Scotland's governmental system to the forefront of political conflict in the 1970's
should have, in general, campaigned less actively during the Referendum than was
normal practice at general elections (even where it had little hope of electoral
success, as in Edinburgh). Like the other parties, the SNP had its own party campaign during the Referendum period. Every Edinburgh constituency actively engaged
in campaigning for a Yes vote. There were no Nationalist No campaigners at all,
let alone organisational splits on which side to support. But a combination of
factors seemed to create some self-doubt and general uncertainty about the role the
Nationalists should play in the Referendum. SNP activity took place much more
through activism in the Yes for Scotland organisation than through purely party
campaigning. Indeed, throughout the city it was clear that the majority of active
Nationalists shied away from the official party campaign to concentrate on helping
in the Yes for Scotland campaign. It would seem that SNP activists campaigned under
the banner of Yes for Scotland at about twice or more the level of their involvement in the official SNP campaign. And the style of Nationalist campaigning was
drab in comparison with the excitement and flamboyance associated with their campaigning of the late 60's and early-to-middle 70's. On the last Saturday before
polling a rather pathetic car cavalcade of no more than a dozen cars swept through
the centre of Edinburgh. In no constituency, whether operating under the guise of
Yes for Scotland or SNP, did the Nationalists manage a full constituency canvass.
And some areas of the city received no more than one Yes for Scotland leaflet.

If the Nationalists did not display the enthusiasm which might have been expected
of them, it is not surprising that the general public did not work themselves into
a frenzy of excitement either. But it would be wrong to attribute this lack of
Nationalist effort purely to the fact that they sought independence rather than
mere devolution, although this of course was one factor. The SNP was in pessimistic
and embattled mood during the Referendum campaign. From a situation a few years
earlier when the SNP stood at well over 30 per cent in opinion polls, the Nationalists had seen their support decline. Three by-election successes for Labour had
drained Nationalist optimism, and the SNP collapse in opinion polls to a trailing
third behind Labour and the Conservatives made the forthcoming General Election
seem a much greater ordeal than was once imagined. Indeed, the imminence of the
General Election cast into sharp relief the growing tensions within Nationalist
ranks centring around devolution. The so-called "hawks" amongst the Nationalists -
the Independence Nothing Less brigade - were becoming more and more resistant to
involvement in the Referendum which might use up resources. As one hawkish Nationalist MP of the time was heard to aver, "I told my constituency association that
the most important thing this year is to get me re-elected". It was becoming too
easy to explain Nationalist decline in terms of the long-running devolution saga,

thus confirming a sort of Nationalist machismo, and this helps to explain the rather slight involvement of a number of Nationalist MPs during the Referendum. In Edinburgh this was to some degree counteracted by two of the most articulate Nationalists of the 1970's, Stephen Maxwell, SNP candidate in Edinburgh Pentlands, and Professor Neil MacCormick, SNP candidate for Edinburgh North. But even in their cases, involvement in the Yes for Scotland campaign was a convenient option. Tactically, with SNP support seemingly on the wane and opinion pollsters suggesting that an even smaller percentage of the electorate believed in the SNP's independence platform, it seemed useful to many Nationalists to cover themselves with the moderate and respectable image of devolutionists. These Nationalists wanted devolution to hasten the break-up of Britain, of course, a fact recognised by other political activists which no doubt added to the worry of those who saw Edinburgh's Yes for Scotland committee become increasingly dependent upon SNP organisation and manpower. But despite the available camouflage supplied by Yes for Scotland and the presence in Edinburgh of highly active and articulate protagonists of the Yes case, SNP activism was seriously affected by the embattled condition of nationalism and the growing disquiet with the whole devolution saga. Like the parties they so vehemently opposed, the SNP leadership increasingly focussed on Westminster representation and the general election at the expense of the Referendum. British parliamentarianism seemed to be overtaking even nationalist preoccupations.

An adequate discussion of the Referendum campaign in Edinburgh must mention the contribution made by the Scottish Communists and the Scottish Labour Party. Two parties of small membership and slim organisational resources, they none the less fought hard during the Referendum. Both produced and distributed in selected areas their own literature and, while this was inevitably restricted, it did confirm their commitment to devolution. Perhaps more importantly, both parties seemed quite assured in their campaigning for a Yes vote, avoiding the damaging splits of the Labour Party and the schizophrenic niceties of the Nationalists. Their most important contributions came as part of the Yes for Scotland campaign. In Edinburgh they helped by way of planning, campaigning, speaking and organising to an extent which outweighed their numbers.

The Umbrella Organisations: Yes for Scotland and Scotland Says No

The umbrella organisations of Yes for Scotland and Scotland Says No were the most significant campaigning organisations on either side of the Yes-No divide. They seemed in general to attract the most committed protagonists from the parties (excepting the Labour Party), as well as supplying the organisational focus for committed non-party individuals. In a number of ways the organisations in Edinburgh were similar. Both sought as far as possible to present themselves as truly multi-party organisations. For the No side, Robin Cook MP as a Labour man complemented the Tory MPs and Peers who could be relied upon. For the Yes side, great play was made of the all-party profile of the organisation, even though not a single Edinburgh MP was associated with Yes for Scotland. Both organisations relied heavily upon the organised help of one particular party: in the case of the No side on Conservative aid, on the Yes side on SNP organisation. And both groups were organised for the sole task of mobilising support during the Referendum period and were to be wound up after the vote.

There the similarity ends. The Yes for Scotland organisation had their national headquarters in the High Street in Edinburgh, from where the co-ordination of the national campaign took place and where the leading national figures in the campaign regularly met. The spin-off for the Edinburgh campaign was real enough. Leaflets and posters could be had at short notice. Speakers were easily available, and access to national organising officials always possible. As a result there tended to be a close liaison between Edinburgh's organisation and the national one. The Scotland Says No organisation had no organisational base of its own in

Edinburgh.

In terms of the mechanics of the campaigns too there were stark differences. Whereas the Conservative network in Edinburgh was largely responsible for the distribution of literature supplied by the Scotland Says No organisation, on the Yes side the local distribution network was often built around SNP branches and relied upon local committees buying nationally produced leaflets. And as this might suggest, the Yes organisation had to devote some of its energies to fund raising, even during the period of the campaign. One such event, an auction of donated wares, realised one thousand pounds and, good as this was for funds, the man hours involved in organising and running such an event were very considerable indeed. The valuable time of activists spent in fund raising ventures inevitably cuts into time available for general campaigning. The No side, on the other hand, were much more comfortably off and this not only freed the organisation's activists for campaigning purposes, but also enabled them to buy professional assistance. Ian Grant Cumming, public relations manager of SSN joined the campaign on a professional basis, or, as he put it "the No side made the first approach for my services". YFS were dependent upon volunteers to run their public relations. Buying the expertise of an Edinburgh-based professional was never within their compass.

While it was almost wholly Conservatives who manned the Scotland Says No organisation, the Yes for Scotland group, while having a majority of Nationalists as activists, was much more all-party in make-up. This led to a more effective, because more united, campaign on the No side. Whereas the multifarious character and interests of Yes for Scotland led at times to a public profile which appeared inconsistent - nationalist spokesmen pointed to the possibility of the Scottish electorate using the Assembly as a means of squeezing more powers out of Westminster, while others claimed that devolution was a means of preventing the Nationalists from realising their aim of independence - the Scotland Says No side tended to speak much more as one. "We knew Robin Cook, the CBI and Tory spokesmen could be relied upon to have the same message", was how Ian Grant Cumming made the point to me.

The No side of course did not eschew the possibility of having spokesmen who on occasion could appeal to one section of the Yes side - the pure devolutionists who wanted a settlement wholly worthy in itself and not as part of some tactical ploy for the realisation of other aims. This was most significantly done at a meeting organised in Edinburgh University by students supporting a No vote. Lord Home made a speech which was extensively covered in the media claiming that to vote No might in the end make for a better devolution deal (see chapter 2). However cynically the Yes side regarded this appeal, it seems to have played a part in routing the Heath-like appeal for a Yes vote on the part of other Conservative spokesmen.

The lasting impression of the umbrella organisations then is one of greater door-step activity on the part of the Yes campaigners, but a more consistent public campaign on the part of the No side.

The General Impact

In Edinburgh, the campaigners made little impact compared with elections in terms of grass-roots campaigning. The major benefit both sides had was in easy access to the local population through *The Scotsman* and *Evening News* newspapers and Radio Forth, the local independent station. While the newspapers were supporters of devolution - *The Scotsman* in particular having a long and respected tradition of support for Home Rule - both sides were accorded significant coverage. Radio Forth, of course, was obliged to maintain a balanced treatment of the Referendum (as I make clear in chapter 7). Newspaper coverage seemed important at the time in maintaining a public focus on the devolution issue. Even the No supporters in general

appreciated that they were given considerable publicity through pro-devolution
newspapers.

Since such coverage was important - and both sides laid great stress on generating
press coverage - it must be said that the Yes side were unable to use it as coher-
ently and effectively as the No side. Three reasons may reasonably be offered in
explanation. Firstly, the Scotland Says No organisation was well-served by a professional public relations officer. Secondly, the multiplicity of organisations on
the Yes side meant that there was a flood of press releases at times reaching news
desks throughout Edinburgh. This then left the effective overall press strategy in
the hands of news desks rather than in the hands of the Yes side. The No side,
through having fewer organisations, had tighter control over the development of
their press campaign. And finally, the No side were much more united in their overall purpose. Their task was to point out the inadequacies and dangers in the legislation - to run a critical, negative campaign, not having to argue for any change
but merely attack what was on offer. The Yes side, on the other hand, were faced
with the task of arguing for change which, however, meant different things to different factions: the Yes campaigners had no single aim. The variety of strategic,
tactical and ideological perspectives amongst the Yes campaigners made it inherent-
ly much more difficult to project a united approach. It is understandable that the
No campaigners saw it as an advantage to have so many organisations operating independently on the Yes side. But this view was rarely appreciated by the Yes side.
Indeed, at one stage, to generate another platform for the issuing of press releases, some Nationalist members of YFS in Edinburgh started to issue press releases under the name of SCARR (Scottish Campaign Against the Rigged Referendum)
whose slogan was that old Irish cry "Vote early, vote often". But there are no
signs that this "organisation" had a membership which ever exceeded three people or
that it was able to organise the "dead vote" in Edinburgh. On the contrary, the
major problem for the Yes supporters was how to organise the live voters!

And whatever happened to Edinburgh's special interests during the campaign? One
leaflet was produced by Edinburgh's Yes for Scotland committee on the question of
why Edinburgh citizens should vote Yes, giving arguments peculiar to Edinburgh. It
was not very widely distributed; on the Saturday before polling one group of supporters was seen issuing it indiscriminately in Princes Street.

It must be concluded that the overall resources of the Yes side were so poorly organised that the No side, although smaller in terms of available manpower, was
given a tactical advantage. If an effective umbrella organisation had existed, encompassing all the parties and having their commitment, it might have been possible
to organise a more coherent and effective campaign. That this did not happen certainly contributed to the low-level and rather unexciting campaigning in Edinburgh.
It was a question set by MacDiarmid which prefaced this short piece on campaigning
in the capital; his poetry also provides an apt conclusion:

> *There is no one really alive in Edinburgh yet:*
> *They are all living on the tiniest fraction*
> *Of the life they could easily have,*
> *Like people in great houses who prefer*
> *To live in their cellars and keep all the rest sealed up.*

V. ONE MAN'S REFERENDUM: AN ACCOUNT OF THE LOTHIAN LABOUR YES CAMPAIGN
Christopher Harvie

My treatment of Labour's Referendum campaign in the East of Scotland must be qualified by a recognition of the distortions which arise from my own point of view - that of a fairly central participant. For someone to return to Edinburgh after ten years and then take the chair at meetings of the Lothian Labour Yes Campaign may suggest either a flattering degree of charisma, or total institutional break-down. In reality, it meant neither, simply the great organisational axiom of British socialism: "Last out of the room becomes minutes secretary". Yet this personal experience does dramatise some basic problems of the Labour campaign. Devolution was a new and contentious issue for Scottish socialists, bound up, for those who supported it through conviction, with original and somewhat intellectual conceptions of politics. It was difficult to square it with the traditional routines of the Labour Party. But, although a distinctive organisation with a momentum of its own needed to be created to fight the campaign, party unity had still to be maintained in the run-up to a general election. The question which must be asked in retrospect is: did the inevitable compromise weaken the impact of the campaign and, because of tensions which grew throughout, ultimately imperil Labour's traditional solidarity?

The looming election undoubtedly circumscribed Labour's possibilities of action. Party divisions on devolution - with most local government members hostile - meant, so most pro-devolutionists argued, that to join a "devolution coalition", like Yes for Scotland, would provoke intra-party conflict. But the allocation of funds and responsibilities to the election meant that there was precious little to use for a separate campaign. In Edinburgh, with only South, West and East Constituency Parties in favour of a devolution campaign, Pentlands and North hostile, Leith torpid and Central neutral, Labour pro-devolutionists had to proceed very cautiously to create an organisation which would mobilise all available support in the constituencies without spurring the antis into action. But playing it by the book took time. While an Edinburgh branch of Yes for Scotland was organised on November 13 at a meeting in the Appleton Tower, George Square, the Labour Committee was not set up until a meeting on January 20, at the Trades Council.

The Yes for Scotland organisation, whose November meeting I observed, would have confirmed many Labour doubts. The meeting certainly reflected the ecumenical spirit of John MacCormick's Scottish Convention more than the SNP (and, as Yes for Scotland included the Communists, later to be represented on the Labour Committee through the Trades Council, there was some organic connection between the two bodies). But Labour's notion of "solidarity" could not have responded to the inclusion of prominent Conservatives, nor to the active role played by several members of the breakaway Scottish Labour Party, nor, most crucially, to the Secretary of YFS's Edinburgh branch, Ian Hoy. Hoy had, three years earlier, somewhat ostentatiously quitted Labour for the Conservatives, and co-operation with him would have been valuable ammunition for the antis. My own impression is that Hoy's own consciousness of the constraints of his position may have inhibited his own organisation, until quite late on, from building up the informal contacts which were ultimately made.

Constraints of a different sort affected the main personality associated with the Labour campaign in the East of Scotland, Gordon Brown. The former student Rector of Edinburgh University, editor of the *Red Paper on Scotland* (1975) and prospective candidate for Edinburgh South, Brown had been elected to the Labour Party's Scottish Executive in March 1977, and the next year became Chairman of its campaign sub-committee. In this position it was impossible for him to be unaware of the strong anti-devolution feelings of the Chairman of the Scottish Executive,

Mrs Janey Buchan, and his desire to preserve peace on the Executive possibly made
him pursue - and thus transmit directly to Edinburgh - an over-defensive line. No
one worked harder than Brown for the Labour-devolutionist cause, but the tragedy
was that explicitly anti-devolution groups like the Conservatives and Scotland Says
No were all too frequently the least of his worries. His fears were, I think, enhanced by a debate with Tam Dalyell at the Trades Council Centre on January 23,
when a majority, largely composed of councillors and veteran activists, was
aggressively hostile and responded enthusiastically to Dalyell's amazing combination of the folksy and the Olympian - "Yes, I'm glad you asked me that about extra
taxation, Betty, because as Willy Brandt told me ...". At this level, Brown could
not compete, however lucid and impressive his arguments, and the experience may
have led him to overestimate the opposition, which was content to come to meetings,
pass resolutions in the Labour group, and leave it at that.

The initiative for setting up an Edinburgh campaign committee came from South Edinburgh, where the Secretary, Nigel Griffiths, had been empowered to co-opt members
on to a "devolution sub-committee". This met on January 7 and, although only five
strong, commemorated itself with a press release. (Subsequently, Brown was liable
to transform almost any drink with his friends into a "meeting addressed by" for
the benefit of the papers and the bafflement of future historians.) It allowed
Brown, myself and Griffiths to make informal contacts and find out how matters
stood in other parties, and convene the first, and not terribly successful, meeting
of pro-devolutionists in the Trades Council on January 20. The problem was that
both of us were burdened by other - although linked - commitments: Brown with his
Scottish Executive worries and I with the publication of a pamphlet we had written
jointly with Carol Craig of the University Politics Department. Originally stimu-
lated by a perceived lack of simple explanations of the Scotland Act (the antis
having vetoed an official government leaflet), this pamphlet emerged early in February in two forms: *Speakers' Notes* published by the Scottish Council of the Labour
Party, and *The Voter's Guide to the Scottish Assembly*. Given the almost total use-
lessness of meetings and the pamphlet's low sale (about 60 per cent of copies
printed), this was, on reflection, so much wasted effort. Further, on January 19, I
left for Paris to brief Professor François Bedarida's seminar at the Ecole Nationale
d'Administration and to lecture at the Sorbonne, both on Scottish nationality.
Deserting the ship? Possibly; but it was for academic reasons that I was supposed
to be in Edinburgh as a Fellow of the School of Advanced Studies, anyway. Returning
North, I went along to the campaign's second meeting on January 27 at the Trades
Council and, in Brown's absence at Scottish Council, found myself chairing it.

The meeting was instantly faced with a problem: how to get into the Trades Council
offices? This was solved only in a material way by the arrival of the Trades Council Secretary, Des Loughney. His predecessor, John Henry, a much-loved Labour Party
stalwart and strong devolutionist, had gone to the STUC as Assistant Secretary,
whereupon Loughney, a member of the Socialist Workers' Party, had been elected
through a brief entente of the far Left. Although nationally the SWP was pro-devolution, its Scottish Committee was against, and Loughney's lack of enthusiasm was
all too patent. Similarly obvious was the absence of the Edinburgh Labour Party
organiser, Joe Hill, who had been allowed by the City Party Executive to treat the
Referendum as a special campaign, outwith his usual duties. Being hostile to devolution, he had nothing to do with it. The "Lothian Labour Yes Campaign", as the
meeting later constituted itself, gained the use of the Trades Council duplicator
and of Ruskin House, and personal relations with the two dissenting officials were
always friendly, but the Committee had virtually to set up an organisation from
scratch.

That the meeting was a success cannot be attributed to a chairman who had been absent from Edinburgh Labour politics for a decade, but to the personal motivations
of the members who were to take on leading roles and execute them with great competence. These personal factors meant that a neutral chairman was a positive asset.

Don Robertson, who took on the organisation of meetings, and Ian Millar, who did the same for street leafleting, had both been involved with the Scottish Labour Party, and in a sense were "working their passage back"; Jim Boyack, who handled posters and leaflets, had always been a strong Home Ruler within the Labour party; Trevor Davies and Ron Hurley, who handled publicity, were both English, and participated primarily out of a sense of party loyalty. Their enthusiasm meant that decisions in principle about funds, appeals, meetings, leafleting, headquarters and constituency contacts were rapidly taken, a timetable was worked out, and then the constituent elements devolved to individuals for executive action. This left the problem of organisation in the various Edinburgh constituencies. East had been contacted, and informed us that they were well-organised. South and West could be left to themselves. In North, which was run by a far-Left crowd of antis, the moderate minority could be counted on to organise leafleting; a somewhat similar situation obtained in Leith; in Pentlands the party was hostile but the candidate, Arthur Johnstone, and a minority of members were helpful and energetic, while we could count on increasing support in Central as its MP, Robin Cook, took a more and more prominent share in the Conservative-sponsored Scotland Says No campaign. For all of these constituencies as well as for some of the actively devolutionist ones, we had to arrange leaflets and posters.

Leafleting was crucial. There was neither time nor manpower available for canvassing - although this would have been valuable in yielding poster sites. And the supply of literature was less than masterfully handled by the central organisations of the Scottish Labour movement. The STUC leaflet was a crabbed little piece of typography, while the Labour Party one was an unmitigated disaster - less than 100 words along the lines of "All say yes or Tinkerbell will die". Even more tragic was the admirable special issue of *Highway* issued by the Transport and General Workers' Union: the size and format of a *Daily Record* sheet, only about 200 could be carried at a time, and in no way could it be used as a poster, despite its bulk. As for posters, the beaming grin of Uncle Jim coexisted ill with streets of ungritted frozen slush, the result of the public service workers' strike, while the STUC offering had to be read through binoculars at distances of over five feet. We printed our own. But however bad these publications were, our problem was that they never seemed to be where we wanted them. We asked for about 32,000 of the Labour leaflet and got about 15,000, while around the same number of *Highways* found their way to our headquarters at Ruskin House, frequently from union or party offices where they had simply been dumped. Some, for all I know, may still be there. Eventually, we got them all out before Referendum day, but only by making informal contact with Yes for Scotland and the SNP to ensure that Yes literature in general was well-distributed throughout the city. For this I take responsibility, as well as for the fact that the last 2000 *Highways* (a late windfall) were actually distributed in Pentlands by Stephen Maxwell, the SNP candidate, and his helpers on the evening of February 28 when Labour was having its final rally.

Our publicity was well-organised. There were press releases, press conferences and every evening we would sit and feed Gordon Brown with "new lines" for his Glasgow press conferences on the following day. To what end? My own view now is that it simply made our arguments too diffuse: Tam Dalyell, by hammering away ceaselessly at three or four points, remained the personality of the campaign, simplistic and deeply reactionary though I think the tendency of his "anti-government" propaganda was. As for meetings, God knows we tried. Our own promotion at the Trades Council on February 21 was, in terms of numbers, a near disaster although the standard of speaking - from Ronald King Murray, the Lord Advocate, and Hygh Wyper of the T&GWU - was better than what was to come in the final rally organised by Labour in the North British Hotel. The strikers had closed the Assembly Rooms, so the venue had to be moved to this ominously named palace. The speeches of Bruce Millan, John Smith and David Owen, stupefyingly dull, were dutifully applauded by a capacity audience of well-dressed Edinbourgeois. The only man in a kilt there proved to be hostile. I cannot recollect that a word of thanks was expressed by the platform

party or the Transport House officials to any of the Edinburgh volunteers. But by
that time we had other things on our minds.

Referendum day was, almost inevitably, an anticlimax. Jim Boyack and his squad got
poster boards out to schools in Labour areas (no mean feat given the non-partici-
pation of half the constituencies) and I manned the Labour Party office at Ruskin
House. But for most of the time there was little to be done as, without canvassing
returns, we had little information on needs for cars, babysitters, etc. I spent
more time dealing with a stream of foreign journalists and Bedarida's ENA students.
Most of our effort was put into four hired loudspeakers which were transferred from
car to car as these became available. We covered pretty constantly the main Labour
areas and shopping centres, overlapping as little as possible with the other Yes
loudspeakers. In the intense cold of the evening we concentrated on Wester Hailes
and Leith. Yet phone queries from areas like Craigmillar and Dunfermline seemed to
indicate that assurances of efficient campaigning in "solid Labour" areas were
false, and pro-devolution organisation non-existent. But by then there was nothing
we could do. Polls closed at 10 and we all trooped over to the pub to watch ITN,
where a poll suggested a lead for devolution in Scotland of 57 per cent : 43 per
cent. Angus Calder, who had been driving a loudspeaker car for most of the day,
persuaded himself after several pints that it was 1945 all over again. Thus exhila-
rated we went home. Next afternoon, when the results came in, the Yeses had it
in Lothian by a whisker - 187,221 to 186,421. A report from the count suggested
that Craigmillar, an area of council housing, had polled 45 per cent; Morningside,
a middle-class area, 75 per cent. While our efforts might just have managed to turn
a narrow defeat into a tiny majority, they were patently useless in overcoming the
relative apathy and indifference of the Labour heartlands.

Who was involved in the Labour campaign? Estimating numbers and judging social
background is difficult, and the sketch that follows is based only on the details
I kept of the 56 who helped at Ruskin House in the last week. Up to 30 more must
have been involved in those constituencies which organised their own campaigns.

TABLE 4.3   Occupations of volunteers

1. Members of the teaching profession		19
a. University teachers	7	
b. Higher education teachers	4	
c. Schoolteachers	8	
2. Members of other professions		14
a. Media, public relations, voluntary societies organisers	9	
b. Other professions	5	
3. White collar (secretarial, clerical)		5
4. Skilled trades		4
5. Union organisers		2
6. Housewives		2
7. Students		3
8. Unidentified or unemployed		7
Total		56

The two most significant groups were from the teaching professions (34 per cent)
and from the other professions (25 per cent), among whom those involved in the
media, public relations, voluntary bodies and publishing yielded 16 per cent. The

dominance of the teachers probably had something to do with the closure of schools and colleges, both through the strikes and on Referendum day.

Table 4.4 Constituencies of volunteers and Ages of volunteers

South*	13	under 20	1
Central	12	21 - 30	16
West*	8	31 - 40	21
North	7	41 - 50	10
Leith	5	51 - 60	7
Pentlands	5	61 - 70	1
East*	4		
Other	2	Total	56
Total	56		

*organised own campaign

The age distribution peaked in the early thirties (although it was significant that students took virtually no interest in the campaign, the University Labour Club being both hostile and moribund). Eighty-five per cent were Scots, 70 per cent were men and the overall political complexion - a very rough and ready subjective judgement, this - seemed to work out just to the right of the Tribune group.

Overall, a paradox emerges. Working-class areas seem to have voted for devolution, middle-class areas against, yet the support for the Lothian Labour Yes Campaign was overwhelmingly middle-class (almost 60 per cent of volunteers had degrees). The local working-class support that a general election involves - lapsed members turning up at temporary offices in housing schemes, offers of windows for posters, old ladies making tea - was almost totally lacking, although it was back in evidence at the General Election two months later. This was plainly the consequence of the failure to mobilise the constituencies as such. Our *Ersatz* campaign, drawing strongly on individual expertise and enthusiasm and personal contacts and well-heeled enough to liquidate £400-odd in debts, generated roughly the effectiveness of a single constituency party at election pitch. It was physically impossible to do more, given the constraints under which we operated.

The most crippling of these and the one which, in retrospect, caused most bitterness, was the lack of strong leadership from the Labour Party organisation. At the very least, the fact that it delayed action until into the New Year meant that the chance of recruiting large-scale trade union and work place support was virtually thrown away. Such support might not have amounted to much anyway - my own view - but by January it was too late to appeal to branch meetings for funds, manpower and factory contacts. Some of us would have gone further and demanded an early warning to dissident councillors, Party officials and MPs, that sustained opposition to devolution would lead to expulsion. At stake, after all, was not simply devolution but the only major piece of legislation the Callaghan government had carried, whose failure would more or less guarantee defeat at the Election. Yet this necessary *Realpolitik* - every bit as much as the subtle arguments for a decentralised socialism - still ran counter to the traditional "solidarity" of the Labour Party, despite the latter's destructive implications. It was evident, however, after Referendum and Election, as divisions - both pro- and anti-devolution and left-right - continued to widen within the Party, that solidarity was wearing very thin.

In the middle of the campaign I ran into Norman Buchan at Waverley Station. He was sceptical about devolution, but reputedly rather less so than his wife. "Yes", he sighed, "Naomi Mitchison wrote to me that the one reason for voting for the Assembly was that it would be interesting to see what happened"; I agreed on that much. He went on: "It would be interesting if you, or (he mentioned a prominent broadcaster) got elected, but it will be the old gang who run it". Well, to revert to the personal: I would have been prepared to serve in the Assembly for a fraction of my salary out of conviction about the need to reconstruct Scotland's economy and society, and to experiment with new forms of democratic socialism - taking on the "old gang" if necessary, but with some hope that the Assembly experience and its attendant publicity, would break them for good.

I finish this piece as a civil servant of another devolved government, Baden-Württemberg, enjoying resources and privileges far greater than I could have hoped for in Britain. This appointment may, I hope justifiably, denote some confidence in my own abilities, but it does nothing to lessen the bitterness that I feel at the dissipation by the old political order in Scotland of all the ability and altruism that was evident in the campaign for devolution.

REFERENCE

Brown, G. (1975).   (Ed.) *The Red Paper on Scotland*. EUSPB, Edinburgh.

CHAPTER 5

THE LOCAL PRESS

John Bochel   and   David Denver

Scotland has a network of more than one hundred local weekly papers which covers
the country, outside the four cities, pretty comprehensively. Each of the nine
local government Regions is served by a number of papers ranging from 41 in Strathclyde to six each in the Lothian and Fife Regions, while the three Islands Areas
have one paper each. The combined circulation of these papers is close to one
million, which compares with a total circulation of about 1.5 million for the six
papers comprising the Scottish morning daily press.

Local papers are, of course, quite different from the national press. They have
neither the resources nor the pretensions of daily papers but circulation figures
suggest that they remain an important channel of communication in local communities.
As such, they constitute a potentially important stimulus to voter mobilisation and
medium of political communication. In a previous study of the Scottish local press,
we showed that local papers print a good deal of political news, attract and publish
a lot of correspondence on politics and are extensively used for political advertising (Bochel and Denver, 1977). In the three weeks of the February 1974 election
campaign the Scottish local papers, between them, devoted considerably more column
inches to reporting major party activities than did the whole of the British national daily press, (national dailies 16,000 column inches, Scottish weekly papers
20,817 column inches); they also printed 305 letters (2,222 column inches) and contained 1,621 advertisements for candidates (15,780 column inches). The local weeklies, moreover, reported the campaign in a markedly different way from the national
dailies. There was, naturally, the local perspective, but they were also more calm
and serious, more thorough in reporting what candidates were saying and less partisan. Taken together, they showed a diversity of style, of message and of character
which belies a common impression of media homogeneity in Britain.

Social scientists are uncertain as to the precise effect of the press (and other
media) in influencing political behaviour. This chapter is not, however, intended
as a contribution to the literature on media effect. Rather we simply accept the
common assumption that the press has *some* influence, however vague, and are concerned to describe and analyse the ways in which the Referendum campaign was handled
by local papers.

If the press has any effect on voting behaviour, it seems safe to hypothesise that
that influence will be greater in a referendum than in an election. In a referendum
the cohesion of the parties is almost certainly more tenuous, and the motivations
of their activists more likely to be weaker than in an election. For voters in a
referendum the normal cues of class, party identification, parental guidance and

99

habit are less likely to be helpful in making decisions about whether and how to vote. Together these factors will probably make it more difficult for partisan groups to maintain campaign momentum in a referendum. In the particular circumstances of the Scottish Referendum some of these features, as demonstrated elsewhere in this volume, assumed considerable significance. In addition, the absence of partisan broadcasts on radio and television during the campaign added to the potential importance of the press.

We are concerned here with the Scottish local weekly press during the four weeks of February 1979, which we defined as the Referendum campaign period. Our discussion is based on an analysis of 458 issues of the 112 titles which we identified as being in circulation at the time.[1] We deal with four aspects of press coverage, namely, editorial comment, news of the campaign, correspondence and the uses which the various partisan groups made of paid advertisements. In order to provide some perspective, we compare our findings, where possible, with those of our previous study of the February 1974 election.

EDITORIAL PREFERENCE

Local papers were far less likely than were national papers to produce editorials[2] on the Referendum debate, and when they did so they were far less likely to be partisan (see Brown, chapter 6). As we found in our study of the February 1974 election, so again in 1979 about half of the papers (55) had no editorial on any subject during the campaign period. Of the remaining 57 papers, 13 did not have one on the Referendum. Thus, only 44 papers (39.5 per cent of the total) made editorial comment. They did so in 60 leading articles, giving an average of less than 1.5 per paper in a four-week period. Slightly fewer papers had editorials on the Referendum than had them on the February 1974 election, but the latter attracted a mean of 1.8 leaders in a three-week campaign.

It was not always easy to classify the orientation of editorials, and Table 5.1 is necessarily based on subjectively derived data. In some cases editors were apparently bemused or confused by the debate, and the intent of their sermons was obscure. The categories Weak Yes and Weak No in Table 5.1 include cases of editorials which, on the face of it, seemed to take a neutral line, but which, on a careful reading, could be said to lean one way or the other.

Although the greatest number of papers advocated a No vote, the numbers of neutral and No editorials were almost equal. The proportion of neutral editorials is almost the same as that in our general election study and the proportion of No editorials is not very different from that of pro-Conservative ones. The Yes cause fared relatively badly, for almost half of the editorials on this side were in the "weak" category. In terms of column inches devoted to advocacy, the No cause attracted nearly as much space as the neutral and Yes points of view. Editors who favoured a No vote were more vociferous and loquacious than the rest. It is noteworthy, too, that most of them wrote in papers which apparently did not regularly have editorial comment. In contrast, most of the papers which supported the Yes cause or were neutral apparently had regular editorials.

We commented, in relation to the general lack of editorial partisanship in 1974,

---

[1]The total number of issues is more than 112 X 4 because a few bi-weekly papers are included.

[2]We categorise as editorials not only conventional leading articles, but items that were sometimes called "diaries" or other features that seemed to be an expression of editorial preferences.

TABLE 5.1 Orientations of Local Papers and Leading Articles [a]

Orientations of papers with leading articles on Referendum		Leading articles		
	N	%	N	%	Column inches
Neutral	11	25.0	22	36.7	191
Yes	9	20.5	9	15.0	90.5
Weak Yes	5	11.4	8	13.3	106
No	17	38.6	19	31.7	288
Weak No	2	4.5	2	3.3	34.5
Total	44	100.0	60	100.0	710

a. Included in the Yes and No totals are newspapers which had, at different times, what we judged to be neutral and Yes leaders (1) and neutral and No leaders (3).

that our findings were something of a surprise. We speculated about whether this was a function of a peculiarly confused and controversial election but obviously this was not the case. For whatever reason, a large proportion of local papers do not go in for editorial pontificating on any topic and an even larger proportion decline to make comment on topical and controversial political issues. It is not for us to judge whether they are right or wrong to do so, but our findings still surprise us. The issue of the Referendum - devolution - was one that, whatever the result, was bound to affect the local communities which the papers served. To take one example, if a Scottish Assembly were set up, one almost inevitable consequence would have been a reorganisation of local government with the likely disappearance of the allegedly unpopular Regional Councils, whereas the *status quo* meant their retention. It seems strange that most local papers, based as they are in the much lamented former burghs, did not feel moved to comment even on this aspect of the debate.

Whether it is the duty of newspapers to structure arguments and give a lead on political issues is an open question. It could be argued, on the basis of our previous study, that local papers by reporting in a more or less even-handed way the speeches and activities of the partisans, fulfil this duty. Perhaps a more interesting question is whether, on the Referendum, Scottish local papers better reflected the position of a rather confused and unconfident Scottish opinion than did their daily counterparts. They certainly, on the whole, did little to alleviate the confusion or raise the confidence of their readers.

COVERAGE OF NEWS

If the editorial columns of newspapers generally failed to give guidance to voters on the Referendum, a partial substitute, and perhaps a preferable one, might be found in their coverage of campaign news if, as we found on the whole in 1974, this was respectable in quantity, reliable in reporting and fairly evenly balanced amongst the partisans.

On the face of it, the Referendum campaign seems to have been less newsworthy for local papers than a general election. For the three weeks of the February 1974 election we recorded, from 301 issues, a total of 20,817 column inches devoted to the campaign (defined in a broad way to include reports of speeches, press conferences, interviews, statements, invited contributions, biographical materials, party activities, features and photographs). For the four weeks of the Referendum

TABLE 5.2   Coverage given to their Campaigns
by Number of Meetings held by Yes and No Groups.

	Meetings		Coverage		Mean coverage per meeting
	N	%	Column inches	%	column inches a
Yes	312	73.8	6,476	64.0	20.7
No	111	26.2	3,642	36.0	32.8
Total	423	100.0	10,118	100.0	

a. This column includes all news of the various campaigns, not
   just meetings.

campaign we recorded, from over 400 issues of local papers, only 10,118 column
inches on the same matters (Table 5.2): that is, just under half of that for the
shorter general election campaign. There were in addition 515 column inches reporting debates and 2768 column inches on other matters relating to the Referendum.

Why did a longer campaign apparently produce less news? Did the local papers fail
in their task of reporting the activities of the partisans? The answer to the
first question is clearly that there was less activity during the Referendum campaign than during the general election. For one thing there were far fewer public
meetings, the staple of local political reporting. Whereas we identified just over
2,000 meetings advertised or reported during the three week 1974 election campaign,
we were able to find only 423 meetings plus 35 debates for the four weeks of the
Referendum campaign.[3] It is natural, and probably right, that newspapers should
devote less space to less activity. But in one sense the Referendum seems to have
been regarded by the local papers as *more* newsworthy than an election. A division
of the number of column inches of news on all aspects of the Referendum by the number of meetings and debates held produces a figure of 29.2 column inches per meeting for the Referendum and 10.4 column inches for the election. Whether consciously or not, local newspapers actually promoted the Referendum in default of activity. We do not, of course, know whether the papers would have devoted space in the
same proportions if activity had been comparable to that for an election. News
coverage should, other things being equal, be contingent upon the amount of newsworthy activity. But space has to be filled, pride satisfied and deference
accorded.

Not only were there fewer meetings than for a general election, but there seems to
have been less activity of all kinds, certainly on the basis of the kinds of calculation we were able to make from newspapers sources. There were virtually no advertisements announcing walkabouts by prominent personalities; there were few
announcements about the organisation of motorcades, the availability of stickers,
posters and so on. And, as other contributions show, these conclusions from our
study of papers are confirmed from the field.

The absence of unity in the Yes and No campaigns is commented upon elsewhere (see

[3]There is considerable discrepancy between the number of meetings we found advertised in the newspapers and that reported by parties and groups. There are two
  plausible explanations for this. Firstly, not many local weekly papers circulate
  in the larger urban areas where there were undoubtedly many meetings. Secondly,
  some meetings were publicised in other ways.

chapter 2) and there were, of course, bitter recriminations from some quarters about the fragmentation of the Yes side. And yet, purely from a news point of view, this fragmentation could have contributed more rather than less. In different places the Labour Party, the SNP, the Liberals, the Yes for Scotland and Alliance groups all had separate organisations and activities but their local impact was unimpressive. If the Referendum was given less attention than an election, then much of the responsibility rests with the campaign groups.

If the weight of such editorial comment as was made tended to favour the No cause, this cannot be said about news coverage. Taken together, the various factions on the Yes side obtained almost two thirds of the space devoted to news of the partisans (Table 5.3).

TABLE 5.3   Number of Meetings held by Individual Yes and No Groups
by Coverage in Local Papers

	Meetings		Total coverage	
	N	%	Column inches	%
Yes for Scotland	121	38.8	1498	23.1
Labour Movement Yes	79	25.3	1602	24.8
SNP	73	23.4	2396	37.0
Liberals	27	8.6	533	8.2
Alliance for an Assembly	2	0.6	-	-
Other Yes	10	3.2	447	6.9
Total Yes	312	99.9	6476	100.0
Scotland Says No	78	70.3	1184	32.5
Conservatives	25	22.5	1690	46.4
Labour Vote No	8	7.2	243	6.7
Other No	-	-	525	14.4
Total No	111	100.0	3642	100.0

In our previous study we did not establish a relationship between the number of meetings advertised or reported and the amount of news space allocated to them. We attributed this partly to the desire of editors to maintain something of a balance between parties. But there are circumstances in which it would not be reasonable to give equal coverage to campaigns that varied greatly in the intensity of their activities. Unlike coverage of the 1974 election campaign, there was, for the Referendum, a positive relationship between the amount of activity by groups, as measured by the number of meetings, and the amount of coverage they obtained.

Study of Table 5.3 shows that *parties* as opposed to *ad hoc groups* did comparatively well. The large difference between the proportion of meetings held by the SNP and the proportion of coverage that its campaign received is partly explained by a much higher level of ordinary branch activity than was apparent in the Labour or Liberal Parties. Very many more SNP branches existed, and, as it happened, during the Referendum period a large number of them held their annual general meetings or had other activities such as Burns suppers. Their prospective candidates, councillors, chairmen or others who were the main speakers at those meetings that were reported usually took the opportunity to exhort members and electors to support the Yes cause. The main *ad hoc* group on the Yes side (YFS) did comparatively badly and the Scotland Says No group even worse, whilst the Conservatives did even better than the SNP. Again, the disproportionate amount of space allotted to the

Conservative case is partly attributable to the other activities of local Conservative Associations. But in the case of neither the SNP nor the Conservatives does it account for the largest part of the difference. An explanation might be that parties had contacts with local reporters and editors that the *ad hoc* groups did not have and that they made good use of them. In addition, it does indeed look as if the greater heterogeneity of the Yes campaign may have been beneficial as far as publicity was concerned.

As in 1974, the largest amount of space was devoted to reports of speeches, debates, interviews and statements by protagonists. Reports of speeches made up 37.6 per cent of news coverage, statements 22.5 per cent and interviews 1.0 per cent, making a total of 61.1 per cent. Again, reports of speeches were apparently *verbatim*, but abbreviated versions of the originals; comments were sometimes made about attendances and this time there seem to have been healthy numbers attending, particularly for debates.

There were a few pieces explaining "What Devolution Means", a number of straw polls (usually showing a Yes majority) and interviews with "men in the street". Other news items included challenges from one side or one person to debate with another, polling and counting arrangements and news about various organisations' doings and plans for the campaign. Only two "national" items attracted significant attention. One was the controversial Church of Scotland letter to be read from pulpits which seemed to recommend a Yes vote, and a statement from the CBI in Scotland which predicted that devolution would damage the Scottish economy.

A good number of local papers used some imagination in drawing attention to the devolution debate. Frequently whole pages, and sometimes two pages, with special headings, were used to attract readers. But, although over 90.0 per cent of the papers printed news on their front page, Referendum news appeared on the front pages of only 55.0 per cent of them.

Three papers, the *East Lothian Courier*, the *Grangemouth Advertiser* and the *Turriff and District Advertiser* (which in one leading article managed a timid Yes recommendation), ignored the Referendum altogether in their news columns, although they all benefited from campaign advertisements; but they did print letters on the debate. The *Dumfries and Galloway Standard*, which is published twice a week, devoted most column inches to the debate (557). Of the weeklies, the *Border Telegraph* with 386 column inches had most. The mean number of column inches per paper was 115.

As in the 1974 election, therefore, local papers provided their readers with a fairly full account of local campaign activity and in doing so helped to publicise the issues at stake. Given the extensive reporting of speeches, readers had the opportunity to be well-informed about the main arguments being put forward by the two sides in the debate.

ADVERTISING

There is, in Britain, a statutory prohibition on political advertising on television and radio, but partisans are free to place political advertisements in newspapers. Comparatively few of these appear in national newspapers, presumably because of the cost, but this campaign "technique" is common in local weekly papers. It is easy to understand advertising to give notice of public meetings or to appeal for help or to make other announcements, but such advertisements constitute a minority of the total, and other political advertisements account for more than four times the space. The motives for inserting propaganda or, as we label them, partisan advertisements, are more obscure. It seems unlikely that this is conceived of as an attempt to put across a message unadulterated by editorial selection because few extended and cohesive arguments are presented in this form and in any case, as we have indicated, local newspapers are pretty fair in their reporting. Nor (because many advertisements are placed by small local organisations) does it seem likely to be intended as part of a sophisticated "Saatchi and Saatchi" type conditioning process. Two explanations seem more likely. Firstly, organisations advertise because others do so and this is one way to publicise the political equivalent of a brand image. Secondly, political advertising might be used as a supplement to, or in place of, conventional campaign techniques because manpower resources are inadequate or the techniques impractical or ineffective. Advertisements might be thought to give an impression of activity, of strong support, of a bandwagon rolling.

Whatever the reasons, political advertising is an example of partisan groups using the medium of the press to communicate directly with electors and must be considered in any study of elections or referendums.

The lower key in which this Referendum seems to have been fought, compared with a general election, is reflected in the smaller amount of political advertising in the former. The longer, four week Referendum campaign produced only 13,724 column inches against 15,780 for the three week election campaign of February 1974. As we noted earlier, there were fewer meetings during the Referendum campaign and consequently there were fewer advertisements for these. The greater activity of the Yes side generated more advertisements for meetings and, as we have seen, greater news coverage. It seems likely again that the so-called split in the solidarity of the Yes campaign resulted in more meetings and advertisements than a united campaign would have done. The main "umbrella" group (YFS) held only 40.1 per cent of the meetings on the Yes side whilst the Scotland Says No group accounted for 78.1 per cent of the meetings on the No side. It is worth noting that (whatever happened in densely populated areas) in the parts of Scotland covered by this survey, the Labour Movement Yes campaign held slightly more meetings and had a slightly greater number of advertisements for them than the SNP. The figures for the SNP are also interesting. They demonstrate that SNP efforts were not entirely channelled through the Yes for Scotland group and that in a good number of places they fought quite independently (see also chapter 2).

TABLE 5.4 Press Advertising by Campaign Groups [a]

| | Partisan advertisements | | | | Meetings advertisements | | | |
	N	%	Column inches	%	N	%	Column inches	%
YFS	69	17.1	1,577	13.9	92	25.1	573	23.9
SNP	55	13.6	538	4.8	57	15.6	306	12.7
LMY	14	3.5	180	1.6	60	16.4	267	11.1
Liberals	4	1.0	62	0.5	9	2.4	42	1.7
AFA	-	-	-	-	4	1.1	9	0.4
Other Yes	7	1.7	48	0.4	7	1.9	40	1.7
Total Yes	149	36.9	2,405	21.2	229	62.5	1237	51.5
SSN	230	57.1	8,640	76.3	107	29.2	1012	42.1
Conservatives	16	4.0	146	1.3	19	5.2	104	4.3
LVN	3	0.7	108	1.0	7	1.9	31	1.3
Other No	5	1.2	24	0.2	4	1.1	17	0.7
Total No	254	63.0	8,918	78.8	137	37.4	1164	48.4
TOTAL	403	99.9	11,323	100.0	366	99.9	2401	99.9

a. For abbreviations see the list at the beginning of the book.

The greatest number of advertisement was concerned with partisan points or slogans, and of these nearly two thirds (63.0 per cent) were inserted by the No side, almost all by the Scotland Says No organisation. Taken along with the smaller number of meetings, this suggests that No activists were thinner on the ground than those on the Yes side but their greater financial resources enabled them to back up their more meagre campaign in the field with newspaper advertisements. Not only did the No side have more partisan advertisements (1.6 times more) than the Yes side, they also accounted for far more of the space devoted to these (3.7 times more). The great majority of local papers carried, during the campaign, two or more 40 column inch advertisements inserted by the headquarters of the Scotland Says No organisation. There were well over a hundred of these and they accounted for well over half of the partisan advertising on the No side. There were two versions of these No advertisements (appearing in local newspapers), neither of them very exciting.

None of the headquarters organisations on the Yes side seems to have launched a similar campaign, and the advertisements inserted by local organisations were smaller and, if anything, less sophisticated. Even the SNP, whose newspaper publicity we admired in the February 1974 General Election, showed little variety or originality on this occasion.

Finally, it may be worth noting that the sponsorship of some advertisements was not always clear and we suspect that in some cases this may have been deliberate. George Reid, SNP MP for Clackmannan and East Stirling and a Vice-chairman of the Yes for Scotland group, advertised his public meetings under neither a Yes for Scotland nor an SNP heading but instead under the more ambiguous "Scotland Yes" heading. This is but one example.

The 40 per cent rule was, as can be seen elsewhere in this volume, highly controversial. It made voter turnout critical. Although not always noted by commentators and thus little appreciated, official bodies did something, in a rather formal way, to publicise the Referendum. Almost every local newspaper carried rather spectacular full-page advertisements on postal voting and these could hardly be missed by readers. Indeed, official advertisements accounted for more column inches (14,586) than those of all campaign groups together.

CORRESPONDENCE

Correspondence columns are a prominent feature in many local papers. They serve, amongst other things, as a means of political participation and as a channel of communication. In the context of a referendum, where voting may be less determined than in an election, and the debate more open, correspondence columns may serve as a genuine forum for electors for asking questions, making partisan points and for presenting a reasoned case. It may also be used as a substitute for at least part of a conventional campaign.

That this may be the case is suggested by our finding that letters were the only feature of local newspapers that showed an increase for the Referendum as against the February 1974 General Election. In the first place the Referendum seems to have encouraged more editors to open their columns to partisans. Only a few local papers (eight out of 112) did not have letters relating to the campaign (50 out of 121 in February 1974). Secondly, many more letters, covering many more column inches appeared. The increase over the 1974 General Election was five times in terms of both number and column inches.

Table 5.5 shows that the Yes side had a clear lead in the number of letters published and in its share of column inches. Again it seems likely that the heterogeneity of the Yes campaign may have resulted in more publicity although the

largest number of both Yes and No letters were, as far as we can tell, the result
of "private enterprise" on the part of individuals. A feature of the correspondence
aspect of the campaign is the extent to which a few leading figures on each side
intervened. On the No side seven people accounted for 316 letters, or almost 48.0
per cent of those published. On the Yes side there were only three persistent
"official" correspondents and between them they had just over a hundred letters
published or just about 12.0 per cent of the total.

TABLE 5.5   Origins, Orientations and Column Inches of Letters
to Local Weekly Papers [a]

	N	%	Column inches	%
SNP	148	9.6	1,514	12.4
Yes for Scotland	88	5.7	694	5.7
Labour Movement Yes	50	3.3	428	3.5
Liberals	21	1.4	196	1.6
Alliance for an Assembly	2	0.1	22	0.2
Other Yes [a]	564	36.7	4,345	35.4
Total Yes	873	56.8	7,199	58.8
Labour Vote No	208	13.5	1,612	13.2
Scotland Says No	123	8.0	764	6.2
Conservatives	56	3.6	520	4.2
Other No [a]	276	18.0	2,163	17.6
Total No	663	43.1	5,059	41.2
TOTAL	1536	100.0	12,258	100.0

a. Letters labelled Other Yes and Other No are those which did not
   indicate that the writer was formally connected with one of the
   campaign groups.

We suggested earlier that the No side may have advertised heavily partly to make
up for a comparative shortage of manpower in the field. The same might be said of
their letter-writing campaign, particularly for the Labour Vote No group. Three
leading personalities, Tam Dalyell, MP, Brian Wilson and Allan Campbell McLean had
202 letters published in all. Dalyell conducted a veritable marathon of letter-
writing and he, alone, had 140 letters published in 66 papers. One paper printed
seven letters from him and several others printed at least five. Alone of the
prominent letter-writers, he seems to have composed individual letters for individual papers. His letters were usually in reply to others which had appeared in
each paper. We do not know how many letters he wrote which were not printed, but
they must have been numerous. Given that Dalyell was the leader of the Labour Vote
No campaign, participated in 16 public debates with Jim Sillars, MP, and addressed
very many meetings and debates all over Scotland, his correspondence campaign
alone merits the adjective "remarkable". Brian Wilson and Allan Campbell McLean
seem to have sent a standard letter to most local papers, as did the Scotland Says
No correspondents Lord Wilson, Adam Fergusson and Ian Grant Cumming, the Press
Officer. Their lower success rate may well have been due to the reluctance of some
editors to print circular letters.

Another notable correspondent on the No side was George Cunningham, MP, the author
of the 40 per cent rule. His standard letter appeared in 19 papers. Perhaps he had
two disadvantages compared with Dalyell. Firstly, he sent standard letters and

secondly, although a Scot, he represented an English constituency.

Jim Sillars MP (Yes for Scotland) was a leading correspondent for the other side with 55 letters published, followed by Dr Robert McIntyre (SNP) with 30 and Helen Liddell (Secretary of the Scottish Council of the Labour Party) with 19. All of them seem also to have sent standard letters.

A good number of others, some well-known in Scotland, some not, conducted a letter-writing campaign of varying intensity, e.g. Iain Sproat, MP (No), Winnie Ewing, MP (Yes), David Graham of the AUEW (No), and there were numerous letters to papers all over Scotland from Mr W.A. Small of Forfar, Mr A.J.C. Kerr of Jedburgh and Dr J. Wilkie from Vienna (all Yes).

Local newspapers do not regularly receive and publish shoals of letters from out-side their circulation areas, so the Referendum period was exceptional. It seems unlikely that editors printed these letters from outsiders to fill space, since there was no shortage of correspondence on the Referendum. An interest in promoting a genuine debate is not an over-generous view of their motives. They were certainly liberal in the amount of space they allocated to Referendum letters - almost equal to that for news on the subject. Frequently a whole page, and sometimes two pages, were devoted exclusively to Referendum letters and a good deal of imagination was used in presentation in these cases.

It is difficult to comment on the content of letters to the press without seeming to be condescending, but the majority of those that we read made important and often original points to the debate, a feature helped by many editors' tolerance of quite lengthy contributions.

CONCLUSION

We have no doubts at all that the Scottish electorate were well served by their local papers during the Referendum campaign. Partisanship, where it existed, was usually moderate, coverage of news was generous in quantity and balanced in content, correspondence columns were open to many points of view. It could not be said that the local press contributed to the campaign by mobilising opinion on one side or the other. That is not, on the whole, how they see their role. What can be said at a minimum is that their coverage helped to air the arguments pro and con and pro-vided a medium through which partisans could communicate with voters. In these ways local papers made their own contribution to the Referendum debate and it is a con-tribution not to be underestimated.

REFERENCE

Bochel, J.M. and D.T. Denver (1977). Political Communication: Scottish Local News-papers and the General Election of February 1974. *Scottish Journal of Sociology*, 2(1), 11-29.

CHAPTER 6

THE SCOTTISH MORNING PRESS

Michael Brown

"Definition: National Newspaper ... a technical term meaning
a regional paper produced in London." Alwyn James, editor,
Scotland, *December 1973.*

Scotland has its own distinctive morning press. This is worth emphasising, since
some writers imply there is one British press, based on London and serving the
whole of Britain (Blondel, 1977, p. 22 - among others). The major London titles are
indeed sold throughout Scotland but in some parts of the country they arrive only
in the afternoon or even a day late. They account for only a fifth of the morning
papers read in Scotland. The remainder, the vast majority, are edited in Scottish
cities. In every category of morning paper - apart from the quality Sundays which
experience no indigenous competition in Scotland - Scottish readership patterns
differ sharply from those of the rest of the United Kingdom (McGregor, 1977,
pp. 105-107).

The nine titles in the Scottish morning press are made up of two quality dailies,
two tabloid dailies, two regional dailies and three popular Sundays. They adopted
a variety of attitudes towards devolution but all, save for the *Scottish Sunday*
Express, gave prominent coverage to the Referendum campaign (Table 6.1).

THE ATTRACTIONS OF DEVOLUTION AS AN ISSUE

The enthusiasm the Scottish press showed for devolution as a topic is in itself
noteworthy. Three factors might be said to have contributed to this. First, the
area to which the devolution proposals applied happened to coincide with or embrace
the papers' circulation areas. Secondly, among some sections of the personnel and
institutions of the press there was a long-standing enthusiasm for devolutionary
ideas. And thirdly, many participants in the devolution debate were in themselves
newsworthy and hence attracted press coverage in their own right.

These three factors deserve to be explored in more detail. Most of the Scottish
press makes great efforts to emphasise its Scottishness. Mastheads sport thistles
and lions rampant and other Scottish symbols. Where the name itself does not make
the connection obvious, legends such as "Scotland's Newspaper" are added. The press
is accustomed to defending Scottish interests and fending off threats, real and
imagined, from London and elsewhere. With distinctive Scottish legal, ecclesiastical,
educational and administrative interest to report and defend, the writers of head-

TABLE 6.1   The Scottish Morning Press: Attitude to Devolution
and Coverage

Paper (Place of publication)	Ownership	Attitude to devolution	Space devoted to Referendum as % of total[a]
Scotsman (Edinburgh)	Thomson Organisation	Strongly pro	13.0
Glasgow Herald (Glasgow)	George Outram, Scottish and Universal Investment Trust[b]	Pro	5.0
Daily Record (Glasgow)	Mirror Group, Reed International	Strongly pro	4.7
Scottish Daily Express (Manchester)[c]	Express Newspapers, Trafalgar House	Strongly anti	4.4
Dundee Courier & Advertiser (Dundee)	D.C. Thomson	Strongly anti	2.5
Press & Journal (Aberdeen)	Thomson Organisation	Little commitment	4.4
Sunday Post (Glasgow)	As *Courier*	Suspicious of Bill but wanted change	3.6
Sunday Mail (Glasgow)	As *Record*	Strongly pro	5.0
Scottish Sunday Express (Manchester)	As *Express*	Anti	1.1

a. This is the percentage of editorial space in the paper, i.e. all of the paper other than that devoted to advertising. The period covered is the month of February and March 1, 1979. This represents 25 issues of the daily papers and four issues of each Sunday.

b. During much of the campaign Scottish & Universal Investment Trust was unsuccessfully fighting off a take-over by the multi-national, Lonrho.

c. But edited in Glasgow.

lines, editorials and letters to editors look instinctively to the Scottish angle in the story (Webb and Hall, 1978, p. 13). This attitude pervades the press and is at its most strident on the sports pages. In a nation which "reads its papers from the back", this is of no small significance (Harvie, 1977, p. 38).

Devolution provided an opportunity to write up UK politics from the Scottish angle. It was an issue which coincided with circulation areas. When journalists assess the news value of a story, one of the rough and ready criteria employed is whether the issue is of relevance to all or most of the readership. Devolution fitted neatly. In these circumstances it was not surprising that even those opposed to the devolution proposals were at great pains to demonstrate that their opposition was in Scotland's better interest. Just how much prestige was placed on this Scottish identity was revealed by the bitter exchanges between the two tabloids. In a slanging match conducted on rival front pages they debated which was better fitted to "speak for Scotland" - the anti-assembly *Express* published in Manchester or the pro-assembly *Record*, edited in Glasgow by an Englishman!

Within the Scottish press itself there had been a long history of sympathy for what once was known as "Home Rule". *The Scotsman* had long espoused this cause and even the *Scottish Daily Express*, devolution's most bitter opponent, had flirted with nationalism in its early days under Beaverbrook and was still inveighing against "traitors" and, shortly before it was taken over by the Trafalgar House flag, opposed devolution. Many journalists themselves were plainly attracted to the idea of a Parliament in Edinburgh. The prestige it would have brought to the capital city would have elevated the press and its practitioners from provincial to national status (Wilson, 1976, p. 28; Macdonald, 1978, pp. 12-17). Many Scottish journalists were active in devolutionary politics, especially in the Scottish National Party, and many others were influential in forming the Scottish Labour Party, a breakaway from the Labour Party over the question of devolution which favoured a maximalist approach (Drucker, 1977, pp. 19-22). In some papers, particularly the *Daily Record*, *Sunday Mail* and *Scotsman*, leading staff writers and columnists campaigned on the subject. In this, Scottish newspapers and journalists were maintaining the link, traditional in nineteenth-century Europe, between journalists and nationalist movements (Kiernan, 1976, p. 111).

While the first two factors suggest that devolution was given prominence because it met the traditions and interests of newspapers, the third suggests a more accidental explanation of its prominence. An analysis of Referendum coverage, dealt with in more detail below, reveals that the issue rarely received prominent treatment in its own right but rather because of its association with individuals, institutions or events which would anyhow have received attention. These categories included politicians, political parties, churches, trade unions, the courts, pressure groups and the media themselves. The events involved include splits, rows, legal actions and allegations of shady practice. There were, for instance, splits within political parties and unions on policy and tactics; there was a feud within the Church of Scotland on what, if anything, should be said from the pulpit; there was legal action against the broadcasting authorities and there were visits to Scotland by prominent politicians. These are events which tend to receive extensive coverage whatever the issue at stake. During the Referendum campaign they were widely reported, and in the process devolution was headlined.

Thus, the press displayed considerable enthusiasm for devolution, and this despite a lack of evidence of popular interest in the subject. This popular apathy is borne out not only by impressionistic evidence but by the concern, widely expressed by campaigners, that there would be a low poll. Indeed, pollsters found that respondents regularly rated devolution low in their priorities with *The Scotsman*, as late as February 19, only 10 days before the Referendum, reporting that only five per cent of those surveyed in an ORC poll regarded devolution as one of the "most important issues" of the day. The same poll found three out of 10 respondents unaware of the "40 per cent" rule which had featured prominently in the Referendum coverage.

THE STYLE OF COVERAGE

The Scottish devolution Referendum was a unique event and it might have been expected that the press would adopt special techniques to cover it. In the event, the various Scottish papers employed the usual mixture of news reporting, features,

comment columns and readers' letters that is adopted in covering any major political story. The innovations which were made are dealt with below. They were not
numerous. In essence the Referendum campaign was about a complex piece of legislation designed to implement an abstract concept. This is not the stuff of which
front page stories are made, particularly in the mass circulation press. As has
been remarked, the subject was generally given prominence only when it was linked
to another topic which met the traditions of news-worthiness. Thus it was as late
as February 13, a fortnight before the poll, before as many as five of the six
morning dailies carried the same devolution story on their main news pages. (The
exception was the *Dundee Courier*) The occasion was the visit to Glasgow by the
Prime Minister, James Callaghan. The purpose of his trip was to put his political
weight behind the call for an Assembly. As it happened, his appearance coincided
with a nadir in his political prestige, but that is an intriguing connection to be
returned to. It is worth mentioning at this stage that Prime Ministerial visits
usually receive prominent treatment in the press - whatever the purpose.

While the style of coverage was conventional enough for the most part, the extent
of that coverage was considerable and this was particularly so in the case of *The
Scotsman*. In the month of February, 13 per cent of the editorial space (defined as
all the space in the paper less display and classified advertising and advertising
features and supplements), was devoted to devolution and the Referendum. The rest
of the press devoted around four or five per cent to the topic with the *Dundee
Courier* trailing slightly and the *Scottish Sunday Express* scarcely touching the
subject (Table 6.1).

Table 6.2 illustrates the different editorial styles used in covering the Referendum campaign, breaking down the total of items on the subject into various categories of treatment. The term "item" includes news stories, features, opinion columns
and letters. The front page lead is the main news story on page one, or in the case
of the *Courier*, which carries only advertising on page one, the main news page.
There is no evidence to suggest that the reader allocates any particular importance
to an issue which is given the lead position but it is a decision which is given
much attention by editorial executives and hence the allocation of stories to this
category gives a useful insight into editorial priorities. In fact, the Referendum
rarely occupied this position. The allocation of other positions on page one provides further evidence to the same end. There is of course more space for such
stories on the broadsheet papers which can carry a dozen or more items than on the
tabloids which are usually restricted to two.

Inside news was treated differently even in otherwise similar papers. *The Scotsman*
devoted a news story to each aspect of the day's Referendum events, while the
Glasgow Herald tended to run each day's Referendum news into one report. This
difference in attitude is reflected of course in the totals.

The feature category embraces a wide range of items. In some cases events treated
as straight news by some papers were written up in the more interpretive feature
style by others. The *Daily Record* did this frequently. In the *Sunday Post* the bulk
of the political news was presented through the anonymous political column in a
chatty and intimate style.

The *Sunday Mail* brought a rare edge to the coverage thanks to its Mailstrom column
which, in a style more reminiscent of *Private Eye* than Scotland's staid and defer-
ential journalism, delved into the personalities and incidents behind the devolution news stories and published the inside gossip which most journalists merely
swap among themselves. The feature, which caused so much unhappiness to many in
the Scottish establishment, has since been dropped. Most papers made use of the
contributed column by outsiders who were usually partisan to the debate and quite
often opposed to the paper's own views. The *Glasgow Herald* has long used this

TABLE 6.2 Press Treatment of the Referendum [a]

Paper	Total Items	Page One Lead	Other Page One	Inside news	Editorial	Feature & Diary	Column & View	Letters [b]			
								Total	Pro	Anti	Other
	N	%	%	%	%	%	%	%	%	%	%
Scotsman	476	1.5	4.4	38.6	3.2	6.5	–	45.7	19.3	10.5	15.9
Glasgow Herald	160	1.8	8.8	17.5	3.7	9.4	5.0	53.7	18.1	23.7	11.9
Daily Record	131	2.2	0.8	22.0	2.2	58.8	2.2	10.0	9.9	0.8	–
Sc. Daily Express	120	5.0	7.5	21.7	5.0	21.7	2.5	36.6	3.3	32.5	0.8
Dundee Courier	100	2.0	3.0	18.0	4.0	2.0	2.0	69.0	31.0	27.0	11.0
Press & Journal	150	1.3	4.0	40.7	1.3	10.7	1.3	40.7	18.7	17.3	4.7
Sunday Post	26	–	3.8	–	7.8	73.1	7.8	7.6	–	3.8	3.8
Sunday Mail	14	7.1	–	7.1	7.1	64.3	7.1	7.1	7.1	–	–

a. The period covered by the Table is the month of February 1979 and March 1. This embraces 25 issues of each daily and four issues of each Sunday paper. The *Scottish Sunday Express* made insufficient references to devolution to merit inclusion. It carried only five items on the subject.

b. The percentage of total items on the subject represented by "letters to the editor" is further broken down into categories - pro, anti and other - for those letters favouring the devolution proposals, opposed to them and for those letters dealing with the subject in general or whose meaning was obscure.

---

device and others took it up for the campaign. The *Sunday Post*, in its last edition before the poll, devoted two pages to rival spokesmen. In other cases non-partisan experts were brought in to analyse the implications of the devolution legislation.

The editorial or leader column carries the paper's official line on the affairs of the day and most of the press made some use of the space to air their views on devolution. *The Scotsman* in particular explained its views at some length and analysed the arguments of its opponents. The *Daily Record* and the *Daily Express* editorialised on the front page on polling day, as did the *Scotsman*. Letters to the editor proved a major source of coverage of the campaign - though only in some papers. *The Scotsman* on occasion devoted as much as a page and a half to readers' views. There was no correlation between a paper's stance on devolution and the predominant view expressed in the letters carried (Brown, 1979, p. 69).

In its style of coverage of the campaign the Scottish morning press displayed no major innovation. As with any major political story, coverage increased as polling day approached. The expansion of *The Scotsman*'s letters page was noteworthy, as was the occasional series of editorials entitled "Agenda for an Assembly" which sought to develop the ideas and policies an assembly could carry out. The exchanges between the *Express* and the *Record* have already been mentioned but they represent in extreme form the competitiveness prevailing among the tabloids. The *Express* was the subject of comment when it introduced a competition with a £100 prize for the best anti-assembly letter - a gesture which tended to reinforce the impression that devolution was of less than burning concern to the population as a whole, the zeal of *Scotsman* letter-writers notwithstanding.

                    THE EFFECTS OF COVERAGE

It is common practice for studies of elections to record the behaviour and orientation of the press during the campaign. Data on the space devoted to various
issues and personalities is recorded and much attention is devoted to calls by the
mass circulation press to support this or that party. While most writers appear to
be agreed that this is somehow important enough to be reported, little attempt is
made to establish the actual effect the behaviour of the press might have had on
the outcome.

In the case of the Scottish devolution Referendum the Scottish morning press devoted much space and energy to the subject and argued for and against the devolution proposals. But what effect did this have on the result?

The political effects of the mass media are incompletely understood. Save for a
prevailing sense that the media must be significant, the understanding is fragmented
and on occasion contradictory. It is, however, worth emphasising that in a modern
mass society few people can witness politics at first hand, and even those who are
active in politics cannot survey the entire political environment unaided (McQuail,
1969, p. 63). Most people, most of the time, use the mass media as their major
source of information about the political world, either directly, or through discussion with those who have used the mass media.

Theories on the political effects of the mass media have gone through numerous
fashions, including periods which have under-rated their effectiveness, particularly towards change. The 1970s, however, saw an extensive re-assessment of their role
and a growing awareness that their powers might be considerable. Not only is the
concept of powerful media being re-admitted but possible effects are being sought
in a wider range of directions (Blumler, 1977, pp. 3-13). In colloquial usage,
however, the "effects" of media coverage are taken to refer to effects on individuals. In the absence of any comprehensive model relating press activity to voter
behaviour, there are no grounds for saying that the Scottish morning press caused
any particular result in the Referendum. But it was undeniably an actor on the
scene at the time of the Referendum and it would be reckless to write it off. In
the wide ranging research under way on media and politics generally two themes can
shed some light on events in Scotland in February 1979. They are the concepts of
"agenda setting" and the "spiral of silence".

One of the earliest adages on the subject is the observation that the media are not
very good at telling people what to think but very good at telling them what to
think about. This is the notion underlying agenda setting. From an infinite potential pool of material the news organisations select and package a very particular
sample (Kraus and Davis, 1976, p. 213). Much research on the subject is designed to
demonstrate that an audience exposed over time to a particular agenda of issues
adapts its own priorities to match those of the media. Instances of this have been
demonstrated but the point has not been proved on any large scale. But whether or
not the audience internalises the media's priorities, the items on the agenda constitute the arena in which a contest between political groups is fought. Commentators on political campaigns usually note the contestants' enthusiasm to promote
certain issues - which show them in a favourable light -, and to avoid other issues
- which might show them up unfavourably. Given the limited opportunity of individuals to survey politics other than through the media, the potential of agenda, or
arena setting becomes apparent. In the case of the devolution Referendum it is
therefore interesting to determine which issues formed the arena and then to assess
which side might have benefited or suffered.

The agenda of the Referendum campaign can be broken down into three distinct areas: first, items concerned with the detail of the devolution proposals; second, items concerned with the consequences of devolution going ahead or not; and third, the progress of the campaign itself.

The first category was also the smallest. All the papers, as a public service, outlined the basic details of the Scotland Act. This coverage was divorced from other devolution coverage and the evidence of the ORC poll published in the *Scotsman* (February 20, 1979) suggested that even among supporters of devolution there was a fair degree of ignorance on the details of the proposals. There are no indications to suggest that this category influenced the outcome in any way.

The second section of the agenda, concerning the consequences of the Scotland Act being implemented, was dominated by the arguments of the No camp. Their arguments were negative in tone: the Bill (as No campaigners frequently referred to the Scotland Act) was a bad piece of legislation, the assembly would generate more bureaucracy and cost money, and it would lead to the break-up of the United Kingdom, this last often summarised as the "slippery slope" argument. The Yes campaigners had answers to these charges and they were vociferous in presenting them - but in doing so they were fighting the campaign on the terrain chosen by their opponents. They could argue, for instance, that the cost of an assembly would not be great, but in doing so they were conceding that cost was an issue and giving credence to the concern. In other instances they were in a more dangerous trap. By highlighting the "slippery slope" argument, the No campaign were able to emphasise the contradiction within the Yes lobby between those who were there to use the assembly as a step to independence and those who saw the assembly as a means of thwarting the Nationalists. The positive line of argument favoured by the Yes camp was that an assembly would increase democracy by providing a means in Scotland of supervising those powers already long devolved to the Scottish Office in Edinburgh. This, however, was a concept unlikely to fire the enthusiasm of headline writers, although there was a limited attempt to explore the possible workings of an assembly, spurred by the publication of a collection of essays on the theme (MacKay, 1979, passim).

And so, left with the uninspiring prospect of promoting the limited innovations of the Scotland Act, the press found it much easier to resort to the emotional appeal of Balmorality - a synthesis of tartan kitsch, spurious nostalgia and selectively rewritten national history. This was true of the tabloids in particular but in the "qualities" the letter pages maintained the theme, albeit with a veneer of erudition. *The Scotsman*, for instance, had a lively correspondence on the way Sir Walter Scott would have voted in the Referendum. The style was well illustrated by the *Daily Record* headline on the eve of poll: "Now's the day, and now's the hour!" (The quotation is attributed by the national poet, Robert Burns, to the national hero, King Robert the Bruce, on the eve of the Battle of Bannockburn, the much celebrated clash of 1314 which ended in the defeat of a more numerous English army.) But when it came to indulging in Caledonian clichés, fanciful history could too readily give way to kailyard excesses. The day after the result was declared one columnist was so dismayed by her compatriots' verdict that, she confided to her readers, she felt unable to eat porridge for breakfast.

In terms of arena, three topics can be identified: in one arena it was argued that the proposals were expensive and divisive, in the second it was argued that the proposals provided a limited degree of democracy, and in the third support for an assembly was linked to a sense of Scottishness.

No data exists by which to determine which contestants benefited from the contest being held in these particular arenas but certain informed assessments can be made.

On the evidence of opinion polls conducted over a lengthy period, the prospect of
the break-up of Britain and independence for Scotland would attract the support of
only a minority of voters, the vast majority of whom, it might be supposed, would
already be firmly established in the Yes camp. It is therefore difficult to see
how the focusing of attention on the prospect of devolution leading to independence would provide additional benefit to the Yes vote: it could be argued that it
would be more likely to move middle ground voters, opponents of independence, into
the No camp.

In the aftermath of an extensive and controversial reorganisation of local government, the argument that further change would lead to further cost and confusion
might have appeared all too credible. Disputes on the actual cost only emphasised
the question. Concern for the cost of the innovation might not have perturbed the
enthusiasts for devolution but it would scarcely attract the less committed. It
was no coincidence that the question was raised and promoted by the Act's opponents.

The Yes campaign did put over the point that devolution, by providing an assembly
to supervise the Scottish Office, would further democracy. But at no time did even
the pro-devolution press adopt the prospect with any burning enthusiasm. Indeed it
presented something of a problem. How does one enthuse over limited devolution?
There is not much mileage in promoting a souped-up regional council with the power
to quarrel over budgets with Westminster and quiz junior Scottish Office ministers
over educational spending. The more that attention was focused on the proposals,
the more apparent it became that the powers were limited; nor was there much hope
of appeasing the devolution maximalists with a hint that further devolution would
follow, because this would only confirm the "slippery slope" arguments of the anti-
Assembly lobby!

Lastly, the appeal to Scottish consciousness would appear to be a powerful one and
yet, given the many manifestations of Scottishness which have long featured in
Scottish public life - from law courts to sports meetings - there has been a marked
failure of Nationalist politicians to harvest, in full, this awareness. Researchers
into urban Scottish politics have noted this missing connection between Scottish
identity and its expression at the polls (Budge and Urwin, 1966, p. 163). The
Scottish National Party's years in the political wilderness were eloquent testimony
to the fact that pride in national myths and cultural trappings is no guarantee of
political commitment. It may have been easy for the press to play the tartan card;
there are no indications that it was effective. One possible consequence of the
attempt to link patriotic fervour to a Yes vote may have been the campaign tactic
of listing the names of well-known supporters. This will be discussed below.

The third major theme in the coverage was the campaign itself. This was coverage
which implicitly regarded polling day as an end in itself and was thus concerned
with covering the "horse race" between the competing campaign groups. The category
includes details of the campaigners, their groupings, splits, tactics and conflicts.
It also embraces the role of politicians and political parties, the administration
of the Referendum, opinion polls and speculation on the outcome, and the controversial 40 per cent rule (see Chapter 1 for a discussion of its provisions).

The 40 per cent rule was to become a focal point of the campaign. In many respects
this was surprising. Any group arguing that there was in Scotland a burning desire
to have a greater say in the running of Scottish affairs, could scarcely go on to
suggest that only a minority of the population might care enough to vote. When the
Scotland Bill was negotiating its final stages through Parliament, the opinion
polls were reporting that 70 per cent of the electorate favoured the idea. The
requirement to get little over half this total out to the polls should scarcely
have taxed or alarmed the Yes campaigners. But at the same time the 40 per cent
rule exerted a fatal fascination. It was, by all standards, an unusual requirement

to impose. It savoured of gerrymandering, it caused *The Scotsman* to describe the
event as a "rigged election", and, given the appetite of the Scottish press for
grievance, this Westminster device was seized upon greedily. Quickly it proved
popular with the writers of leaders, headlines and letters. From the journalistic
point of view it enjoyed all the characteristics of a good "running story". Almost
every day someone was available to answer charge and countercharge while the complexity of its implications - would an abstention count as a No vote? or was the
electoral register accurate? - kept the issue in the headlines.

This obsession focused attention on the 40 per cent rule and there was much calculation and discussion on whether the requirement would be met. In a conventional
election politicians are usually quick enough to publish optimistic canvasses and
claim there is no risk of defeat. But with the press maintaining the 40 per cent
rule prominently on the agenda, the optimistic tone with which the Yes campaign
had begun was soon confused by the clatter of slide rules and cries of foul play.
The requirement, from being an unfortunate hurdle of little consequence, began to
take on the appearance of an alibi for failure. The intense debate on whether the
hurdle would be cleared contrasted strikingly with the tone of the press a year
before when it regularly discussed the political future in terms of when (and not
if) devolution took place.

At this point the concept of the spiral of silence can usefully be introduced. The
concept postulates that public opinion is based on a "quasi-statistical sense",
whereby people try to integrate themselves in society by identifying the prevailing
climate of opinion and giving voice to those views they believe to be gaining support (Noelle-Neumann, 1977, pp. 144-145). The concept should not be confused with
bandwaggoning, the process whereby a successful movement gains support from those
who wish to be associated with its success or novelty. Rather the idea is that
most of the population has a range of predispositions held with no high degree of
commitment: the public expression or endorsement of a view is likely to be related
to the individual's assessment of the prevailing trends in public opinion. In
integrating with the prevailing climate of opinion they are likely to give expression to those views they perceive to be on the ascendancy and less expression to
those they believe to be on the decline. The theory concedes that there will be
some who hold views with a high degree of commitment: they will be far less sus-
ceptible to changes in the opinion climate.

It is worth stressing that this concept is still being investigated by researchers;
there has been some supportive evidence but, given anyhow the limited data available in the Scottish case, there is no prospect of drawing any firm conclusions.
The spiral does, however, provide a tool with which to examine the course of the
campaign in the press.

Over the period during which Parliament was debating the Scotland Bill (and its
predecessor which dealt jointly with Scotland and Wales), opinion polls suggested
that more than 60 per cent, and on occasion up to 80 per cent, of the committed
samples favoured devolution. Once the campaign was under way, however, and particularly in the final month with which this chapter is concerned, commitment for
devolution was below 60 per cent (Macartney, 1979, pp. 227-228). By eve of poll,
it appeared that opinion was evenly split (*Scottish Daily Express*, February 28,
1979). The opinion polls, in as much as they were news, indeed widely reported
news, presented an image of a climate of opinion which was going against the idea
of an assembly. The point has already been made that, in terms of the arenas in
which the campaign was contested, the opponents of devolution had been successful
in determining a major part of the arena - on their terms. The Yes campaigners
were on the defensive.

A feature of the later stages of the campaign, of relevance at this point, is the

enthusiasm both sides showed for listing the well-known names endorsing their cause.
Latterly the No camp made particular use of the device, perhaps understandably,
given the Yes camp's strong pursuit of the Scottish culture and patriotism theme.
The *Daily Record* grumbled at one point about impressionable voters hitching themselves to a star. The complaint missed the point. Ardent devolutionists were not
going to change the beliefs of a lifetime to follow a pop-star, football hero or
captain of industry. But for the less certain, these public declarations demonstrated that numerous well-known people, many patently Scottish, nevertheless
doubted the wisdom of the proposed devolution scheme. The publicity demonstrated
that Scottishness could be divorced from support for an assembly. In the early
stages of the devolution legislation, with all the national dailies favouring
devolution (before the *Express* changed policy), the anti-assembly reader might well
have felt he was on his own. By the end of the campaign that impression would have
been dispelled.

Other aspects of the newspapers' agenda may also have been relevant to the spiral
process. There is always a risk in studies such as this, which are devoted to a
particular topic, that attention will be too narrowly focused. A newspaper
presents news as a composite or mosaic of juxtaposed items and there is no evidence
to suggest that the reader employs the clinical distinctions of the researcher in
separating them.

The point has already been made that the Referendum campaign received prominent
coverage whenever the Prime Minister or other prominent members of the then Labour
Government became involved in the campaign. One of the reasons for the number of
Yes campaign groups was the refusal of the Labour Party in Scotland to mount a
joint campaign with devolutionists from other parties (see Chapter 2). Apart from
natural antipathy to rivals - particularly the Nationalists - the Labour Party
regarded the Scotland Act as its own distinctive achievement. The Bill had been
born after not a little distress on the part of its Labour parents and, as is often
the case in such circumstances, the parents might well have expected outsiders to
show an unrealistic level of admiration for the offspring; at any rate Labour
believed the Act promised electoral rewards and it planned to be the sole benefi-
ciary.

As a result Labour's Yes posters emphasised visually the link between devolution
and the Labour Government. Prime Minister Callaghan loomed large on the hoardings.
In the process a link was being forged with another spiral: the popularity of the
Prime Minister and the Government was in decline through the later stages of the
campaign.

The major British news story of February 1979, even in the Scottish papers, was not
the Referendum but the widespread series of strikes in the public sector. Even in
the case of the *Scotsman*, that most enthusiastic publicist of devolution, a breakdown of the 25 front page lead stories from February 1 to March 1 shows that devolution did not enjoy priority.

Strikes/pay disputes/union conflicts	10	
Devolution/Referendum	7	
Foreign news	3	
Natural disasters	2	
Budget forecast/Royalty/Leyland	1	each

Most of the strikes concerned the public sector and hospitals and schools were
among the institutions affected. Public health officers warned that if the strike
by grave-diggers continued, bodies would have to be buried at sea: mourners were
reported to be digging graves for their own relatives. It was emotional material
for the press and the writers of headlines and leaders, rarely well-disposed to

to unions at the best of times, set to with zeal to point out the failings of the Labour movement – and of course the party of government with which it was so close-ly linked. In the *Scotsman* the cartoonist Dewar pictured a tombstone inscribed 'LAB' and alongside it a shovel labelled 'NUPE' – one of the public service unions involved in the disputes. And so, while the unions were effectively interring the hopes of the Callaghan government, the Referendum campaign was being fought by the Labour Party in Scotland with a campaign which sought to identify devolution with the prestige of the Prime Minister. The idea might have worked, had Mr. Callaghan maintained the prestige he enjoyed when the plan was devised. But throughout the troubled winter his stock fell: the System 3 monthly survey for February 1979 showed Labour at its lowest for a year and well below the peak of the previous autumn (Macartney, 1979, p. 225).

RETROSPECT

The Scottish press thus presented the Referendum contest in the form of an arena of issues which appear either to have offered little positive advantage to the Yes campaign – by emphasising the symbols of Scottishness – or which may have been detrimental – the questions of cost, the effectiveness of the proposed system, the prospects of the "slippery slope" to the break-up of the United Kingdom, and the obstacle posed by the 40 per cent rule. At the same time the Yes campaign, already on the defensive compared with the strong position of the devolutionists a year before, was also locked into the fortunes of the Government, which happened to be in decline.

It is important to emphasise that this image of the contest was conveyed by the press regardless of the orientations of the individual papers. There are complex processes operating in the media which lead to this homogenising of the agenda (Brown, 1979, p. 76). Thus, a paper could and did argue for devolution in its leader columns while at the same time giving prominence to news which was detri-mental in implication to devolution. Media intentions may bear no relationship to media effects. To assume that a paper has benefited a cause or party because it has declared its support would be naïve in the extreme.

The information available in this study allows no more than an informed assessment to be made and some potential tools for further study to be introduced. Bearing in mind that the media do provide the arena in which such contests take place, the study of any future referendum would usefully determine not only which issues featured in this arena but also the predispositions of the public to each issue. In addition steady monitoring of public opinion would be required to determine which contestant groups or policies were perceived to be in the ascendant and which in decline. Much requires to be done before the effects of the press can be declared with any assurance; but the customary caution of confining observations on the press to a catalogue of contents and allegiances is not only inadequate but can also be misleading.

REFERENCES

Blondel, J. (1977). *Voters, Parties and Leaders*. Penguin, London.
Blumler, J. (1977). The intervention of television in British politics. In Lord Annan (Chairman), *Report of the Committee on the Future of Broadcasting, Appendix E*. H.M.S.O., Cmnd 6753-1, London.
Brown, M. (1979). The Scottish morning press and the devolution referendum of 1979. In N. Drucker and H.M. Drucker (Eds), *The Scottish Government Yearbook 1980*. Paul Harris, Edinburgh.
Budge, I. and D. Urwin (1966). *Scottish Political Behaviour*. Longmans, London.

Drucker, H.M. (1977). *Breakaway: The Scottish Labour Party*. E.U.S.P.B., Edinburgh.

Harvie, C. (1977). *Scotland and Nationalism: Scottish society and politics 1707-1977*. George Allen & Unwin, London.

Kiernan, V. (1976). Nationalist movements and social class. In A.D. Smith (Ed.), *Nationalist Movements*. Macmillan, London.

Kraus, S. and D. Davis (1976). *The Effects of Mass Communication on Political Behaviour*. Pennsylvania State University Press, Pennsylvania.

Macartney, W.J.A. (1979). Summary of Scottish opinion polls relating to voting intentions and constitutional change. In N. Drucker and H.M. Drucker (Eds), *The Scottish Government Yearbook 1980*. Paul Harris, Edinburgh.

Macdonald, M. (1978). The press in Scotland. In D. Hutchison (Ed.), *Headlines: The Media in Scotland*. E.U.S.P.B., Edinburgh.

McGregor, O.R. (1977). Attitudes to the press. As supplement to *Report of the Royal Commission on the Press*. H.M.S.O. Cmnd 6810-3, London.

MacKay, D.I. (Ed.) (1979). *Scotland, the Framework for Change*. Paul Harris, Edinburgh;

McQuail, D. (1969). *Towards a Sociology of Mass Communications*. Macmillan, London.

Noelle-Neumann, E. (1977). Turbulences in the climate of opinion: methodological applications of the spiral of silence theory. *Public Opinion Quarterly*, 41, 143-163.

Webb, K. and E. Hall (1978). *Explanations of the Rise of Political Nationalism in Scotland*. Centre for the Study of Public Policy, University of Strathclyde, Glasgow.

Wilson, B. (1976). Devolution is appeasement that is doomed to fail. *Journalism Studies Review*, 1, 28-30.

CHAPTER 7

BROADCASTING

I. TELEVISION

John Fowler

Although there are occasional squabbles and accusations of bias, television coverage
of general election campaigns in Britain is guided by a generally acknowledged set
of ground rules. The Committee on Party Political Broadcasting, consisting of
representatives of the BBC, the IBA and the main political parties, determines the
number, timing and distribution of party political broadcasts (the content being
left to the parties concerned) and other campaign coverage is expected to be
"balanced" in accordance with statutory obligations laid upon the television companies.

In this field, however, as in others, a referendum poses novel problems. Lacking a
tradition of referendums, Britain lacks also a generally agreed set of procedures
for determining the role of television in referendum campaigns. The arrangements
and procedures which had worked out satisfactorily in the EEC referendum were not
acceptable in the devolution Referendums and the result was that the whole question
of broadcasting during the campaign became a matter of considerable controversy.

The Controversy over Ground Rules

From the time of the Parliamentary debate on the Order for the Referendum to the
end of the campaign there was bitter argument over the content of the ground rules
which were to apply to broadcasting coverage. The most significant episode in this
battle arose from the fact that four party political broadcasts had been scheduled
for transmission in the last week of the campaign on BBC and ITV. At least three of
these broadcasts, those of the SNP, Labour and Liberal Parties, would be in favour
of a Yes vote, while the attitude of the Conservative Party was uncertain. This led
to allegations of unfairness and imbalance which culminated in a court case.

The episode over the party politicals was, however, merely a symptom of a more basic
problem arising from the ambiguous nature of the concept of balance, and this in
turn was linked to fundamentally conflicting views about the status and purpose of
the Referendum itself and its relationship to the normal political process (see pp.
4-6 above).

Everyone agreed that the main purpose of the ground rules was to ensure fair balance in coverage. However, there were two totally different conceptions of balance and these were incompatible, in that the conditions of one could not be satisfied without violating the other. The first can be called proportional or representative balance which is the standard applied at election times. According to this, privileged access to broadcasting and radio facilities is given only to political parties insofar as they have earned the right to act as articulators of public opinion. This right is earned by the support given to them at general elections and by the seriousness of their electoral challenge as measured by the number of candidates they put forward. The essence of this sense of balance is that it is numerically unequal. Very small parties have no right of access to the medium because their views are unrepresentative. Each party is free to use its allotted slot as it thinks best. It does not have to be guided by broadcasters or by the other parties' ideas of the main issues of the day. The balance involved is one between the different weights given to politicised public opinion in the country. On this basis it is seen as fair that orthodox views should be given preferential status over eccentric, minority or deviant views.

The second standard of balance could be called the debating or competitors' principle of balance. A specific issue is artificially extracted and isolated from normal context and is structured so that two teams compete against each other. In this situation balance is something quite different. It entails providing precisely the same conditions, opportunities and facilities for each side. The classic example is the debate. Unlike the first case the past history or status of the competitors is irrelevant. What is essential is that at the beginning and during the competition equal facilities should be provided to the two competing sides.

Although these two concepts of balance were incompatible, the Government seems to have wanted to apply both criteria. They did this on the one hand by segregating the question of party political broadcasts from all other media treatment of the issue. As Under-Secretary of State for Scotland Harry Ewing explained, "party political broadcasts are something apart", and "the material used in a party political broadcast is a matter entirely for the party concerned". The Government was intent on defending the "time-honoured formula" of PPBs (Hansard, 958, cols 1331-1332). On the other hand, Secretary of State for Scotland Bruce Millan applied the other concept of balance to the rest of the media's coverage of the campaign by referring to the precedent of the EEC campaign where both broadcasting authorities had adopted a meticulous balance in their allocation "for" and "against". The same distinction was made by Labour backbencher Donald Dewar, who argued that "the normal all-party machinery should decide the allocation of party political broadcasts, that each party should use them as it saw fit, and that otherwise politicians of both parties should rely on the professional integrity and competence of the broadcasters to ensure that there is a fair spread of representation and that the issue is fairly argued out" (Hansard, 958, cols 1309-1310).

The reference made by the Secretary of State to the 1975 referendum muddied rather than clarified the situation. The White Paper of February 26, 1975, on the conduct of the EEC referendum (Cmnd 5925, para 33) refers to the need to "ensure that there is a fair balance between opposing views in news and feature programmes". There is no reference to party political or ministerial broadcasts, for the simple reason that in their proposals made to the semi-official Committee on Party Political Broadcasting the broadcasting authorities presumed that there would be no requests for party politicals during the period of the referendum. Instead, the broadcasting authorities in 1975 offered 40 minutes of television time to each of the two umbrella organisations. Each organisation prepared programmes, paying all expenses apart from studio facilities, production staff and technicians, which were provided by the BBC (Smith, 1976, pp. 197-198).

In 1975 the decision to allow the umbrella organisations to take over this function of the political parties was arrived at through the normal channels, i.e. through discussion by the whips in the Committee for Party Political Broadcasting. So, even in the act of relinquishing their rights to free broadcasting slots, the parties retained control of the decision-making process itself. The CPPB remained the only channel whereby the vague concept of balance could be translated into the concrete details of programme making, even though the IBA were "somewhat sceptical about the validity of the PPB committee's jurisdiction" during a referendum (Smith, 1976, p. 196). In the end they were convinced by the arguments of the BBC. The referendum could well be a unique event and the umbrella political alliances were necessarily transitory while the BBC had to depend upon the continuing goodwill of the Government. The BBC were therefore loath to make arrangements which would antagonise the major parties; besides, the BBC thought that by getting the CPPB to ratify their proposals they were binding the party whips to recognise both the umbrella organisations and the allocation of time 50:50 for and against the issue.

Ironically the very arrangements which absolved the BBC from the burden of making a decision proved to be their downfall in 1978. The 1975 EEC agreement suited both the Government and the media. Because of powerful opposition within the cabinet, the Prime Minister had had to release ministers from the obligations of collective responsibility. In these circumstances it would have been impossible for the Labour Party, without an agreed line, to present party political broadcasts. On the other hand, there were umbrella organisations which were wide enough to carry the burden of arguing the case before the public. It was not a question of the Government giving up its traditional advantages to promote a fair campaign. It was an arrangement based on the self-interests of all concerned. In 1978 neither of these conditions held. The Prime Minister was able to make devolution the official policy of the Government and the Labour Party in Scotland and Wales, so that there was no longer any obstacle in the way of party political broadcasting. Furthermore, the Labour Vote No groups in Wales and Scotland made it clear that they intended to campaign independently and would resist any attempt by the broadcasting authorities to push them into a combined campaign with Conservatives and other opponents of devolution. So the BBC were hoist with their own petard. The means they had used so cleverly, as they thought, to bind the Government, were now used to bind them. The BBC were committed by the 1975 precedent to use the Party Political Broadcasting Committee, and innovations in the allocation of broadcasting time could be made only by agreement of the political parties. When the Government vetoed the BBC's plans for a 50:50 arrangement, the BBC had no alternative but to adhere to the *status quo*. So the Government got what it wanted. PPBs and ministerial statements would go ahead as normal during the campaign despite the advantage that this gave to the Government and the Yes cause.

At first sight it would appear that the Government's desire to reintroduce party political broadcasts was an attempt to obtain a party advantage out of a fortuitous conjunction of events. But a closer look at the evidence revealed that party politicals were merely part of a systematic government strategy which could be summed up as reintroducing the political party as the main channel for the conduct of the Referendum and therefore reclaiming the ground that had been lost by default to the umbrella groups in the 1975 campaign. The key to the Government's strategy was given by Alec Jones, Under-Secretary of State for Wales: "This is nothing to do with the General Election. This is a Government in the course of its lifetime advocating certain policy which the House has accepted. It seems reasonable that they should use the normal machinery of government" to do this (Hansard, 958, col. 1393).

At the heart of the struggle over the ground rules lay two fundamentally irreconcilable conceptions of the status and significance of referendums. These divergent models can be labelled "isolationist" and "integrationist", respectively. The former sees the referendum as an equivalent to or extension of the principle of the free vote in parliament. By mutual agreement the normal procedures and alliances are suspended. A specific question is abstracted from the routine of party warfare and government business. In this context the referendum becomes a self-contained independent process, an alternative to the normal procedure of decision making. Abstracted from the normal areas of political conflict, it has its own logic, its own procedures and hence its own rules of fairness and balance. This argument was tersely put in 1975: "If we are to have [a referendum] it will be because Parliament has decided in effect to waive its rights. Once it has taken that decision, logic and public expectation demand that the rules offer an equal chance to both sides" (cited in Smith, 1976, p. 194). However, it is important to remember that while this was the view of commentators in 1975, it was never stated or implied in the Government's White Paper itself, which, in the tradition of British pragmatism, stuck to the nuts and bolts of referendum arrangements without broaching or even implying any of the basic propositions about the actual status of referendums (Cmnd 5925).

The integrationist model, on the other hand, sees the referendum as just another channel supplementing but not substituting for the normal means of conducting political controversy. This view assumed the primacy of political parties in the decision making process. The proponents of this view argue that, as the options offered at a referendum have been expounded and defended on the official platforms of political parties and have been incorporated into government business as an integral part of the government's programme, it is futile to pretend that the referendum process can be isolated from the normal decision making process. This would fly in the face of facts and provide an excuse for parties to shuffle off the responsibility of taking a stand on the issues of the day, thus undermining the justification for the existence of political parties.

Now it was obviously in the interests of the Conservative Party to encourage the first view, while the Labour Party had every incentive to identify itself with devolution schemes which it was certain would be successful while placing all the odium of opposition to legitimate nationalist aspirations firmly on the Conservative Party.

Although, therefore, everybody agreed that coverage of the Referendum should be fair and reasonably balanced, what constituted a fair balance would depend on what one thought the function of a referendum was. There was a neat and inevitable congruence between the two concepts of balance - the representative and the competitive - and the two models of a referendum, the integrated and the isolated. Obviously, if the Government held that a referendum should be integrated into the normal process of party warfare and government decision making, then the balance demanded would conform to the standards of balance already accepted by parties and enshrined in the time-honoured formulae of the PPB committee. From this point of view the fact that three party broadcasts might be in favour of devolution and only one against was neither unfair nor anomalous. On the contrary, any attempt to rectify the situation artificially would hit at the basic principle of a party's jealously guarded right to use its broadcasting facilities as it saw fit. Thus the Government saw themselves as defending a clearly established and just *status quo*.

On the other hand, if one took the view that the referendum process should be isolated from normal Parliamentary practices, then the 3:1 allocation of slots was patently unjust. The only reasonable rule to apply was the 50:50 principle applied in the 1975 referendum. The balance should be between those advocating Yes and those advocating No, as in a debate. The past electoral performance and the present policy of political parties were irrelevant because the political parties were not legally recognised entities in the referendum process. They had waived their rights and the only relevant category of participants were those persons and organisations campaigning for a No vote or a Yes vote. This was the view of all the Government's opponents including the Labour Vote No campaign committee who sought the interdict against the IBA and it was this view that provided the basis for Lord Ross's judgement in their favour.

The Court Intervenes

On February 9, 1979, Brian Wilson, Tam Dalyell, MP, and the other officials of the Labour Vote No committee brought a petition to prevent the IBA going ahead with its scheduled programme of party political broadcasts, on the grounds that these arrangements breached the statutory duty of the IBA under the Independent Broadcasting Authority Act 1973, which stated that the IBA should ensure that programmes broadcast by them maintained, *inter alia*, a proper balance "having regard both to the programmes as a whole and also to the days of the week and the times of day at which the programmes were broadcast" (IBA Act 1973 Sections 55 (2)(b) and 22(3)). However, the battle lines had been drawn up earlier during debates on the Referendum Order in Parliament. Opponents of the Government complained about the "monstrous unfairness" of the consequences of normal procedures and felt the Referendum campaign was being rigged, but they could offer no solution to the problem except to demand that the Government should intervene and somehow or other ensure parity. The Government fiercely resisted this. Intervention would mean undermining the rights of the parties to control their own broadcasting arrangements and would endanger the autonomy of the broadcasting authority.

The Gordian knot was cut by Lord Ross's judgement. Following the Labour Vote No petition on February 9, Lord Ross allowed the IBA time to present their own case. This they did on February 14, raising fundamental questions about the interpretation of the IBA Act of 1973, the right of the petitioners to sue and the competency of the Court of Session in this area. The first objection of the IBA was that all the relevant parties had not been involved, as a petition had been issued against the IBA alone, whereas the content of the party political broadcasts was a matter solely for the political parties, and therefore the petition should have been made against them as well. Lord Ross rejected this claim by making a distinction between a referendum and a general election. He asserted the "disengaged" model of referendums: "Voters are not being invited to vote for members of political parties but to answer the question: 'Do you want the provisions of the Scotland Act of 1978 to be put into effect?'" (Wilson *v.* the Independent Broadcasting Authority. Reports, *Scots Law Times*, 1979, p. 282).

The issue was not, therefore, a party political issue and so the four major political parties did not have the sole prerogative of attempting to persuade the voters. Lord Ross's interpretation of the Referendum was fundamentally opposed to the assumption on which Government strategy had been based. According to the disengaged view, once the Government had decided to allow a referendum, they had given up all their rights and the issue was to be lifted completely out of the political context which had given birth to it. For the Government, the Referendum was about whether the voters agreed with the provision made by the Government in pursuance of electoral promises; the public were being invited to participate in a vote of confidence in the Government. From Lord Ross's view of the referendum as a process apart from the normal conventions of party government, it followed logically that any voter or organisation had a legal interest in ensuring that the IBA did not breach its statutory duty. Furthermore, Lord Ross upheld Lord Denning's ruling (Reports, *Scots Law Times*, 1979, p. 284) that it was the court alone and not the relevant minister who was competent to judge whether a breach of a statutory duty had occurred and to take appropriate action. On the substantive issue the IBA repeated the Government's case that there had been no impropriety because the normal rules for balance which had already been upheld by the courts had been followed, but Lord Ross's definition of a referendum made the normal rules totally irrelevant: "I do not consider that the method of arranging party political broadcasts, which is normally employed, is appropriate when the party political broadcasts are to be devoted specifically to the questions to be put to the electorate in the

Referendum" (Reports, *Scots Law Times*, 1979, p. 285). The petition brought by the
Labour Vote No committee was, therefore, upheld.

The decision did not completely settle the battle over the party political broadcasts. The injunction did not bind the BBC, who were therefore still legally entitled to go ahead with the scheduled transmission. Nor did it rule out a new
arrangement agreed by the parties and conforming to Lord Ross's criteria for
balance based on a 50:50 split between Yes and No. But by February 19 the different
groups were rapidly ruling out whatever few options remained. Labour Vote No made
it quite clear that they would take out a similar interdict against the BBC if they
did not cancel the arrangement, while the Yes for Scotland campaign threatened
legal action if the Labour Party attempted to substitute a ministerial broadcast
for the four blacked-out ITV broadcasts. Only the official Opposition was entitled
to a right of reply to a ministerial broadcast and Jim Sillars complained that
"this would mean the two political parties getting a monopoly of air time; it
would run counter to both the letter and spirit of Lord Ross's judgement" (*Glasgow
Herald*, 19.2.1979). In the House of Commons the following day, in an oral answer
to Alexander Fletcher, the Prime Minister repeated the Government's position
(Hansard, 963, vol. 249). Totally at cross purposes to Lord Ross's view of a disengaged referendum, the Prime Minister re-asserted the "primacy of the political
parties" view. Personally he hoped that the BBC would go ahead with the broadcasts,
despite the ban on the IBA. That Callaghan could advocate such an extraordinary
situation, could only be accounted for by assuming that his view of the Referendum,
as a public battle between the major parties, was so strongly and deeply held that
he was quite incapable of grasping the alternative view of the Referendum asserted
by Lord Ross.

At a meeting of the Chief Whips at Westminster, a new inter-party agreement failed
to emerge. As *The Scotsman* cynically commented, "the parties concentrated on
manoeuvres designed to pin the blame for the shambles on each other" (*Scotsman*,
22.2.1979). The Government Chief Whip, Michael Cocks, proposed a ministerial
broadcast but this was rejected by the Conservatives. In turn, the Conservatives
repeated their formula of two Yes and two No programmes. This proposal had already
been rejected by the Labour Party, which had no intention of giving an official
platform to the Labour Vote No dissidents. However, the issue was closed that very
evening when the BBC announced that, although they did not have the same statutory
obligation to ensure balance as the IBA, they, nevertheless, felt that they should
comply with the spirit of the judgement. In their statement to the press they repeated the charge made by Leon Brittan, MP, in November 1978 that the absence of
clear guidelines in broadcasting was very unsatisfactory and that it would now be
necessary to have discussions with the political parties on guidelines for any
future referendums.

The court decision ended the Government's chance of a dramatic campaign climax,
which would identify the Tories as the villainous opponents of the legitimate aspirations of the Scots. The broadcasting authorities had already intended to concentrate their programmes in the last week of the campaign, so the absence of the
party politicals was not significant. The public, in turn, were spared another
Saatchi & Saatchi production, a no-holds-barred phone-in organised by the SNP, another dose of popularist sentimental nationalism from the Labour Party, and whatever offering the Liberals had prepared. The only clear victors were the judiciary,
who had emerged as the people's champions against the wiles of the politicians.

The intractability of the problem of ground rules was revealed by the fact that,
despite Lord Ross's judgement, another quarrel blew up during the last days of the
campaign. On Monday, February 22, the Prime Minister was interviewed at Downing
Street by Robin Day for the "Panorama" programme on BBC 1. The hour-long programme
was designed to cover the state of the nation, giving the Prime Minster an opportunity to explain and defend his policies in detail. Early in the programme almost

10 minutes was devoted to the issue of devolution. Callaghan was concerned to calm voters' fears and to urge them to vote Yes. Although technically the programme was not specifically on Scotland, and although the format implied that the Prime Minister was being fearlessly interrogated by the interviewer, the substance and tone of the Prime Minister's exhortations were no different in quality or quantity from a party political or a ministerial broadcast. In fact, the "propaganda" was more effective for being in a supposedly neutral context. Robin Day's questions were little more than cues for the Prime Minister to expand at length on his message of calm and reassurance.

The Conservatives were furious and the Conservative Central Office, led by Lord Thorneycroft, spent the next day arguing with Sir Michael Swann about the unfair advantage the BBC had given the Prime Minister (*Scotsman*, 27, 28.2.1979; *Financial Times*, 28.2.1979). The Conservatives argued that the interview was a *de facto* ministerial broadcast and that, therefore, they had the right of reply. They asserted that a senior Conservative should be given an equally prominent spot on television on February 28, i.e. on the eve of the poll. The BBC would not agree to this, but "under great duress" the Referendum Unit in Glasgow agreed to screen a six minute interview with Lord Home by Donald MacCormick. This interview was slotted in as a curtain-raiser to the already scheduled devolution programme of Tuesday night. As a piece of programming it was singularly clumsy and one can understand why the Glasgow producers were unhappy, but, as one BBC source in London was quoted as saying, "the big guns were wheeled in" (*Scotsman*, 28.2.1979). The interview served as an *ad hoc* unofficial reply by the Opposition to the ministerial statement that never was. Once again the BBC had come up with a diplomatic solution which satisfied the interests of all and yet saved face by avoiding any question of principle.

The Problem of Balance in Campaign Coverage

In addition to the problems over party political broadcasts, the television companies had to cope with a number of attacks on their professional integrity and impartiality peculiar to the Referendum campaign. Two major challenges were made, for example, during the Parliamentary debates on the Referendum Order. Firstly, it was alleged that the BBC would be biased towards the Yes case. Tam Dalyell argued that, as the BBC Controller in Scotland, Alistair Hetherington, was strongly in favour of an Assembly, it was "not satisfactory that a player should also be the referee who blows the whistle" (Hansard, 958, col. 1293). He asserted that the Controller's attitude would inevitably permeate the whole organisation and suggested that Hetherington be given a sabbatical during the campaign (*ibid.*, col. 1294). A far more fundamental objection was also made by Dalyell when he pointed out that BBC Scotland, as an institution, had a considerable interest in the outcome of the Referendum, since a devolved Scotland would lead to an enhanced status for it, with inevitable promotions for executives and increases in the number of jobs (*ibid.*, col. 1354). Dalyell was of course aware that there were mechanical rules which had already been used in the 1975 referendum and in elections to ensure a temporal equality in news and documentary coverage by use of the stopwatch. What worried him was the qualitative bias, conscious or unconscious, which could affect the campaign but which would not be amenable to proof. For example, the attitude of the presenter could affect the tone and hence the impact of a programme (*ibid.*, col. 1391). Other MPs were quick to add their own scenarios. It was suggested that the use of emotive locales, like the old Royal High School in Edinburgh, which was to become the home of the new Assembly, would lead to bias (*ibid.*, Col. 1328). Also the level of attention given to the debate (*ibid.*, col. 1303) could affect turnout and hence the decision. Finally the selection of speakers for both sides could lead to unconscious bias. This was not merely a Scottish problem: the Welsh MP, M. Roberts, stated bluntly, "the people of Wales don't believe that the professional ethic of the BBC/HTV will ensure impartiality in the coverage of the campaign"

(*ibid.*, col. 1354). The debate proved that, once one left the safe ground of mathe-
matical equality, a bottomless pit of unending possibilities opened up.

The debate merely strengthened the Government's resolve to stick to its policy of
dual responsibility based on a division of labour. The parties would be responsible
for the content of their broadcasts; in all other areas the broadcasters would be
in control. The Government steadfastly refused to encroach on the professional
responsibility of the medium by intervening in the conduct of broadcasting, while
at the same time assuming that political broadcasts were solely a matter for the
party whips and the PPB committee. The Government could legitimately claim that
this clear division of jurisdiction provided the only viable ground rules for
broadcasting in this kind of referendum. Their opponents could claim that this very
division of labour created anomalies which could only be solved by a mutual set of
ground rules which co-ordinated both politicians and medium.

The second major problem arose out of the basic differences between this Referendum
and the 1975 EEC referendum. In the earlier referendum it had been assumed that
there were only two points of view, and it was, therefore, possible to concentrate
on presenting a clear statement of both sides of the case, despite the large number
of bodies engaged in the campaign. In other words, the common allegiance of the
pro-European overcame the differences of party allegiance. Labour, Liberal and
Conservatives were by and large putting forward the same kind of argument for or
against the Market because there was no distinctive party perspective on the issue.
However, quite the reverse was true in 1979. Both the official Labour Party and the
SNP were urging a Yes vote, while the Labour rebels and Conservatives wanted a rejection of the Scotland Act, but in both cases the nominal allies asserted voci-
ferously that what divided them was much more important that the fact that they
shared a Yes or No position. The theoretical arguments for this distinction were
put clearly and impressively by Leo Abse, MP, but also supported by the Labour Vote
No group in Scotland. Abse argued that the reasons the Conservatives and Labour
rebels had for opposing the Bill were more important than the result that both were
in the same camp, and, therefore, the motivation or reasoning behind those groups
was of more importance than the consequence of their action (*ibid.*, cols 1359-1361).
For example, the Labour Party in Scotland had every reason to dissociate itself
from the SNP, particularly as one of the main motives for devolution was to undermine the appeal of separatism. Consequently Abse argued that the broadcasting
authorities had an obligation to select spokesmen not merely to balance the Yes or
No advocates but also to recognise "the existence of substantial independent bodies
of opinion". In other words, the broadcasting authority had an obligation to make
clear the difference between advocates nominally on the same side, and to bring
out clearly the independence of the various groups, with their different motives.
Any presentation which obscured or ignored these differences would be unbalanced
and unfair, even if a nominal balance between Yes and No was maintained. This, of
course, automatically ruled out the kind of programmes sponsored by the umbrella
groups in the 1975 campaign.

The response of the BBC to these challenges to its professional ethic of impartiality was to set up an autonomous Referendum Unit. The task of this Unit was to
co-ordinate all devolution programmes and to protect the BBC from any allegations
of bias, while at the same time avoiding boring programmes. The Unit was under the
control of two senior editors, Matthew Spicer, the overall Editor of Current
Affairs, and David Martin, senior producer. A director, Linda Howard, a journalist
and two research assistants were also attached to this team. For the presentation
of programmes the BBC relied mainly on James Cox. His style was an important contribution to, and a consequence of, the overall strategy of the Unit. Whereas presenters like Walden and Dimbleby participate actively in discussions and have a
style similar to the positive stance taken by committed investigative journalists,
Cox preferred the self-effacing image of the political host. The role of the
neutral umpire, whose only concern is to facilitate the access to the media of as

many of the participants as possible, certainly was effective in eliminating any suspicion that the BBC favoured devolution. In fact, both during and after the campaign none of the participants had any complaints about the political bias of any of the programmes mady by this Unit. It is true that David Steel consistently blamed the media as a whole for being Glasgow- or Strathclyde-centred (BBC programme "Tonight", 8.3.1979). This was, however, partly deliberate in order to avoid any association with Edinburgh as the proposed capital and partly logistic because of the difficulties of covering rural campaigns.

The cost of this self-effacing strategy, which was designed to avoid errors rather than to make a positive contribution to the debate, can only be guessed by imagining what opportunities were lost. In contrast to the two London-based programmes presented by Dimbleby and Walden for ITV, Scottish programmes gave an overall impression of a very complex and confusing campaign dominated by politicians intent on protecting their weak spots, while putting the best gloss on their intentions. In the absence of a strong framework forcing their participants to concentrate on a few central issues chosen by the presenter, the *laissez-faire* Scottish policy allowed the debate to fragment into a bewildering kaleidoscope of personalities and opinions.

STV had neither the resources nor the problems of the BBC, as they had already received the Dalyell seal of approval for impartiality in the Parliamentary debate on the Order for the Referendum. They relied therefore on their existing team of Russell Galbraith as overall co-ordinator and Colin MacKay as presenter. By and large their strategy for handling the debate was very similar to that of the BBC, as a breakdown of the programmes revealed. The benevolent, avuncular image of Colin MacKay performed a similar function to that of the quizzical, ironic detachment of James Cox in distancing themselves, and therefore their institutions, from any sense of involvement in the outcome of the issue. The contrast between the interventionist presenters like Dimbleby and Walden, and the cool, neutral, disengaged couple showed the importance of Dalyell's assertion that the qualitative imponderables were far more crucial in determining the balance of programmes than the mere mechanical quality of the stopwatch.

Campaign Coverage

The coverage of the campaign by BBC and STV will be considered under four headings, viz.

(i)   Normal, early evening news programmes. On BBC 1 the magazine "Reporting Scotland" follows the National News at 5.55 p.m. During the campaign there were five special "Nationwide" programmes replacing and extending this spot. On STV the Scottish News at 5.45 p.m. is followed by "Scotland Today".

(ii)   Special programmes. The BBC used their normal Scottish current affairs programme "Tuesday Night" for a series of three related programmes devoted to devolution. STV's normal current affairs programme "Ways and Means" was supplemented with three special Referendum reports.

(iii) BBC's "Referendum Reports". This was a round-up of news and events broadcast late every night of the week, except Sunday. STV had no equivalent.

(iv)   London-based programmes. Several of these were devoted wholly or in part to devolution - "The Money Programme", "Westminster", "Panorama", "Weekend World".

Early evening news: montage effect. Perhaps the most decisive contribution of television to the Referendum campaign was one which had not been foreseen by either the politicians or the media professionals. This was due to what could be called the "montage effect" - which derives from S. Eisenstein's dictum that the meaning of a screen image is not discrete and self-contained but that each image is affected by those contiguous to it. Two images deliberately juxtaposed can create an overall impression not found in either separately. In this case the montage effect results from the fact that the news reporting of the campaign could not be isolated from the general reporting of political news during this period. Afterwards, the Secretary of State for Scotland, Bruce Millan, was to complain that a long-term constitutional issue had suffered from being associated with the short-term unpopularity of the Government (STV "Scotland Today" interview with Colin MacKay, 2.3.1979). Whether this association was unfair or not, its existence cannot be doubted, although the evidence of its effect is indirect and speculative.

The montage effect can be clearly seen when we consider the television coverage of the opening of the Yes campaign in Glasgow on February 12 by the Prime Minister. The TV cameras showed Callaghan pushing his way through a forest of NUPE placards as he tried to enter the McLellan Galleries. The juxtaposition of the images of the Prime Minister besieged by his own supporters and the immediately following images of the Prime Minister as the benefactor of Scotland created a new message: that devolution was the party policy of a Government which had already made a drastic miscalculation about the attitudes of its own supporters. Devolution itself acquired guilt by association. Before Christmas, there had been a close correlation between the popularity of Callaghan, the 28 per cent Labour lead over the Conservatives and the corresponding popularity of the devolution scheme, which would satisfy the Scottish feeling of grievance, while at the same time avoid the dangerous possibilities of separation. Now, with the beginning of the campaign proper, there was an equally close correlation between the collapse in the status of the Labour Party and the Yes vote. The McLellan Gallery sequence faithfully placed the two opposing images side by side: Callaghan the statesman conducting a low-key campaign to ratify a *fait accompli* as the only Prime Minister able to solve the Scottish riddle, and Callaghan the Party leader swept along by a current over which he had no control.

The problems arising from this twin focus were also graphically illustrated the next day. On the six o'clock "Scotland Today" news journal on STV the leading item was a report on the NUPE threat to schools, rubbish collection and hospitals. Almost as an aside it was revealed that NUPE did not intend to close the schools during the Referendum vote. This was the only reference to the campaign in the programme. However, in the BBC programme "Reporting Scotland" the NUPE item was presented towards the end of the programme as part of a section on the campaign. Incidents like this were rare as news editors on both BBC and ITV were careful to avoid any blatant juxtaposition of devolution news with other political reporting, something which was made easier by the division between UK and Scottish news programmes. Editorial decisions of the relative newsworthiness of industrial and devolution items turned out to be of much greater import for influencing public opinion than the much debated question of party political broadcasts.

Only the appearance of major political figures, like the Prime Minister or Lord Home, earned the Referendum campaign a place in the London news bulletins, and then only at the tail end. More surprisingly, this was also true of the early evening Scottish news. Apart from the rare interventions of the political magnates, the only times the campaign became "newsworthy" were on February 16 when Lord Ross's High Court decision was announced, February 22 when the Church of Scotland appeared to withdraw its support for devolution and finally on February 19 when the numerical target for the 40 per cent hurdle was announced. All these issues, while eminently newsworthy and dramatic, were of only tangential relevance to the substantive issue.

Though devolution set pieces appeared regularly in the magazine sections following the news, it is difficult to assess the adequacy of, for example, the five special "Nationwide" programmes as vehicles for informing the public. Certainly there was

no systematic exploration of themes, no continuity either within individual programmes or through the series. The only points of sharp engagement, apart from the
Sillars/Dalyell debate, were a violent quarrel over whether the No campaign had
been funded by Arabs or Dutch landowners, and vehement protests from Yes and No
campaigners alike at a satirical slot by Richard Stilgoe as part of one of the programmes.

An analysis of the news topics covered during the last three weeks of the campaign
suggests that Scotland was in the grip of a minor crisis. With the exception of the
particularly bad weather, which merely added to the gloom, strikes and industrial
unrest monopolised the news. Strikes hit at the most sensitive domestic areas,
while signs of a withdrawal of American firms from Scotland suggested long-term,
incurable unemployment, as the Government policy of replacing traditional, heavy
industry by light industry seemed to be collapsing. Not only did these topics crowd
out everything else but more importantly the message they implicitly carried was
monotonous: the inability of the Government, whether culpable or not, to provide
explanations or even consolations, let alone solutions to these problems.

Following the patterns of general elections we would expect the Yes and No groups
to capitalise on the situation by attempting to create a montage effect favourable
to their cause by, for example, suggesting that devolution would mitigate Scottish
economic problems. However, neither in the news reports nor in the special devolution programmes did this occur. As a result the campaign kept a hermetically sealed
atmosphere. The arguments of both sides were technical, constitutional or philoso-
phical and this tended to isolate the campaign from the great economic and industrial issues of the day. Intentionally or not, devolution was firmly relegated to
the second division.

While in my opinion the reporting and editing of the economic scene was the single
most decisive contribution of television to the campaign, there were (with one
exception) no complaints from either the public or the parties about news coverage
or editing during this period. Janey Buchan, the chairperson of the Scottish Council of the Labour Party, blamed the media for "trivialising the debate" (BBC
"Tonight", 8.3.1979), which should have concentrated on substantial argument rather
than the drama of court bans, Kirk politics or inaccurate electoral rolls. But
otherwise people accepted that, given the fateful conjunction of the campaign with
the economic hurricane, the editorial priorities of both channels, which led to the
demotion of devolution as an issue on the agenda, were the right ones.

Special programmes. At the other end of the scale from the early evening magazines,
both networks produced a series of specialised programmes for late evening viewers
prepared to take a more sustained interest in the Referendum argument. The BBC's
contribution replaced the regular Tuesday night current affairs programme on
February 13, 20 and 27. STV's "Referendum '79" programmes were on February 18, 21
and 23. In general, the BBC conveyed factual background information more adroitly,
while the STV interviewer Colin MacKay was more adventurous in directing discussion
than his BBC counterparts, but otherwise the tone and contents of both were remark-
ably similar.

The first of the BBC's programmes, on February 13, was technically well-executed
in the sense that a large number of facts were packaged covering the history, administrative and constitutional arrangements and the projected effect of devolution.
The first two sections of this programme concentrated on facts and avoided any
interpretation that might be controversial. Only the next section, on the supposed
consequences of devolution, was both polemical and focussed on a specific issue
but even here issues were not developed because, in the interest of balance, the
viewers were offered a series of juxtaposed experts. Admittedly the programme was
meant to be introductory but it introduced a kaleidoscope of issues, personalities
and facts with no centre.

The BBC's second programme, on February 20, followed a formula already used during the EEC referendum campaign. Under the chairmanship of Sir Myer Galpern and using the Speaker's Committee rules, the Referendum Unit reconstructed the type of debate which had occurred in Parliament over the Bill. The selection of speakers managed to square the circle by achieving both a numerical balance of four Yes and four No speakers but also a balance reflecting party strength in the House of Commons. Technically the production was superb and the debate, though it lacked the bravura and atmosphere of the later Oxford debate, was decidedly the best organised and most informative of the campaign. As a result it highlighted clearly the diversity of motives and the fragmentary nature of the discussion which made a real debate impossible.

The BBC's final programme, on February 27, was a variation on the debate formula – a contest between two legal politicians, Lord McCluskey, who had been responsible for piloting the Scotland Bill through the House of Lords, and Nicholas Fairbairn, a Conservative legal notable. Each was allowed to defend his case by calling three expert witnesses to be cross-examined. The programme suffered from the stilted legal procedure and the absence of professional communicators, but it did extend the debate beyond the politicians, if not into the community at large, and it did concentrate on a few vital issues.

The first of the STV's "Referendum '79" programmes was shown on February 18. Like its BBC counterpart, it was designed to provide a basis of information about the Scotland Act, and it similarly floundered in a morass of unrelated facts. There were no themes, no connections, no investigations of controversial issues such as nationalism, the motives of the parties or the real status of the Assembly. The facts were strictly neutral, that is, ultimately uninformative and often trivial or irrelevant.

The second STV programme attempted to reproduce the conflict between the parties over devolution. Like the BBC, the producers found that only two teams of four enabled them to square the circle of representing all the political interests, official and unofficial, and at the same time ensuring that there was an equal number of Yes and No speakers. Such an unwieldy number representing such diverse positions made a coherent, developing debate impossible from the start. However, instead of using a neutral speaker, as the BBC had done, the STV presenter Colin MacKay put each of the speakers on the defensive by tackling them at their weakest point. This certainly helped to sharpen the issue and the outcome was in that sense more successful than the unstructured BBC debate. It helped create openings and force damning admissions which resulted in a sharper and tougher debate in the second half of the programme when the presenter withdrew.

The final programme, on February 23, used the same format – eight speakers chaired by Colin MacKay, but this time mixing regional with national politicians. The presenter hoped to steer the speakers to the "heart of the debate": whether there was a real function for the Assembly apart from providing opportunities for bureaucrats and politicians. Again, the sheer number of speakers necessitated by the dictates of balance made this impossible. Predictably, discussion disintegrated as the SNP, CBI, Labour Party representatives etc. paraded their Sunday-best arguments.

The broadcasters had obviously come to the conclusion that the debate was the most successful way to cope with the conflicting demands made by the campaigners and to protect themselves from any dangers of involvement. On the eve of polling day, viewers were offered a choice of any or all of three different debates. The most ambitious was a film of the debate held at the Oxford Union on February 26. This debate had received some publicity because of a walk-out by Tam Dalyell who was incensed that it should be held outwith Scotland. Despite the fancy dress atmosphere (reminiscent of the last night of the proms), the debate did at least break out of the narrow circle of Scottish combatants repeating the same arguments from the safety of their political dug-outs.

The second debate of the evening was an additional Referendum programme improvised
to fill the gap left by the absence of party political broadcasts. This debate,
organised by the STV current affairs team, came live from the Glasgow studio at
nine o'clock and, unlike the Oxford debate, was an exclusively Scottish affair. The
presenter, Colin MacKay, encouraged a free-for-all. Unfortunately, apart from paying off old political scores, few of the participants were prepared to venture into
the opposition's territory. The debate ended as it had begun - fragmentary and
solipsistic - as each speaker held firm to his interpretation of devolution - its
advantages and dangers.

Finally, on BBC, 10 minutes before midnight came "Referendum Reports"'s extracts
from a debate held at Glasgow University.

In preparing their special Referendum programmes broadcasters had to cope with
genuine dilemmas. Firstly, as far as simple provision of information was concerned,
they could not apply the experience of elections to the Referendum and, therefore,
had to work in ignorance of the need and expectations of their audience and without
any co-ordination with other channels of communication. It was understandable that
they should start from a clean slate and educate their viewers in the ABC of the
issues involved. Nevertheless, there was an unfilled gulf between these elementary
facts and full-blooded political controversy - a gap which the medium itself could
have filled by an investigation in depth of specific controversial issues. The contrast between the information programmes described above - diffuse, comprehensive
and neutral - and the intensive and selective treatment of issues by "Weekend
World" could not be greater.

Secondly, there was the need to maintain balance between the different parties and
factions. After the campaign some suggested that much confusion could have been
avoided by prior agreement between politicians and the media to fix an agenda, define the areas of disagreement and establish a consensus about the issues at stake.
However, some of the politicians were determined to disagree about the terrain upon
which the battle would be fought and expected the media to register this disagreement. To draw up an agenda would have been to take sides in the debate itself. In
these circumstances broadcasters could either decide themselves what they thought
were the significant issues or stand back and let the political groups define the
issues. In the main, both Scottish broadcasting institutions chose the latter
course and could claim that they were merely reflecting the confusion and muddle
intrinsic in the campaign. The "safe" way out of these sorts of problems was a
heavy reliance upon debates but, although debates have superficial drama and obvious convenience in representing a large number of views, this served to confuse
rather than illuminate the issues at stake in the Referendum.

Late-night "Referendum Reports". The most successful innovations in broadcasting
during the campaign were the series of late-night "Referendum Reports" produced by
the BBC's Referendum Unit, which began on February 18 and were presented by James
Cox and John Milne on BBC 1. Each programme ran for 40-50 minutes and was divided
into three sections. The first part consisted of a political essay, occasionally
an attempt to probe party attitudes by an extended interview with a party dignatory
and often an analysis of the latest poll figures. Items included the problem of
financing the Assembly and the attitude of the Church of Scotland. These long reports were similar to the ones in the early evening news journals but of greater
depth and complexity. The second section, the longest and most original, consisted
of reports direct from the hustings. Up to a dozen campaigners were interviewed
briefly. This section gave a vivid impression of the atmosphere of the campaign
without the artificiality of the debate convention. In the final section, the presenter gave a summary of the editorial and devolution news in the following morning's newspapers. This series of "Referendum Reports" was designed for the politi-

cal *aficionado* and was characterised by verve and sophistication. The presenters'
dry, sceptical wit fitted the intellectual tone of the series perfectly; also, because these programmes appeared nightly (except Sunday), they had a topicality
which was absent from the set piece productions.

London network programmes. In addition to the specifically Scottish programmes
produced by the BBC Referendum Unit and STV, Scottish viewers could also see national network programmes emanating from London. This was a mixed blessing as, in order
to appeal to a British audience, some of the programmes had to cover ground already
over-familiar to any Scot with even a vestigial interest in the issue. On the other
hand, being further away from the combatants, the London based producers could
afford to be more controversial. A good example of this was BBC 2's "The Money
Programme" on February 28, which covered a number of important controversial issues
which had not been fully treated in the Scottish programmes, such as the role of
oil in fuelling nationalist aspirations, the complex financing of the Assembly and
the problems arising from raised expectations as a result of the Assembly. These
BBC programmes were necessarily specialised as they were oriented to minority
audiences. This is not true of London Weekend Television's hour-long "Weekend
World". The edition of February 25 was shown on STV and Grampian TV and it certainly lived up to its claim that it offered "expert analysis of the news *behind* the
headlines by a top team of journalists". Presented by Brian Walden, "Weekend World"
had a very successful approach which neatly sidestepped the BBC's obsession with
balance and bias and the accompanying assumption that the role of broadcasting
would be limited to that of acting as a gatekeeper or referee, leaving the task of
presenting a substantial view on politics to the party partisans or the independent
experts. The unstated conclusion that devolution was bound to exacerbate rather
than relieve Scottish problems was certainly biased in the sense that it gave
powerful support to the No case without a glimmer of consolation to the Yes people.
The Yes for Scotland organising secretary felt bitter enough to label the programme
as the "most heavily biased from any TV company and virtually in contempt of court
given Lord Ross's decision that the IBA should remain impartial" (*Scotsman*, 26.2.
1979). In fact, the ability of "Weekend World" to present a dramatic, consistent
and unified thesis depended entirely on its rejection of any formulae of mechanical
balance and bias, its lack of interest in political impartiality as an end in itself and its resolute selection of material to suit the purpose of its conviction.
It could defend its policy by pointing out that the tests of balance were not meant
to be applied to each individual programme but only to coverage of the campaign as
a whole, and that, if impartiality meant giving a monopoly of positive comment to
politicians, the broadcasters were failing in their duty to present an independent
contribution to the debate.

The only BBC programme to approach the independence and frankness of "Weekend
World" was also London based and had the added protection of being a post-mortem on
the campaign. "Referendum: Yes or No" was shown on BBC late on March 2 and consisted
of David Dimbleby interviewing a spectrum of politicians. Dimbleby's interviewing
was the most effective of the Referendum coverage. The Scottish interviewers and,
for that matter, Robin Day's interview of the Prime Minister on "Panorama", true
to the gatekeeper ideology, used their questions as polite cues, introductions
which allowed the politicians to develop their views in the way most advantageous
to them. Dimbleby's interviewing could be called interrogatory or inquisitorial
without being at all querulous or antagonistic, challenging the interviewee by
forcing him to defend his most vulnerable points. Thus, Dimbleby raised a number of
hitherto taboo subjects, particularly about the motives and attitudes of the parties.

Comparing these two London-based programmes with the other, safer special programmes, it would seem that in the perennial conflict of interests between politicians and broadcasters the overall balance was tipped decisively in favour of the
politicians, with the result that, given the weakness of opposition to devolution

in the press (see chapter 6), important areas of debate were left untouched. This failure of the media to avoid dangerous controversy could account for some of the confusion and disorientation that observers noted even or especially among people who were well-informed on the subject. On the other hand, this could be seen as a rational response by the broadcasters to the complexity and intangibility of the subject itself. In all events, it was only metropolitan teams, led by presenters like Dimbleby and Walden with reputations well-established enough to make them relatively invulnerable to the attack of the parties, who were able to make an independent contribution to the campaign by acting as the devil's advocates or by raising embarrassing subjects.

Conclusion

When the Referendum campaign was over, the media professionals were happy that they had succeeded once again in containing attacks on their ethics and practice. Given the formidable barrage of criticism before the campaign, they had escaped very lightly. Lord Ross had passed judgement against political party scheduling which had virtually been forced upon the broadcasting authorities by the Government and they could now claim that their original idea of a 50:50 split had been vindicated. The BBC could claim that it had developed the magazine format of political reporting to a high pitch of virtuosity. In their role as gatekeepers, both broadcasting organisations could claim that they had provided opportunities for young and relatively unknown politicians and for a number of notables outside the magical political circle. This was true, but one has to weigh the victories against the broadcasters' sins of omission, contributions that they could have made to the debate but did not. While the broadcasters had maintained their independence and public standing, the politicians also got what they wanted. Their pre-campaign attacks had upset and softened up the broadcasters sufficiently to deter them from making an independent contribution to the political debate. The politicians had once again held on to their monopolistic position as the sole authorised diviners of political issues on television.

Reference

Smith, A. (1976). Broadcasting. In D.E. Butler and U. Kitzinger, *The 1975 Referendum*. Macmillan, London.

II.   THE SOUND OF DEVOLUTION

Roger Mullin

Radio coverage of the Referendum campaign highlights the difficulties confronting political broadcasters in the UK. Faced by public and professional demands for independent editorial control, the reality of political broadcasting reflects the need to satisfy politically sensitive masters. The rules and procedures governing political broadcasting arguably prevent an imaginative and critical treatment of campaign politics. In an effort to prevent the party bias so evident in many British newspapers, radio stations, both public and independent, are forced to manufacture "balance" rather than presenting the most interesting programmes possible to the public. This peculiar relationship between the body politic and the media is something with which this short essay seeks to deal.

Scotland was served by a complex radio network at the time of the Referendum. By far the most significant coverage was that of the BBC. Radios 1, 2, 3 and 4 are received in Scotland and prior to the Referendum supplied information to a British audience on the progress of the Scotland Bill and then the Referendum campaign. This was managed primarily through news bulletins, with only a few special programmes being transmitted almost exclusively on Radio 4. It is worth noting that Radio 4's transmission of Parliamentary Question Time and its informative late night programme "Today in Parliament", together with the early morning programme "Yesterday in Parliament", gave significant air time to the issue of Scottish devolution, particularly during the period of the Bill's passage through Parliament. For the Scottish listener, however, it was BBC Radio Scotland which presented the fullest account of the Referendum campaign.

At the time of the Referendum, BBC Scotland had two major studios, one in Edinburgh and one in Glasgow, with four Northern outposts, operating from Aberdeen (Radio Aberdeen), Inverness (Radio Highland), Kirkwall (Radio Orkney) and Lerwick (Radio Shetland). Around 100 hours of Scottish produced programmes were broadcast each week by Radio Scotland, the remainder of its programmes being Radio 4 transmissions. The four Northern outposts had a strictly local audience for the comparatively few hours each week when they opted out of Radio Scotland for local items. But Shetland was a source of considerable interest during the campaign due to the debate which had developed about its future political allegiance should Scotland attain devolution, and Radio Shetland proved a particularly valuable source for Radio Scotland in this period, as the BBC's *Annual Report* for 1979 recognised.

Whereas the BBC had nationwide coverage on a number of stations, independent radio had a smaller coverage as well as fewer resources to call upon. Only two independent stations existed in Scotland at the time of the Referendum: Radio Clyde, based in Glasgow, and Radio Forth of Edinburgh. While independent in name, their role as political broadcasting agencies under the control of the Independent Broadcasting Authority has made them in reality just as much under the control of political forces as the public corporation which is the BBC.

News Reporting

As with the television service, specialist political programmes on radio tend to have a comparatively small audience with a high proportion of politically motivated and committed people amongst the listeners. While programmes of this nature should not be ignored, neither must they be of dominating concern here. The most frequent treatment of politics and the Referendum in the weeks preceding the vote came from the news services of the broadcasting stations. In the three weeks preceding polling, not a day passed without some news coverage of the Referendum, and by the last two weeks of the campaign such news items were included in a high proportion of the many news bulletins produced each day. The number, frequency and timing of news bulletins meant that their audience coverage was much greater than that of any specialist programme.

While no claims can be made about the effect of such news items, it would be fair to say that any influence would in part reflect the content and the personalities involved. It is precisely in such matters that editorial control is critical. But in dealing with major political events, editorial choice may be subservient to such considerable controls and pressures that it would be naïve to imagine that political control of programme content does not exist. The effect of political inter- ference was amply demonstrated by the radio stations' Referendum coverage. Whether on BBC or independent radio, all coverage of the Referendum had to maintain a "balance" in projection of the issues and individuals involved: a task usually attempted through what has been described as a "crude stopwatch conception of 'scrupulous fairness'".

But "scrupulous fairness" has its hazards. The need to be fair, allied to the broadcasters' perception of the importance of the much debated 40 per cent rule, produced a most unusual journalistic briefing by the IBA. On Tuesday, January 30, 1979 Radios Forth and Clyde, together with Welsh independent stations, attended a meeting in London called by the IBA to discuss how impartiality and balance were to be achieved in coverage of the Referendum campaigns. Such was the concern about the implications of the 40 per cent rule for coverage on polling day that a self- inflicted censorship on the biggest news story of the day was proposed. As "Theseus" put it in *The Scotsman*: "The IBA view was that the Scottish and Welsh commercial stations had better spend March 1 avoiding the one central news story of the day - how the polling was going. To say that 'so far, polling has been unusual- ly light' could start the Yes masses from their firesides and out to the polling booth. To say that 'long queues of citizens were jostling to vote' might persuade the doubters to breathe 'Ach, tae hell' and break into the next six-pack" (*Scots- man*, 9.2.1979). As John Fowler has already made clear in this chapter, the nature of balance became a significant issue itself in the Referendum, ending in the court ruling that political broadcasts must reflect not party balance but a Yes:No one.

All radio stations maintained very tight control over the reporting of the views of those on each side of the Yes:No divide. Two measures dominated the control mecha- nism. The air time of each side was matched as exactly as possible and all stations, even after the court ruling, maintained their efforts to give all the political parties involved an appropriate share. Such mechanisms of control involved a com- plex system of recording and planning. For example, Radio Forth operated a log- book in which were recorded the time allocated to a particular Referendum item, the side whose views were being presented, the name of any individual given air time and the political party with which he or she was associated (this even if the in- dividual was speaking on behalf of some other organisation, such as Scotland Says No). The entries for February 12 were typical examples of the logging process:

No side	Yes side
R. Cook (Labour) 38 secs on *Herald* Poll	Preview of PM visit 44 secs
Support for Yes falling 55 secs	S. Maxwell (SNP) *Herald* Poll as Spur 38 secs

Records were kept by all Scottish stations.

As far as generating an appropriate balance in terms of party air time goes, this was made particularly difficult due to party splits on devolution. In this regard, the division in the Labour Party caused most difficulty, the very active Labour Vote No campaigners giving the impression that Labour was more evenly split on the

issue than any other party, even though devolution was Government and official
Party policy. While it may seem that the courts clarified the problem by ruling
that the Yes:No divide should be the focus for generating a balanced view, for the
journalists and broadcasters involved, party balance remained a dominating concern.
As a number of journalists made clear to me, after the Referendum they would still
have to live with and often rely upon political parties. Put crudely, the broadcasters could live with any Referendum result, but life would be decidedly awkward
if the major political parties were alienated to the extent of future non-co-
operation.

One result of all this was that the content of particular items was by no means
always the most important reason why they were selected to be broadcast. Nor was
the adequate coverage of issues of greater importance than stopwatch precision.
The aim was to balance each side's air time to the second. Given such severe constraints and political pressures, the common complaint that political coverage
lacks the flair and incisiveness of other types of programmes is perhaps just as
much the responsibility of politicians who seek to protect their own interests by
shackling broadcasters as it is a lack of imagination on the part of broadcasters
themselves.

In the particular circumstances of the Referendum, the necessity to pay regard to
the interests of political parties inevitably created problems for the umbrella
organisations of the Yes and No sides. For example, Jim Sillars, then Scottish
Labour Party MP for South Ayrshire, was Vice-Chairman of Yes for Scotland and that
organisation's effective political head, but despite his leading role and the fact
that he was one of the most articulate proponents of the Yes case, he appeared less
frequently on the air than might have been expected. As one journalist informed me,
"Sillars would cause difficulties", due to the fact that he was the Leader of the
small breakaway Scottish Labour Party. Here is an obvious example of party align-
ment being an unseen editor of considerable power.

Special Programmes

Special programmes were produced by all of Scotland's radio stations. Regular
current affairs programmes devoted considerable attention to the Referendum, particularly during the final two weeks of the campaign. All stations used similar
techniques of production, with phone-ins and studio-interviewed panels of guests
being regular features of such "specials". Panels were selected so that the Yes:No
divide was balanced for each programme. This normally involved two or three representatives of either side being involved, with party balance being generated over
the series of productions. While some organisations other than political parties
were on occasion included in such programmes - the STUC and Scottish CBI, for instance - the concern to achieve a party balance was of paramount concern. Thus,
the very common format of balanced panels of political guests may hardly have made
for lively and interesting programmes, but it had the great advantage of keeping
the parties satisfied.

While Radios Forth and Clyde gave significant attention to devolution in current
affairs programmes, they could not match the concentration of the BBC on the issue.
Lacking the resources available to the BBC in Scotland and having less scope for
"serious" programmes, this observation does not imply criticism in relation to the
BBC. As John Fowler has already made clear, the BBC had the comparative luxury of
being able to man a special Referendum Unit. Their research back-up, experience and
political familiarity with Scotland should have led to programmes of much higher
standard than could be managed by the independent commercial stations. Such expectations were not fully realised. BBC Radio Scotland put out a major series of three
programmes, each lasting one and a half hours and being broadcast from 6.30 each
evening in the period February 21 - 23. In each programme there were three spokes-

men for the Yes side and three for No responding to phone-in questions and comments
from the public.   Rather than use their chief political reporter in Scotland as
the linkman/chairman, however, the BBC imported for the occasion Professor Robert
McKenzie. There was little to suggest that his expertise in Scottish politics
warranted his importation. Furthermore, the lack of variety in format and presentation was not liable to excite the listener. The BBC did make considerable efforts
to inform listeners about the details of the form of devolution on offer. In a
short series of "briefings", James Cox of the Referendum Unit and Chief Political
Correspondent for BBC Scotland explained the most contentious and important aspects
of the legislation as part of Radio Scotland's early morning "Good Morning Scotland"
news magazine programme. And the General Programmes Department produced one
"factual phone-in" on the nuts and bolts of the proposals as part of the "Jimmy
Mack Show". The influence of such factual programmes is difficult to assess,
although it might not be unreasonable to suggest that their technical nature may
have contributed to the often technical and obscurantist form of debate which
seemed to develop during the Referendum.

Editing out news

Journalists rely heavily upon being alerted to news stories. In politics, press
releases and press conferences are a welcome aid to news reporting. However, with
the need for broadcasters to ensure balance in coverage, neither side was able to
win extra air time by being particularly active or newsworthy. According to the
records kept by Radio Forth, the Yes side sent out many more releases than the No
side (in the three days in which I studied Radio Forth's operation, 10 releases
were received from varying Yes groups and none from the No side), and the Yes side
tended to have more press conferences too. In three days Radio Forth received
press releases from the Scottish National Party, Labour Party, Scottish Liberals,
Scottish Labour Party, Yes for Scotland, Yes for Scotland Youth Committee, Health
for Scotland and the Fabian Society. The effect of this activity in relation to
the need for balance was that the Yes groups were fighting between themselves for
available air time. It did allow the broadcasters a little extra freedom to select
issues from the Yes side, whereas the fewer releases and conferences of the No
side gave the latter more effective control of the issues it sought to raise. If
the additional effort of the Yes side was intended to gain extra air time, this
was a fruitless exercise. It demonstrates wasted energies due to the lack of an
effective umbrella organisation, which could have co-ordinated the raising of
issues and campaigned, one suspects, in a more rational manner. It is worth
stressing, however, that an abundance of items worthy of coverage from one side
will not get air time if the opposing side cannot produce items or responses which,
over time, will create a balance. I do not claim this necessarily happened, but the
possibility seemed a real one at the time. In terms of broadcasting this gives an
element of editorial influence to opposing factions. What, one wonders, would
happen if one side in a referendum refused to appear on the air with the opposing
side? Is it reasonable for one side to have the power to prevent full coverage of
campaign politics by non-co-operation with the media?

It would be fair to say that all stations devoted considerable time and effort to
the devolution Referendum and particularly to the appeasement of the political parties. While resources were limited and political pressures intense, many issues
were aired and much time was spent on explaining the devolution proposals in detail.
Impressive though this was, it is a pity that one of the most significant measures
of success for radio controllers was the lack of complaints from interested political actors. When success revolves around appeasing politicians rather than satis-
fying the demand for an independent and wide-ranging consideration of the issues,
one wonders what price is being paid by the public and in whose interest.

CHAPTER 8

THE OUTCOME

John Bochel   and   David Denver

Votes cast in the Referendum were counted and results announced on the day following polling. Generally, the administration of this aspect of the Referendum seems
to have gone smoothly, although there was some controversy in the Lothian. Region
counting centre over the counting officer's decisions concerning spoiled ballots.
When the results were complete it was clear that the result in Scotland could
hardly have been worse for the Government. A small majority of those who voted had
voted Yes, but the proportion of the electorate that this represented was far short
of the required 40 per cent. Tables 8.1 and 8.2 show the Scottish result in detail.

TABLE 8.1   Referendum Result

	Eligible Electorate	Votes Yes	Votes No	Spoiled Ballots	Turnout %
Region					
Borders	76,742	20,746	30,780	92	67.3
Central	195,673	71,296	59,105	198	66.7
Dumfries & Galloway	104,085	27,162	40,239	114	64.9
Fife	243,485	86,252	74,436	254	66.1
Grampian	339,881	94,944	101,485	415	57.9
Highland	134,997	44,973	43,274	90	65.4
Lothian	561,234	187,221	186,421	324	66.6
Strathclyde	1,750,299	596,519	508,599	1,302	63.2
Tayside	290,076	91,482	93,325	282	63.8
Island Areas					
Orkney	13,789	2,104	5,439	17	54.8
Shetland	14,724	2,020	5,466	18	51.0
Western Isles	22,127	6,218	4,933	27	50.5
SCOTLAND	3,747,112	1,230,937	1,153,502	3,133	63.8

Although a majority of voters were on the Yes side, the majority (77,435) was so
slim and the proportion so far from 40 per cent of the adjusted electorate
(1,498,845) that the results were widely (and rightly, we think) interpreted as a
defeat for the Yes campaign and a triumph for the Noes. Claims by the Yes side,

TABLE 8.2   The Yes Vote

	% Votes Yes	% Electorate Yes
Region		
Borders	40.3	27.0
Central	54.7	36.4
Dumfries & Galloway	40.3	26.1
Fife	53.7	35.4
Grampian	48.3	27.9
Highland	51.0	33.3
Lothian	50.1	33.4
Strathclyde	54.0	34.1
Tayside	49.5	31.5
Island Areas		
Orkney	27.9	15.3
Shetland	27.1	13.7
Western Isles	55.8	28.1
SCOTLAND	51.6	32.9

especially SNP spokesmen, that, because a majority had voted Yes, the Government should therefore proceed with the Act seemed rather desperate and out of touch with the realities of the political situation. In their elation, the No side claimed that many of their supporters had stayed at home in the belief that this was equivalent to voting No and that, but for misleading propaganda by the Yeses, the Noes would have had a majority of votes cast. But, though this claim cannot be properly tested, such poll evidence as we have suggests that non-voters were not significantly skewed to the No side in their preferences. At any rate, the arguments made by the Yes camp during the campaign, that an abstention was equivalent to voting No, backfired somewhat. If all abstentions were indeed to be deemed Noes, then the result was a severe defeat for the devolutionists.

As the above tables show, none of the counting areas crossed the 40 per cent barrier. The Central Region came closest with 36.4 per cent of the electorate voting Yes. Three mainland Regions - the Borders, Dumfries & Galloway and Grampian - recorded Yes votes of less than 30 per cent of the electorate. The figure for Scotland as a whole was 32.9 per cent. Five of the nine mainland Regions recorded a Yes majority amongst those who voted but only in Central, Fife and Strathclyde could the majorities be said to have been decisive. Overall turnout, at 63.8 per cent of the adjusted electorate (62.9 per cent of the registered electorate), was significantly lower than Scottish turnout in the October 1974 General Election (74.8 per cent) or than in the 1979 General Election which took place shortly after the Referendum (76.8 per cent). Interestingly, though, this was a higher turnout than had been the case in the 1975 referendum, when 61.7 per cent of the registered Scottish electorate turned out. In absolute terms, 104,212 more Scottish electors participated in the devolution Referendum than in the Common Market referendum.

Given that the results of the Referendum were declared for 12 counting areas only and that three of these are very small and, in statistical terms, unimportant, there is not a great deal of scope for more extensive analysis. A few points can, however, be made. Firstly, turnout did not vary a great deal from Region to Region (excluding the Island Areas). Only the Grampian Region, traditionally a low turnout area in local and Parliamentary elections, deviated significantly from the overall turnout. Secondly, support for the Assembly appears to have been strongly related to electors' party preferences. If we correlate the percentage of Yes votes in each of the nine Regions with the share of the votes obtained by the parties at the October 1974 General Election, then the coefficients obtained are: -.81 for the Conservative vote, +.81 for the Labour vote and +.60 for the SNP. It is interesting to note that support for the Assembly is more closely related to the Conservative/Labour division than it is to SNP support. With only nine cases, however, we would not want to place too much emphasis on this. What does seem clear is that the level of pre-existing support for Labour and the SNP combined was closely related to the eventual Yes vote. This can be simply illustrated by listing the Regions in declining order of Labour and SNP support in 1974 and comparing that with a listing according to the Yes share of votes in the Referendum.

Labour and SNP 1974	Yes vote 1979
Central	Central
Strathclyde	Strathclyde
Fife	Fife
Tayside	Highland
Lothian	Lothian
Grampian	Tayside
Dumfries & Galloway	Grampian
Highland	Dumfries & Galloway
Borders	Borders

Only the Highland Region is noticeably out of order in the second list, the Yes vote there being larger than expected.

The relationship between party support and Referendum vote is confirmed by survey evidence. All opinion polls taken during the campaign reported large majorities of SNP voters intending to vote Yes, decisive majorities of Labour voters intending to vote Yes, and majority support for No amongst Conservatives. The distribution of Yes support is illustrated in Table 8.3. Though the two polls overestimated the Yes

TABLE 8.3   Voting Intention in Referendum

	Feb. 20-22 (MORI)	Jan.29 - Feb.6 (System Three)
	% Yes	% Yes
All respondents	60	56
Conservative voters	24	32
Labour voters	69	58
SNP voters	94	91
Age: 18-24	69	} 64
25-34	63	
35-54	58	56
55+	55	49
Men	64	59
Women	56	54
Class: ABC1	41	AB 35
C2	71	C1 47
DE	68	C2 60
		DE 65

vote, the pattern of support found is similar and is typical of that reported by all polls.

Support for the Assembly was heaviest among Labour and SNP voters, younger voters and the working class. Even so, a substantial minority – about a third – of Labour supporters were intending to vote against the policy of the Labour Government officially supported by the Labour Party in Scotland.

The result of the Referendum contrasted markedly with the expectations of most people at the start of the campaign. Yes supporters had good grounds for optimism since opinion polls over a long period had shown large majorities of Scottish voters in favour of devolution. As late as the first half of February 1979 three different polls pointed to a decisive Yes majority. The figures, excluding "Don't knows", are given in Table 8.4, together with the dates when the polls were taken.

TABLE 8.4   Early Campaign Polls

	System Three Jan.29 - Feb.6	ORC Feb. 8-11	NOP Feb. 15-16
	%	%	%
Yes	56	60	59
No	44	40	41

In the light of poll results of this kind we ourselves wrote in *The Scotsman* on February 13, 1979: "If the fate of the proposed Scottish Assembly were to be decided straightforwardly by the proportions of votes for and against ... then there would be little doubt about the outcome ... there is no reason to expect anything other than a considerable Yes majority in the referendum. Certainly in any election a political party would feel very confident if opinion was as strongly in its favour as it seems to be for the Assembly".

As the campaign period progressed, however, polls found the Yes majority being steadily whittled away. Table 8.5 shows voting intention at various points in the campaign as reported by two polling organisations – Market and Opinion Research International and System Three. The dates show when the fieldwork for each poll was carried out and "Don't knows" have again been excluded from the table.

TABLE 8.5   Later Campaign Polls

	M O R I			System Three		
	Feb. 12-14	Feb. 20-22	Feb. 27-28	Jan. 8-20	Jan.29 - Feb.6	Feb. 23-25
	%	%	%	%	%	%
Yes	64	60	50	64	56	52
No	36	40	50	36	44	48

Clearly, as the campaign progressed there was a dramatic erosion of the Yes majority. How is this to be explained? Explanations for the outcome of the Referendum have been many and varied and it is doubtful whether general agreement could be reached as to the "real" or "basic" reason for the result. Clearly a combination of factors must be taken into account.

It is important, first, to remember that,although polls had regularly found Scots to be in favour of devolution, they also found that this was a matter of low priority to voters. Devolution did not pre-occupy the voters and it was only during the Referendum campaign that strong arguments against devolution began to be articulated. When faced with a concrete proposal and a decision to be made, voters had to consider the issue more seriously. The decline in support for devolution during the campaign suggests that the No side simply had the better of the argument. They stressed the costs of devolution, the over-bureaucratisation that would result and the potential break-up of Britain. Despite the rather muted nature of the campaign, electors had ample opportunity to hear and weigh these arguments and,although we cannot be precise about their effects in encouraging switching, it is significant that in an ITN Referendum day poll the three most important reasons given by No voters for their decision were the potential break-up of Britain (31 per cent), the cost of devolution (31 per cent) and the creation of another level of government (23 per cent) (cited in Kauppi, 1979).

At various points in this book another important factor contributing to the decline of the Yes support has been noted. This is the fact that during the campaign the two parties most closely identified with the devolution policy - Labour and the SNP - were relatively unpopular with the electorate. For reasons quite unconnected with devolution, the Labour Government was trailing badly in opinion polls. Industrial unrest was the main cause of this. In its February poll (covering the UK), Gallup put the Conservatives 20 percentage points ahead of Labour in voting intentions. For reasons which are less clear, SNP popularity was also slipping in Scotland. From a peak of 36 per cent of voting intentions in March 1977, the SNP had declined steadily and, during the Referendum, polls suggested that they would receive about 20 per cent of the Scottish vote.

In contrast, the Conservatives, who were most clearly identified with the No side, were increasing in popularity in Scotland. In the October election of 1974 the Conservatives had come third with only 25 per cent of the Scottish vote. In February 1979 their support was estimated by various polls at between 30 and 35 per cent. And it was amongst intending Conservative voters that support for the Assembly weakened most markedly during the campaign. As Table 8.6 shows, the proportion of Conservatives intending to vote Yes more than halved in the campaign period. This was a tribute to the success of the Conservative Party in making devolution a party issue. While still claiming to be in favour of devolution in principle, the Conservatives argued that this Labour Act should be defeated.

TABLE 8.6   Referendum Voting Intention by Party (System Three)

	Jan. 8-20	Jan.29 - Feb.6	Feb. 23-25
	% Yes	% Yes	% Yes
Conservatives	46	32	21
Labour	68	58	66
SNP	95	91	91

This was the burden of the argument made by the former Conservative Prime Minister, Lord Home. There is no real evidence that his particular "intervention", of which much was made in the campaign, had of itself any significant impact. It may have put heart into the No camp, but is unlikely to have had any effect on Labour or SNP supporters. Sir Alec's view was, however, consistent with that being promulgated by the Conservative Party in Scotland and the latter does seem to have influenced Conservative voters.

Although the campaign period was decisive in determining the outcome of the Referendum, this was a campaign in which neither set of protagonists had any decisive advantages despite the apparently superior financial resources of the Scotland Says No group. It is routine for a defeated side in an election to place at least some of the blame for defeat on the media. This is, however, a difficult charge to sustain this time. The case for the Assembly was supported by a majority of Scottish daily papers which together had majority circulation, and which favoured the Yes side in the amount and nature of their coverage. Although the majority of local weekly papers which expressed editorial opinion were against the Assembly, they represented less than 40 per cent of the total. In any case, the Yes side had much higher coverage than their opponents and, almost without exception, it was favourable. The treatment of the campaign by radio and television was almost painfully egalitarian and otherwise fair. Although a great deal of fuss was made about the banning of party political broadcasts, neither side can legitimately claim that it was disadvantaged in relation to the other.

It is true that the No side was, centrally at least, better financed than the Yes side, but it was not overwhelmingly so. Indeed, the Yes side issued many more leaflets for house-to-house distribution than did their opponents and the printing of other campaign material, where it differed in quantity, seems to have reflected different priorities rather than differing resources. The superior financial resources of the Scotland Says No group enabled them to make far greater use of poster hoardings and newspaper advertisements, but this could also have been a matter of strategy or even necessity, given their weaker manpower resources in the field.

On their own claims and on more objective evidence, the local Yes groups together spent more money, distributed more literature, held more meetings, did more canvassing, had more workers and were generally more active than the No groups.

So in terms of resources, and particularly of those that are important in election campaigns, the Yes side was not, if at all, significantly inferior. It may have been, but we doubt it, that the No side deployed their resources more efficaciously. We are not persuaded that their poster and newspaper advertising had the effect of swinging many votes. It has not been demonstrated by political scientists that this kind of propaganda is effective.

In the immediate aftermath of the Referendum there were bitter recriminations from some sections of the Yes side about the lack of unity among those in favour of an Assembly and the consequent damage caused by the divisions. It is true that the Labour Party's decision to go it alone was a blow to unity, but whether it was even damaging, let alone fatal, is not at all clear. Certainly it seems to have been inevitable. Even if the Labour Party nationally had recommended its members to join the Yes for Scotland group, to make it an umbrella organisation, it is doubtful whether most activists, or even large numbers, would have done so. There was too much recent bitterness, sometimes of a personal nature, between Labour and the SNP for genuine co-operation to take place. Even the title of the group was too strident for some, - "another version of the selfish 'It's Scotland's Oil'" - as one activist put it. We do not know either whether Labour involvement would have prevented SNP branches from conducting a separate campaign under their own banner, as many of them did. As it was, both SNP and Labour had different motives for campaigning for a Yes vote. Consequently, the messages from the Yes side reaching the voters were sometimes conflicting (as, to a lesser extent, were those from the No side). It could be argued that, as a matter of strategy, Labour and the SNP, by appealing to their own voters, on their own terms, could maximise support for the Assembly, for between them they obtained nearly 67 per cent of the votes in the October 1974 election. This argument is unlikely to be settled one way or the other now.

What we do know is that, for one reason or another, no party or group on either side put great enthusiasm into the Referendum campaign, and their efforts compared poorly with those that they mount in general elections.

We have mentioned the coincidence of the Referendum with a decline in support for Labour and the SNP, but only weeks later, in the General Election, Labour increased its share of the vote and, although the SNP lost a lot of ground, between them they held on to 60 per cent of the total vote. This suggests that, for many Labour voters at least, the question of devolution was decided upon independently of their normal vote. Survey evidence (Strathclyde Area Survey Devolution Survey) supports this interpretation, showing that 38 per cent of Labour voters thought that the Labour Party was very much in favour of the Assembly, 56 per cent thought that the Party was somewhat in favour and only 6 per cent thought that the Party was against. Clearly, many Labour supporters knew their Party's position on the issue but, having considered it, decided to differ from the Party.

In seeking to explain the Referendum result, some commentators have talked about (only partly frivolously, we suspect) an "Argentina syndrome" - a reference to the débâcle suffered by the Scottish football team in the 1978 World Cup. This is a psychological explanation of the result of the Referendum encapsulated in a letter to *The Scotsman* which suggested that Scotland's mistake was to go and play in Argentina. The Cup was won before we went, it argued (and those of us who lived in Scotland had almost been persuaded of this) and it was a risky business to go all that way for the formality of picking it up. Political analysis on the basis of national character is out of fashion today, but the question must be asked: Were the Scots prepared to ask for devolution, to take actions which made it seem likely that it would be granted, but when it came to the point of decision, did they lack the self-confidence to clinch it? The main headline in *The Scotsman* on the eve of the Referendum poll, reporting last-minute appeals from politicians, seemed to accept that there was something in this diagnosis: "Appeal to Scots for courage in voting", it read. Bruce Millan, Secretary of State for Scotland, asked Scots to "take courage in their hands and vote Yes". David Steel, the Liberal leader, warned against "failure of nerve", and Jim Sillars, a leading Yes for Scotland figure, assailed "the fearties" (those who were afraid). The *Scotsman*'s own editorial (unusually on the front page) called for "an affirmation of faith in the ability of Scots to deal with their domestic affairs ...".

Such an affirmation manifestly was not made. Whether this was due to the particular events of the winter of 1978/79 or to more enduring features of the Scottish character and situation will remain a subject for debate. We ourselves believe that the genuine demand for devolution in Scotland was never as strong or as widespread as SNP support and opinion polls might have suggested. None the less, had the Government been less unpopular when its proposals came before the people, they could well have received endorsement. In that case there would have been set in motion a train of events quite different from those described by James Kellas in his account of the aftermath of the Referendum (see chapter 9).

REFERENCE

Kauppi, M.V. (1979). The 1979 Scottish Referendum results: explanations, rationalisations and protestations. Paper presented at the sixth annual meeting of the Rocky Mountain Conference on British Studies, October 26-27, 1979, Colorado Springs.

CHAPTER 9

ON TO AN ASSEMBLY ?

James Kellas

The Referendum result of March 1, 1979 was a critical event in the history of devolution. It had the effect of stopping further progress on the Scotland Act. Although
a bare majority of the votes cast favoured the Act, this was interpreted widely as
being insufficient for a major constitutional change, in particular because it fell
well short of the target of 40 per cent of the electorate set by Parliament, against
the wishes of the Government.

Now, however, Government leaders seemed almost too ready to admit that they did not
have a strong mandate to proceed with implementing the Act. Publicly they were in
favour of advising the House of Commons to vote against an Order repealing the Act.
But Bruce Millan, Secretary of State for Scotland, said shortly after the Referendum
that the narrowness of the majority was a serious impediment, even if the 40 per
cent rule could be ignored. The Executive of the Labour Party in Scotland issued a
statement on March 3, 1979, which affirmed the devolution commitment but did not
call for implementation of the Act. Instead they merely asked that the Government
"in reaching the decisions on how to proceed would do so on the basis of a continuing commitment to devolution". This seemed to reject the interpretation of the
Referendum result as a victory for the Act. Very shortly afterwards the Labour
Party's Scottish Conference met in Perth with a well-known anti-devolutionist,
Mrs Janey Buchan, in the chair. All the emergency resolutions on devolution were
withdrawn from debate, leaving only the Executive's statement that devolution would
"remain at the forefront of the programme" and urging the Government to implement
the Scotland Act, but without specific suggestions as to how this should be done.
Mrs Buchan, as chairperson, refused to call any MPs at the debate, claiming that
they had a platform elsewhere. This roused Dennis Canavan (MP for West Stirlingshire) to fury and he fulminated to the press and TV against the "incredible spectacle of a Labour conference being chaired by a person who voted in the referendum
against Labour Party policy. She had tried to gag her critics, and invited to the
rostrum traitors who had collaborated with the Tories and used court action to gag
their own party during the referendum" (*The Scotsman*, 12.3.1979). He was referring
here to actions of the Labour Vote No campaign but his reference to "traitors" had
later to be explained as "traitors to the Labour Movement" and not "traitors to
Scotland", as the latter interpretation would have placed him perilously close to
the Nationalists in his political language.

It was the SNP in fact which kept the devolution flag flying with a "Scotland Said
Yes" campaign. This was intended to put pressure on Labour MPs to vote in Parliament against the Order repealing the Scotland Act. It was also an attempt to con-

147

vince the people of Scotland that there was a mandate from the Referendum to go
ahead with devolution. Many of the old theoretical arguments were brought out about
majorities and democracy, and analogies were drawn between the 33 per cent of the
electorate voting for the Act and the comparable "mandates" achieved by the Government and anti-devolution MPs in the election. However, such arguments proved feeble
in the face of real politics, for the sober fact remained that neither the Government nor the people of Scotland[1] now believed that there had been a decisive vote
for devolution on March 1. The Scotland Said Yes campaign was made into a purely
SNP affair, and the Labour Party did not co-operate.

The political battle had now shifted to London where in Parliament the Government
and the SNP were faced with very uncomfortable decisions. These decisions showed
clearly how politics at the centre can move in ways distinct from politics on the
ground, in this case in Scotland. In the case of the Government, its majority, composed mainly of English Labour MPs, with the addition of Liberals and Nationalists,
was at stake. The Referendum had destroyed Welsh devolution, so the Welsh Nationalists were prepared to settle for other concessions for Wales in return for support. When a vote of confidence eventually came about, these concessions were
hurriedly provided. The Liberals did not make Scottish devolution a priority condition for their support, and so the Government did not have to promise immediate
implementation of the Scotland Act. David Steel, the Liberal leader, told the Scottish Liberal Conference on March 16, 1979 that the Assembly was "not going to
happen" and that he would settle for the Scottish Grand Committee meeting in Edinburgh. This riled the Scottish Liberals, who voted for the implementation of the
Scotland Act.

Even if the Liberals at Westminster had supported implementation of the Act, this
would in any case not have gone down well with the bulk of English Labour MPs, who
were now ready to shelve the Scottish commitment altogether. That left the SNP, who
could sense that the Government was not serious about pressing its MPs to support
the Act as a matter of confidence. But the SNP wanted to show this clearly to the
people of Scotland and when Prime Minister James Callaghan refused to lay the
Order repealing the Act before Parliament within three weeks, they tabled their motion of No Confidence. This was what the Conservatives had been waiting for and
they tabled their own "official" motion of No Confidence, which was carried by one
vote on March 28, 1979.

The SNP's actions in Parliament seemed perverse to many, even to some in the Party
in Scotland. While it was clear that the Government were stalling on the implementation of the Act, and might well have been unable to deliver a majority of votes
against repeal, this could only have been made clear by a vote on the Order which
had to be laid before the House for that purpose. It would then have been obvious
that it was the Labour Party, and not the SNP, which had prevented the Act coming
into operation. For it would have been anti-devolutionist Labour MPs who had
successfully combined with the Conservatives against pro-devolution Labour MPs,
Nationalists, Liberals and even some Ulster Unionists. The dilemma for the SNP was
that, if the issue was not brought to a head, the Party was in danger of losing all
credibility as the party which "spoke for Scotland". Instead, as things turned out,
the SNP could be blamed for causing the downfall of the Government and with it the
Act. There were quite a few Nationalists in Scotland, as well as a strong minority
of SNP MPs, who saw the ambiguity of their position, yet they had to take the consequences of the actions of the majority vote of the Parliamentary Party.

---

[1]A System Three poll in the *Glasgow Herald* on April 18, 1979 showed that only 26
per cent believed that the Government should go ahead with the Assembly as proposed
in the Scotland Act. ORC in the *Scotsman*, April 26, 1979 gave 28 per cent in
favour of implementing the Act.

For Labour in Scotland, however, things were much more favourable. They could argue that they had almost "delivered" devolution but that it had not been sufficiently supported by a vote of the Scottish people, and had been defeated by the anti-Government combination on the censure motion, itself a result of SNP initiatives. So, according to this interpretation, Labour could not be blamed for the loss of the Act.

In reality, the Labour Party was very much to blame for the way things had turned out. Right from the start of the devolution story Labour had been divided and ambiguous in its actions. It had failed to support an Assembly until the SNP electoral successes in 1974 and had only adopted its policy through devious means, including the over-ruling of the Scottish Executive by Transport House. At least half of the constituency side of the Party was lukewarm or hostile, and most English Labour MPs went along with the policy out of party loyalty and fear of the loss of Scottish seats to the SNP - or worse, a revolt of the Scottish people against the Union. The Parliamentary progress of the Scotland and Wales Bill and the Scotland Bill showed how little discipline the Government was able, or wished, to exert over the rebels in its ranks, such as George Cunningham, who first forced a Referendum on the Government and then the notorious "40 per cent rule". While some of the Government's difficulties can be traced to its lack of an overall majority in the House, with frequent defeats occurring on many issues, a large part of the trouble was recalcitrance on the part of anti-devolutionist Labour MPs and a weak discipline imposed on them by the Party leaders. The Labour leadership did not link their survival to devolution until it was too late. By that time it is questionable whether they wanted to survive anyway.

The General Election campaign in April 1979 showed that devolution had lost much of its urgency as an issue. While one survey showed that nearly half of the respondents named it as an important issue when they came to cast their vote (Brand and Jordan, 1980), as usual it was mentioned much less frequently than economic issues. And this time too the politicians of all parties kept off it during the campaign. Even the SNP did not stress the issue of constitutional change, preferring to insist that the Nationalists were good for Scotland, or for the particular constituency involved. With the prospect of immediate action on devolution receding, there was no credibility about talk of an independent Scotland within five ... ten ... fifty (?) years. It seemed pointless to press on with the Scotland Act when so many Scots seemed either apathetic or hostile towards it. Labour and Conservative were struggling for much higher stakes - control of the British state at Westminster. Most voters in Scotland turned from their purely Scottish political interests to those of the British economy as a whole, and the choice was between rival governments and Prime Ministers. The third force in politics in Scotland seemed to be increasingly the Liberals and not the Nationalists. The Liberals won 14.5 per cent of the votes in the seats they contested in Scotland (43), while the SNP won 17.2 per cent over all 71 seats. The Liberals kept their three seats, but the SNP were reduced to two, the Western Isles and Dundee East. Twenty-nine SNP deposits were lost, including all in Edinburgh and eight in Glasgow. On the other hand, their showing in many rural seats was very strong, and in terms of votes cast they increased their totals in Angus South, Moray & Nairn and Galloway. In Aberdeenshire East, Banffshire, Moray & Nairn, Angus South and Clackmannan & East Stirlingshire, the adverse vote was in three figures only, and it could be surmised that at the next election the SNP would have a good chance of regaining some of these seats, if circumstances were otherwise favourable.

The collapse of the SNP vote in most parts of Scotland benefited both the Labour Party and the Conservatives. Thus Labour's share of the vote rose from 36 per cent to 42 per cent, and its seats from 41 in October 1974 to 44. The Conservative vote rose from 25 per cent to 31 per cent, and its seats from 16 to 22. This showed that the electoral system worked strongly in favour of the Labour Party in Scotland, since its share of the seats (62 per cent) was much higher than its share of the vote. Conversely, the SNP with nearly three per cent of the seats, did very badly.

Devolution was not a completely dead issue. Opinion polls taken during April 1979 indicated that about two-thirds of Scottish electors wished to see some form of devolution resurrected, although as usual there were divisions as to which option was most suitable. This paved the way for a revival of the subject at an "élite" level, namely inter-party talks at Westminster. These were promised by George Younger, Secretary of State for Scotland, when the Scotland Act was repealed by the House of Commons on June 20, 1979. The talks were, however, not really to be concerned with devolution but with "improving the handling of Scottish business in Parliament". This could mean strengthening the Scottish Grand Committee, with possible meetings in Edinburgh, or reviving the Select Committee on Scottish Affairs. The latter was in fact re-established at the end of October 1979, after pressure was exerted by Scottish MPs. They wanted the Committee to take its place alongside the twelve departmental Select Committees announced in June. Thus the talks could not take the credit for that, and attention turned to the Grand Committee, and other forms of Scottish Parliamentary business. The SNP would not participate in the talks, which did not start until April 1980 and finished the following month. Eventually, in August 1980, the Government proposed merely to give more time to debate Scottish affairs in the Scottish Grand Committee and to discontinue the practice of adding non-Scottish MPs to the Committee. There was no recommendation regarding meetings in Edinburgh, although the House as a whole might decide to allow this.

There was little to get excited about in the proposals, and the MPs showed that they valued their activities at Westminster more than meeting in Edinburgh. Thus, there seemed to be no form of devolution available from the Conservative Government.

Despite this, a new "Campaign for a Scottish Assembly" had been founded in Edinburgh on the anniversary of the Referendum, March 1, 1980. Chaired by Dr Jack Brand, a Politics Senior Lecturer of Strathclyde University and SNP member, the Campaign included among its supporters around five Labour MPs, a Liberal MP, the Scottish Liberal Party Vice-Chairman, Mrs Ray Michie, Mr Archie Fairley of the Communist Party and Mrs Helen Millar of the Conservatives. No Scottish Conservative MP was involved.

The General Secretary of the STUC, James Milne, and George Bolton, Vice-President of the Scottish Area of the National Union of Mineworkers, spoke at the inaugural rally. This remarkable cross-party movement committed itself to "working towards a National Convention" - "a gathering of all shades of Scottish opinion" - to consider proposals for setting up an Assembly. In June 1980, it organised a "Festival of the People" in Edinburgh, and sought without success to open the proposed Assembly buildings to the public (they were used for a meeting of the Convention of Scottish Local Authorities at the end of June 1980).

In terms of practical politics, however, the actions of the parties were more significant. The Labour Party's Scottish Conference in March 1980 gave strong support to a resolution from the Miners' and Transport Workers' unions calling for a Scottish Assembly "with meaningful powers over the economy of Scotland", presumably a stronger body than that envisaged by the Scotland Act. (It was the denial of such powers that had led Jim Sillars to leave the Labour Party in 1976 and form the "Scottish Labour Party"; he is now a member of the SNP.) Unlike the situation in 1974, the members of the Scottish Executive of the Labour Party were now predominantly devolutionists, and also demanded greater autonomy for the party organisation in Scotland (*The Scotsman*, September 10, 1980). In September 1980 a "Labour Campaign for a Scottish Assembly" was formed under the chairmanship of George Foulkes, MP for South Ayrshire, who had defeated Sillars in 1979. Initially, 15 Labour MPs gave their support to the Campaign.

Although the Labour Party's National Executive Committee at first ignored devolution in its "draft manifesto" of July 1980, this was rectified when complaints were
received from Scotland. Devolution was not debated at the Labour Party Conference
(September 29 - October 3, 1980), but Michael Foot, the Deputy Leader, told a
fringe meeting that the commitment would be in the next manifesto. Also outside the
ranks of the Scottish Labour MPs, Dr David Owen, the former Foreign Secretary, proposed a complicated scheme of devolution involving an Assembly and a reformed
House of Lords on a regional basis (*The Scotsman*, September 18, 1980). Should the
need arise then, the Labour Party was ready to move once more on the subject.

That need might well be connected with a revival in the SNP's fortunes, although
paradoxically the association with nationalism in the past had probably discouraged
many Labour activists from supporting devolution. For the SNP's part, the lesson of
the Referendum seemed to be that there was now no half-way house to independence.
Gordon Wilson, the new Chairman of the Party, told the Party Conference in May 1980
that the SNP had seen through the "devolution deception" and that "that phase of our
struggle for national freedom is over". In the meantime the Party seemed to spend
as much time campaigning against nuclear waste dumping, and for a Scottish oil fund,
as for independence. Away from the Conference, the party leaders were not uninte-
rested in devolution, and Wilson himself had promoted a devolution Bill in Parliament in March 1980, under the "Ten Minute Rule", which proposed that the terms of a
devolution package would be determined by an elected Scottish constituent assembly.

But the initiative lay clearly with the two big parties, and in particular with the
Conservative Party. However, as long as Mrs Thatcher remained Leader, there was
little prospect of action and the former devolutionists in the Party dared not
speak on the issue. Even the tentative Government proposals on reform of the Scottish Grand Committee were vetoed by the MPs of all parties, and the Scottish Conservative Conference in May 1980 did not debate devolution at all.

Does this mean that there is no future for devolution in Scotland? This chapter is
boldly titled "On to an Assembly?" and even with the question-mark there is an
assumption that devolution is still a live issue and a practical possibility. While
it is true that the Referendum result was a critical event in Scottish history, it
was not quite as decisive as the Battle of Bannockburn (1314) or the Treaty of
Union (1707). It was essentially ambiguous as to its effect and was also based on a
particular preference expressed by voters on a particular day. The ambiguity remains that while Scotland voted Yes by a narrow majority, the "rules of the game"
and the political climate resulted in the repeal of the Act. In the absence of the
Scotland Act there is a vacuum which about two-thirds of the people of Scotland
would like to see filled. How strongly they would like to see a constitutional
change is another matter, for, ever since opinions have been measured in Scotland,
there has been a two-thirds majority in favour of some kind of "Scottish Parliament". This preference has only been strong, and translated into political action,
in the presence of other indicators of Scottish nationalism, especially electoral
support for the SNP. If that support returns, then action should follow.

But this is to put the initiative entirely on to the masses, and the very same
masses who failed to demonstrate great enthusiasm for devolution in 1979. It is
much more usual for constitutional change to come about through "élite" initiative;
in particular, from party leaders and civil servants working through Parliament and
the Whitehall machine. Until now, this élite has been most suspicious of devolution
and has taken action only when forced to do so through the apparent pressure of the
masses and the SNP. But now that that pressure has been removed, a section of the
élite may feel more secure in moving towards devolution, this time as an élite demand and not as a concession to the irrational masses. One of the features of the
1966 to 1979 period in British politics has been that a section of the élite has
been converted to devolution, starting with John P. Mackintosh in the 1960's and
working through to Cabinet members of both parties in the 1970's. There are signs

that in the Labour Party, and especially in the Labour Party central organisation in Scotland, there are now committed devolutionists who wish to push the cause of devolution forward, even without the stimulus of an SNP electoral revival.

The trouble with this analysis is that these élite members lack political weight at the centre of politics in London and gained credibility there in the past only when the masses were apparently howling at the gates. In the Conservative Party, Heath and Home gained support for their devolution views because of this. In the Labour Party, Kitson and the trade union devolutionists did likewise. Now, Heath and Home are otherwise engaged - as is the trade union movement, facing a Thatcher government.

This may throw the initiative back to the masses. Mass electoral behaviour has even now shown a "conflict" between Scotland and England, especially that part of England in the South which contains the "Establishment". The Conservative Party gets nine out of ten of its MPs from England, but Labour badly needs its 44 Scottish MPs to regain a majority. So the territorial divisions of the United Kingdom are still in play. Labour in Scotland sees its function as defending Scottish interests against a South of England Conservative government. This is a kind of nationalism, although it is still removed from a demand for constitutional change. Such a demand must come from the ballot box.

The Scottish electorate chose to give an ambiguous answer on devolution in 1979. But votes are merely political currency and, like the exchange rates and the stock market, they fluctuate wildly. The vote might have been very different in a different month or year. But there was a sense of truth about what happened which makes the event a critical one and not a deviant happening, that is, it was not something that should *not* have happened in the circumstances. What the Scots and the politicians did in early 1979 was to expose the essential ambiguity of the United Kingdom: its multi-national yet homogeneous nature, its conflicts based on nation as well as class; and its balance between élite and mass initiatives in politics. It also exposed the shifting nature of opinion on devolution and the links between that opinion and party support, itself shifting according to the political climate of the day. It will be very difficult to escape from the divisions exposed by the Referendum, and the stalemate produced by them. A very similar spectacle can be seen in the state capitalism/welfare state *versus* free economy/individualism dilemma in the rest of politics. A devolutionary resolution of the territorial divide in politics requires a much greater push towards change in Scotland, Wales and Ireland than at present prevails, just as socialism or a "free market" is unattainable in times of normal politics.

Some kind of change, is however, inevitable. The history of politics and government in Scotland does show movement towards a greater differentiation in electoral behaviour from England, and likewise in the machinery of government, in decentralisation of departments, and in policy-making processes. It seems likely that these will develop, and devolution is a further point along the line. At the same time, people in Scotland are unwilling to contemplate disruptive change and are becoming objectively more alike their counterparts in the South in their economic and social expectations and actions. They match this, however, with various status demands based on nationalism. They want to be Scottish and British at the same time. This means they would like to have (unspecified) devolution to bolster up their national status in Britain, but also an equal status with all other British citizens. This can be called "having your cake and eating it", but in Britain it is the foundation of a stable and evolving polity.

REFERENCE

Brand, J. and M. Jordan (1980). The issue of self-government: Scotland and the devolution referendum. Paper presented to ECPR Joint Sessions, Florence.

CHAPTER 10

THE WELSH EXPERIENCE

Ian Hume

The experience of the Referendum in Scotland and Wales appears, on the surface, to have had many similarities. In each country there was a history of political interest in the issue, a strong Labour Party pledged to support devolution, a national party (SNP and Plaid Cymru) of success and substance, and an electorate which, according to early opinion polls, was favourably disposed to devolution. The conduct of the campaigns, with the various umbrella groups working alongside the parties, was also similar and the campaigns appeared to revolve around many of the same issues. Yet the results were strikingly different. In Wales, only 11.8 per cent of eligible electors and 20.3 per cent of actual voters voted in favour of the proposals while, for Scotland, the figures were 32.9 per cent and 51.6 per cent respectively. Part of the explanation for the differences must lie in the cultural and political history and sociology of both countries.

THE WELSH SETTING

A sense of national identity is an important mobilising basis in a contest of this nature and throughout its modern history Scotland has retained, even developed, the sense of national identity with distinctive legal, educational, religious and other institutions.

In contrast, Wales, in recent times has not had its own legal, educational or governmental institutions. Without an indigenous aristocracy or capitalist class to develop and sustain these institutions Wales has lagged behind Scotland in formal structural expression of its national characteristics. But the unique character of Welsh identity was bound to respond and develop in relation to the alternative models of culture and society brought by industrialisation. A localised society even today, Wales was until the industrial revolution in many senses a parochial society, but the religious and educational movements of the 18th century began to create new links between areas. The 19th century saw considerable national develop-ments such as the University Colleges, the National Library and the National Eisteddfod. These developments encompassed and drew support from all social classes, status and occupation groups, and all geographical areas of Wales; they provided a truly national focus. Thus, without the framework of a state, a nation was able to express and recognise itself as such. This expression was largely via the medium of the Welsh language. It was not until the beginning of this century that the pro-portion of the population speaking Welsh fell below 50 per cent; today over half-a-million people, a little over 20 per cent of the population, speak the language.

153

The process of linguistic decline has several aspects of relevance for politics.
Firstly, the traditional symbols of national identity originally articulated in the
Welsh language have become less accessible and hence are less likely to act as
bases for political mobilisation. Thus, the cultural movement nowadays has lost the
national character it had in the 19th century. Secondly, for some Welsh people the
decline of the language symbolises a process of economic, social and cultural change
which has caused a serious weakening of Welsh identity. It is an indicator of what
Wales has lost in relation to England. Unlike the position in Scotland, the language
question enters into almost every political debate. The existence of a body such as
Cymdeithas yr Iaith Gymraeg (the Welsh Language Society), politically active in all
parts of the country, distinguishes the Welsh from the Scottish situation. In any
country where two languages are spoken there is scope for political differences to
be expressed in relation to language groups. Wales is no exception.

Several factors distinguish the sociology of Wales. There are regional differences
of political significance. The difficulties of North/South communication - much
road and rail traffic goes via Shrewsbury in England - create the possibilities for
regional rivalries, particularly since the decision, taken some 15 years ago, to
designate Cardiff, in the South, as capital city. The opening of the Severn Bridge,
and the upgrading of the A55 road in the North, have in economic terms given the
North and South firmer links with the adjoining areas of England than with each
other. Further, there is a difference between East and West. One can distinguish
the industrial valleys of Gwent and Glamorgan, together with the industrial area of
Clwyd centred on Wrexham, from the Western rural areas. These divides are real in a
geographical sense and in the significance attached to them by Welsh people. As
well as defining themselves as Welsh, they will often define themselves in relation
to other areas of Wales (see Madgwick, Griffiths and Walker, 1973).

Wales has also experienced a much greater influx of newcomers of English origin
than has Scotland. The tendency has been for the incomers to be small businessmen
or upwardly mobile skilled workers and professional people, or those recently
retired. The last category especially has had a substantial effect on the voting
ecology of the North Wales coast in general and certain places such as Anglesey in
particular. The incomers have not usually identified with Welsh culture and in
several staunchly Welsh towns, such as Bangor and Blaenau Ffestiniog in the North-
west, they have been in the forefront of attempts to lessen the amount of Welsh-
medium teaching in schools. They are inclined to be Conservative supporters. All
this is a hindrance to the maintenance of a firmly-based national identity.

For the greater part of this century the Liberal Party, and then the Labour Party,
through their dominance of Welsh politics offered a measure of identification for
those who saw Wales as a nation, symbolised by its adherence to a radical party.
In 1900, for example, the Liberals held 26 out of the 34 Parliamentary seats; by
1922 Labour had overtaken them to become the biggest party and by 1970 it represented virtually the whole of industrial and indeed agricultural Wales, with 27 out
of the 36 seats. Naturally, these two parties in their time of dominance of Welsh
politics acted as powerful mechanisms for integrating Wales into the mainstream of
British affairs (see Jones, 1977), but there is no doubt that they were also a
locus of a national identity.

The rise in electoral favour of Plaid Cymru in the late 1960's and 1970's, culmi-
nating in the gain of the Arfon, Carmarthen, and Merioneth Parliamentary seats in
the October 1974 General Election, signalled a breakup of the hitherto solid
Labour voting pattern. All of Plaid Cymru's actual Parliamentary gains were in the
predominantly Welsh-speaking areas of the North and West[1], which meant that Labour

---

[1]During this period Plaid Cymru also made considerable headway in local government
elections and Parliamentary by-elections in industrial South Wales - traditional
Labour territory.

could no longer expect radical rural Wales to vote for it *en bloc*. Also, the Welsh Labour Party lost MPs who spoke Welsh and were, potentially at least, in favour of a Welsh Assembly. Until this time it was possible to give a measure of credence to the view that Wales was a "proletarian nation" or a "classless society", expressing its solidarity and identifying itself through its support for a radical party. These tenets were now in serious doubt. The voting behaviour of the Welsh in the 1979 General Election saw the Labour Party confined to the industrial valleys of the South, with a small representation in North-east and West Wales, and confirms the breakdown of the stereotype. The experience of the Referendum has to be seen in relation to this process.

However, Welsh political behaviour is made up of a variety of local patterns. Full justice cannot be done to differences of dominant language and regional culture and their influence on political behaviour by the analysis of aggregate electoral data, nor by simply using party political categories. In rural areas the factors which lead an elector of a given background to vote for one party in his own constituency could lead an elector of a similar background in a neighbouring constituency to vote for another party. It is against the background of both a plurality of local cultures and the national political scene (and also susceptibility to British influences) that we must see the Referendum experience.

THE COMING OF THE REFERENDUM

The events of the 1960s and 1970s made a referendum on devolution in 1979 a logical phase in the stream of politics in Wales (see Foulkes, Jones and Wilford, forth-coming). The period of the late 1960s was a time of considerable growth in electoral support for Plaid Cymru, with nationalist feeling in a more extreme form coming to a head in 1969, the year of the investiture of the Prince of Wales, which was accompanied by legal and illegal forms of protests.

The future of Wales as a nation appeared then, as in 1980, as an issue on the UK stage. The protests over second homes, Government broadcasting policy and unemploy-ment are nothing new in Wales. Equally important in the 1970's were the delibera-tions of the Royal Commission on the Constitution and the substantial degree of support for devolution in the Labour Party.

Within the Labour Party in Wales the idea of devolution and an Assembly had long drawn support from those associated with the non-conformist radical tradition (see Jones, 1977). This tradition had, until the First World War, provided the basis for Liberal domination of Wales. Initially, because of its origins and allegiances, it supported the idea of Wales as a cultural as well as a political nation, and it was well-represented in all areas of Wales. In the industrial South-east, in the anthracite fields and agricultural areas of the South-west, in the quarrying areas of the North-west and in the iron and steel belt of the North-east, there was con-siderable support by MPs and Party members for a measure of devolution. Labour's commitment to devolution in Wales in the 1960's and 1970's was based on this sub-stantial grouping, many of whom were Welsh-speaking. Several factors, however, worked to reduce the influence of this group.

The Party had always had a strong sense of internationalism, a concomitant of which was a view of the working class as a powerful force only when consciously united across other loyalties or cleavages. Those who were of this persuasion saw "Welsh-ness" as something to be expressed via (rather than as part of) a united British working class movement. To them the idea of autonomous institutions could endanger the future of socialism based on a cohesive working class. As the process of lin-guistic decline continued, the strength of Plaid Cymru and Cymdeithas yr Iaith Gymraeg increased. For many, both inside and outside the Labour Party, this asso-ciated the Welsh language with nationalism and separatism. As any Assembly for

Wales would naturally have to be bilingual in operation and would, therefore, be supportive of the Welsh language, some people in the Labour Party saw it as a two-fold threat. Firstly, it would divide the efforts of the British Labour movement and, secondly, it would be a vehicle for nationalist agitation and propaganda.

During these two decades, the influence of the old "Welsh radical" tradition was seriously weakened by the loss of some of its stalwart MPs, by either death or ousting by Plaid Cymru; this occurred at a time when "internationalist" feeling in the Party was being substantially promoted by new MPs such as Neil Kinnock and Donald Anderson, both of whom were fiercely to oppose any scheme of devolution which involved an autonomous Welsh assembly.

Two further considerations influenced opinion on devolution in Wales, particularly Labour Party opinion. The local government and Health Service reforms of the early 1970's had not created a good impression; secondly, Margaret Thatcher (despite her own Party's initiation of these reforms) began campaigning vigorously against "bureaucracy" and "waste in local government". To propose a Welsh Assembly in the latter part of the 1970's was to open oneself to an attack on these grounds from a radical Conservative Opposition, which had the support of a substantial sector of British opinion.

A relatively Anglicised party, the Conservative Party in Wales had always set itself firmly against real devolution for Wales. Virtually no Conservatives campaigned for the Assembly. The Liberals, with their Party's commitment to a federal Britain, saw the proposed Cardiff Assembly, with no powers to raise money, as small beer. Whilst they supported the measure - and indeed had a history of support for economic and political devolution - they were not a major or enthusiastic influence on developments.

The 1979 Welsh Referendum appears as a logical outcome of trends, but one must not overestimate general interest in the issue. Wales does not have a long history of popular concern over devolution. Thus, it was the hard task of informing and educating that faced the campaigners, particularly on the Yes side. To them fell the business of explaining and justifying a relatively abstract scheme. In view of the Assembly's lack of fund-raising power little could be said of its potential.

Ioan Evans, Labour MP for Aberdare, summed up the kind of feelings the Yes enthusiasts faced when he declared¨ "The Welsh Assembly is a cross between a red herring and a white elephant. And it will also have the functions of a Trojan Horse" (*Y Faner*, 16.2.1979). Despite the evidence of opinion polls, devolution had not captured public imagination, and generalisations like these were common during the campaign. With the public poorly informed, these generalisations were hard to combat.

                    THE CAMPAIGN

The Referendum campaign in Wales gave rise to two umbrella groups - the Wales for the Assembly Campaign (WAC) and its No counterpart, the No Assembly Campaign (NAC). These differed in that the WAC had several political parties as formal members, giving much less room for manoeuvre than in the NAC where the only political party formally represented was the Conservative Party. Though based largely on the Conservative Party the NAC had support from the National Federation for the Self-Employed, seven of the eight County Councils (Gwynedd, the mainly Welsh-speaking county in the North-west, being the exception), the Country Landowners' Association and NALGO. A smaller and separate, but very vigorous group was based on six dissident Labour MPs[2] who represented constituencies (Map opposite) which were, in the

---

[2]Ioan Evans, Aberdare; Donald Anderson, Swansea East; Neil Kinnock, Bedwellty; Ifor Davies, Gower; Leo Abse, Pontypool and Fred Evans, Caerphilly.

Welsh-speaking population;

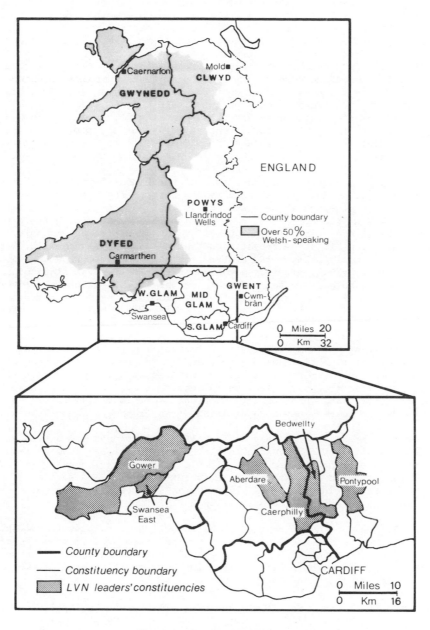

Constituencies of LVN leaders.

main, in the industrial areas of the South-east and had largely lost the Welsh language. Some of the geographical and cultural divisions in Wales were thus re-presented in the Labour Vote No (LVN) campaign at the outset and provided the No camp with the possibility of campaigning on the basis of those divisions.

The WAC consisted mainly of members of the Labour and Liberal Parties, Plaid Cymru and the Wales TUC. The WAC platform membership was predominantly Labour, probably in order to lessen the chances of over-association in the public mind with nation-alism and the Nationalists. Nevertheless, much of the WAC campaign depended on the relatively well-organised branch structure of Plaid Cymru. The existence of the Labour "Gang of Six" acted as a catalyst for anti-Assembly feeling in the Labour Party. As well as leading some constituency parties to campaign for a No vote, it also influenced many others to make what was effectively a withdrawal from the campaign in order to maintain local unity. Within the WAC there could be dis-tinguished among all participants a feeling that the proposed measure was by no means perfect, as it was the product more of Parliamentary compromise than of political initiative in Wales; this obviously affected the level of enthusiasm in their campaigning.

Nor was the other major Yes grouping, that of the Labour Party-Wales TUC, entirely free of such feeling. However, a major reason for running a separate and relatively enthusiastic campaign such as this was, as in Scotland, to fulfil the Labour Gov-ernment's promises without fear of compromise or association with the Nationalists. Despite the existence of two Yes groupings of rather different emphasis, there was between them a significant degree of co-operation and mutual goodwill. Nor did the WAC, despite its politically mixed membership, show any real signs of disunity at the national level of campaigning, although at the local level signs of strain were sometimes to be seen in various parts of Wales. Whilst the Labour Party and Wales TUC organisation obviously put strong emphasis in manpower terms on their own campaign, a cross-section of their membership was also prominently involved in the umbrella Yes group, the WAC.

Funding of these groups was largely as in Scotland, with the additional and contro-versial element of financial assistance voted by the local authorities of Gwent and South Glamorgan. (Almost all local authorities in Wales objected to the Assembly on various grounds, mainly declaring themselves opposed to the "hampering of local democracy" and "unnecessary additional administrative costs". Naturally enough, they also feared the reorganisation of their powers by an Assembly.)

In an election, boundary lines are clear. Allies, opponents and attitudes toward key issues are well-defined. Voting loyalties may be called upon, while a local candidate and a national leader are available to focus the campaign. A referendum is a different form of contest, of which (despite the EEC and earlier, local liquor licensing referendums; see Carter, 1976) the voter, the organised political forces and the media in Wales had little experience.

No Tam Dalyell or John Smith emerged in Wales. With due respect to Leo Abse, Neil Kinnock, John Morris and the Plaid Cymru MPs, their personalities were not national and their appeal remained essentially regional. Perhaps recognising this, the Yes camp tried to increase the public's attention by recruiting prominent Welsh people from the worlds of sport and entertainment.

The pre-campaign literature of both sides had started at the level of principles - stressing words such as "democracy" or "bureaucracy" - but rapidly broadened out during the campaign into more specific issues.

The NAC foreshadowed what were to be the Conservative Party's main arguments in the General Election that followed. They stressed that the organisational prin-ciples of the Assembly would defeat its democratic objectives. A further layer of

government would be costly and would mean more bureaucratic hindrances to the development of a free-enterprise economy; it would also distance a new executive from
democratic control, owing to a diminution of local government powers and functions.
The support given by the local authorities and by NALGO[3] helped to ensure that the
NAC stuck firmly to a critique of the proposals throughout the campaign. They were
on a strong wicket, for before an Assembly existed no one could say firmly and
exactly what it would do and when.

The WAC, however, moved rapidly toward an assumption that the Assembly would have
economic powers; it saw Wales very much as a national entity in its own right, and
a specifically Welsh identity was assumed by their campaign. In its turn, the
Labour Party-Wales TUC grouping saw the economic issue in terms of increased
planning and research functions for the Welsh Office; in contrast to the WAC, their
underlying view was one of Wales as a "Labour Party nation", with its identity
marked not in national, cultural terms but rather in anti-Tory, if not actual class
terms. Within the WAC, although there was a broad area of common concern between
Labour, Liberal and Plaid Cymru, it was understandable that the Labour Party,
particularly that part which was "internationalist" in perspective, should wish to
maintain its own identity in its own campaign. It is similarly logical that the
Labour Party-TUC grouping should present a rather different rationale for the proposed Assembly, based on the increased opportunities for local and democratic control, rather than on the presumption that Wales, having a unique ethnic identity,
needed a means of expressing this in political form.

The two Yes campaign groups shared many areas of common concern and frequently
engaged in similar tactics and it is possible to overestimate the differences of
style and emphasis. Nevertheless, the atmosphere of compromise and negotiation
present at the UK and Wales level at this time in the Labour Government's period
of office also bore considerably on the devolution issue, helping to make an umbrella Yes campaign a virtual certainty. In the case of Wales, where powerful sec-
tors of three major parties, plus the Communist Party, had substantial roots in
the radical Welsh tradition, a firm basic area of understanding - albeit a very
broad one - was already in existence. For the Labour Party this was a reason for
an umbrella campaign. But because it provided a measure of control over the possibility of crossover of its own members to the growing left wing of Plaid Cymru
(owing to co-operation during the campaign), it was also a reason for an additional
and independent Yes campaign.

The Conservative-based NAC is best distinguished by its insistent attack on the
inadequacies and undesirability of the proposed measure itself. Its campaign was,
therefore, well-focused from the outset. Its themes could also be put over to the
public in a more specific way than those of the Yes campaign, it being much easier
to show consequences of the *status quo* than to explain the *possible* courses of
action open to a body whose powers and abilities could be demonstrated only in
practice. Its composition ensured adherence to a basic free-enterprise philosophy.
The free-enterprise economy requires as few bureaucratic hindrances as possible;
the idea of an Assembly "duplicating" existing economic and political powers "at
great expense" offended this philosophy. When coupled with the "bureaucratic and
centralised threat to local democracy" this argument became acceptable even to
much Labour opinion in the County Councils, and to NALGO. Another basic plank of
the NAC was its opposition to any possibility of separation. The Conservative Party
in Wales has always been staunchly Unionist and the County Councils supported this
stand, albeit for different reasons. On the surface it was a coalition including
seemingly disparate elements, but their sometimes different motivations rarely
caused problems because of the narrow and effective focus of their campaign. Unlike
the Yes camp they did not explicitly refer to this contest in party political

---

[3]NALGO indirectly contributed £5,000 to the No campaign.

terms.

An emphasis on cost, bureaucracy and individual freedom figured highly in both campaigns. Opinion polls at the time of the Referendum confirmed that these were matters of public concern and with the recent experience of local government reforms, it was a set of issues of UK importance that it was difficult for the Yes campaign to respond to.

As mentioned previously, hardly any Conservatives campaigned for a Yes result. They thus helped to keep the Conservative vote in Wales firmly on the No side. In contrast, the existence and hard campaigning of the Labour Vote No group gave Labour voters the opportunity to depart from the official Labour line without too much affront to conscience. The decline in Labour support for the measure during 1979 must derive to a significant extent from the activities of LVN. During the last few days of the campaign the Labour Party-TUC group (and to a lesser extent the WAC), sensing from the opinion polls a need for action, turned to a different emphasis, namely that a No vote would be a vote for the Tories and a vote against the Government. The matter was seen almost as one of a vote of confidence on a UK scale. This was a gamble; and because of the scale of the No victory, those who had gone against official party policy had reason to feel vindicated. They also now had reason to doubt the wisdom of the Government, and to consider a shift of voting allegiance in the General Election. As the Conservatives' UK election campaign emphasised several of the same points as the NAC had emphasised, it was easier for voters to defect.

TABLE 10.1   Voting Intention, Wales Referendum, 1978-1979

Date	Organisation/Publisher	Yes %	No %	Don't know %
May 12, 1978	Abacus/BBC	41	41	18
Sept. 22, 1978	Abacus/BBC	38	48	14
Feb. 8, 1979	Abacus/BBC	33	46	21
Feb. 24, 1979	Marketing Wales & West/ *Western Mail* & HTV	22	57	21
Feb. 28, 1979	Abacus/BBC	22	65	13
Feb. 28, 1979	Marplan/*Sun*	22	67	11

The LVN campaign was not the major explanatory factor, but it was of key importance in the battle for the traditional Labour voter's loyalty. They studiously avoided public support for statements of the NAC, but their campaign was one which emphasised the elements of cost, bureaucracy and the opaque nature of the evidence regarding the consequences of an Assembly for the use of the annual block grant from Westminster. The LVN group also brought in the issue of separatism. Most of them had affinity with the "internationalist" side of the Labour Party. One would therefore have thought that this would be one of the prime motivations in their campaign. Surprisingly it figured rather less in their formal campaign than in that of the NAC: only Neil Kinnock really gave this issue consistent emphasis. Whilst their campaign focused on criticism of the measure itself, it also encouraged the public to think in personal terms about the possible consequences of voting for an All-Wales Assembly - an Assembly in which both languages of Wales would be used. The argument was put as follows by Leo Abse (in Erfyl, 1979):

> It is clear, isn't it, that in that Assembly people are
> going to exercise their undoubted right to speak Welsh. And,
> indeed, how could you deny it? Once they speak Welsh it means
> that you have to have interpreters for them, who have in the

nature of things, to speak Welsh. Then all the top Civil
Servants would have to speak Welsh because the same members
who would speak Welsh in the Assembly would speak Welsh in
committees and select committees. So it can't be disputed
that, once there is an insistence on the part of those who
are going to the Assembly that they have the right to use
the language, once that is established, you get the pattern
for a huge and influential bureaucracy and it is one which
will not be open to my people in Gwent.

It is not a great step to spread a fear of domination by a Welsh-speaking élite
into other areas of life. From the letters columns of the Welsh press it was evident that many English-speaking Welsh people became convinced that, should the
Assembly be created, compulsory bilingual education would follow and fluency in
Welsh would become a prerequisite in thousands more jobs. The Yes campaign's
attempts to minimise the consequences of emphasis on the divisive aspects of
language were accelerated during the 10 days preceding the poll, with several prominent campaigners stressing the arithmetic of linguistic representation. Press
statements and campaign literature of the WAC emphasised, for example, the minority
position of North Wales in the Assembly, the purpose being to show that what was
assumed to be solidly Welsh-speaking North Wales would be numerically weaker in
its representation than South Wales.

The Yes campaign was unable, for a variety of reasons, to engender public interest
in the broader principles of democratic control and to emphasise a sufficiently
strong Welsh identity. The No campaigners were able to dominate the debate and to
a great extent set the agenda simply because they stuck solidly to the Act itself
and argued consistently around the kind of issues already in the public mind. With
a UK General Election in the air, the new radicalism of Mrs Thatcher had made it
very hard to argue the merits of what could be portrayed as "more bureaucracy at
greater cost". Whatever the tactics of the campaign, the factors of geography and
political history in Wales, added to the relative lack of generosity of the Act regarding the Assembly's powers, joined with UK political trends to give the No campaigners a considerable advantage.

THE MASS MEDIA

The English-language Press

The English-language press in Wales is very different in nature from that of Scotland. Difficulties of distribution, the relative lack of major regional centres
and a small population are factors explaining this. The Cardiff-based daily, the
Western Mail, and the Welsh edition of the *Liverpool Daily Post* circulate in South
and North Wales, respectively, with little sale outside those areas. The evening
papers, based on Newport, Cardiff, Swansea and Wrexham, are very local in coverage.
Given that Welsh affairs are treated in cavalier fashion by the London-based popular press - virtually no detailed or serious treatment of devolution being given
by them - and that the combined circulation of the *Guardian*, *Telegraph*, *Times* and
Financial Times in Wales hardly equals that of the *Daily Mail*, the majority of
Welsh newspaper readers received little or no hard information on devolution or
the Referendum proposals through these channels.

Of the six daily papers in Wales, the only one with a history of in-depth reporting
and comment on all-Wales issues was the *Western Mail*; it was also the only one to
back the proposed Assembly. In recent years it has tried to develop a role as "the
national newspaper of Wales", but its circulation of around 90,000, restricted to
the Southern area of Wales, foils this ambition. It is not a "popular" style newspaper, and therefore cannot have great impact on readers of the London-based

tabloid press. Like most papers published in Wales it is a Conservative newspaper, albeit an independent one as its support of devolution indicates. Its commitment to the Act was based on a logical and intellectual argument - indeed its Conservative outlook would hardly allow it to become an enthusiastic and fiery supporter on political or nationalistic grounds.

The tendency of the *Liverpool Daily Post* was to restrict the debate to its letter columns until well into February when it carried a series of articles by rival Welsh politicians on the measure; certainly it has no tradition of systematic reporting of all-Wales issues.

The evening papers (which are generally restricted in circulation to the urban and industrial areas of the North-east and South-east) varied in their approach to the provision of information and opinion. The *Evening Leader* (Wrexham), a relatively new paper, ran a series of factual articles and contrasting viewpoints on the measure, and had throughout 1977 and 1978 provided a number of regular features on Parliamentary affairs and matters of concern to Wales as a whole. It did not express a firm editorial opinion, but acted as a forum for exchange of opinion, and urged all electors to use their vote on such an important matter for Wales. In contrast, the papers of the South-east have little tradition of dealing with all-Wales issues, and their readers are accustomed to seeing these presented in relation, almost exclusively, to their locality. The loss of economic and social links with England across the Severn Bridge was never threatened by the Wales Act, yet the reporting and the letter columns of these papers developed the theme of a South-east Wales (often referred to as "South Wales") cut off from its British links and dominated by a Welsh-speaking élite. The *South Wales Echo* (Cardiff) was a particularly vociferous advocate of the notion that an Assembly would be one step along a road that led inevitably to separatism.

Overall, the editorial line of the English-language dailies was anti-Assembly and they tended to report the more sensational and emotive arguments of the No camp. In the hard winter of 1978-1979 the readers of the evening papers in particular had become used to "shock horror" stories about the ferocity of the weather and the strikers alike. This style of reporting was applied in considerable measure to the Referendum campaign. Polarisation and conflict are to many newspapers "good" news. Given their lack of experience on national matters, it is not surprising that the daily press in Wales was generally unable to master the sophisticated business of explaining a relatively abstract issue of national importance.

If the English-language dailies as a whole provided little opportunity for sophisticated debate and information, the weekly press provided even less. To be fair, almost every weekly paper serves a small area and thus survives on highly localised reporting - often aiming for the maximum possible number of local names in each column - backed by a large amount of mainly local advertising. A good proportion do not have editorials and where these are provided, they are sometimes in the nature of a moral homily, with little reference to the political realities of the modern world. Where editorial comment was offered, its sophistication often left much to be desired - the (weekend) *Wrexham Leader*, for example, ended its pre-Referendum leading article by offering "two fingers" to the proposals.

About half of the 60 or so papers had a very small number of readers' letters on the subject. The significance of the geographical distribution of these letters is difficult to analyse; some papers published few letters on the subject, others many. The numbers published may not reflect the numbers received. Some editors wished to keep political argument out of their paper and some others have a policy of publishing few letters. The amount and style of coverage of devolution depended greatly on the nature and the finances of the papers. Despite the fact that large numbers are members of a group and that a complex system of cross-subsidy can operate owing to group advertising, finance is a big consideration and most, therefore, rely on district correspondents, leaving a very small nucleus of full-time reporters who seldom have the time and the experience necessary to develop informative leading or feature articles on all-Wales matters.

The same progression in the letters columns can be observed as in the daily press. Early on, until perhaps January 1979, the concentration was on the more abstract ideas of "democracy" and "participation", but then they moved quickly on to discussion of detail. Some tended to follow the national issues and arguments: "costs", "control of quangos", "effects of additional bureaucracy", "increased participation in government", and so on. Others were cranky, inappropriate, or based on poor logic, some taking their cue from the Gang of Six's references to Welsh-speaking dominance and Leo Abse's particular fears of Gwent people being "foreigners in their own land", while others claimed extraordinary powers for the Assembly, which would heal all ills in Wales. Yet others made tenuous connections, e.g.: "The next time we drive on icy roads, let us reflect on whether we want to take power away from local people who are doing a good job ... If you want to drive on safe winter roads in Brecon and Radnor you should vote 'No' in the referendum ..." (letter by Tom Hooson, prospective Conservative Parliamentary candidate for Brecon & Radnor, *Merthyr Express*, 11.1.1979).

A further category of letters gives a more direct indication of how local issues and ideas affected the aggregate vote. It includes letters from writers who defined their identity in linguistic terms, but also from writers who adopted a more local identity defining themselves against those in other geographical areas. This is particularly noticeable as a North:South divide, with those in the North often concerned at the idea of returning members to a distant and artificial capital city in which there would be a numerical predominance of those who viewed Wales simply as the industrial South-east plus a hinterland; considerable fear was expressed in North-east Wales that traditional social and cultural links, such as those with hospitals in adjacent regions of England, would be broken by a Cardiff-based Assembly. Some letters in South-east Wales were against the Assembly because it would place them under the "dominance" of a Welsh-speaking élite from the North. It is noticeable that relatively few such letters appeared in South-western papers: if the papers are to be taken as evidence, few people saw the Gog or the Taff[4] as a threat. Cardiff is *the* place for a shopping spree for West Walians, so they are not likely to feel antipathy toward the capital city; nor do they feel, in general, any reason to fear the Northerner.

Much confusion about the distribution of Welsh speakers was in evidence in letters to the local press, amounting to a gross over-simplification of the linguistic map of Wales. It was generally only those from the South-east who made the mistake of seeing just North Wales as Welsh speaking, but a substantial proportion based their opposition to Northerners on linguistic grounds, few of these letter-writers apparently realising the extent of the Welsh language in South-west Wales. Letter-writers in North Wales, where they defined themselves against Southerners, generally did so on non-linguistic grounds. They were more inclined to do so if from North-east Wales; there is more indication of opposition to the South on linguistic grounds, as one would expect, from the Welsh-speaking North-west.

An interesting light on the East:West cultural divide can be seen by comparing readers' letters from Dyfed and Clwyd. The columns of the local press in North-east Wales, and around Wrexham in particular, give evidence of a pro:con attitude to the Assembly based on whether or not the writer spoke the Welsh language, but there was far less evidence of this as an indicator in West Wales even though Dyfed (Carmarthenshire in particular) is an area where there is from time to time con-

---

[4]The term often used, somewhat derisively, to describe those from the North (Gogledd in Welsh) or the South-east, respectively.

siderable tension between the County Council and Cymdeithas yr Iaith Gymraeg.
However, in Clwyd - unlike the position in Dyfed - the linguistic boundary is a
particularly sharp one. To many of those associating themselves with the new
pattern of mobility in this area, the Welsh Assembly appeared as a threat and the
Welsh language as a symbol of a "backward" Wales. To many of the Welsh speakers of
the Western parts of the country, on the other hand, English immigration, symbolised by new housing estates and concrete shopping centres, demonstrated just how
far Welsh culture had declined. Thus, language as a distinctly political factor
entered the Referendum debate far more in Clwyd than in an area such as West Wales,
where the language is relatively secure and the threat to traditional ways of life
is less, owing to poor access to alternative cultures.

These are examples of the kind of variations one can find in local political and
social composition through an examination of the English-language press. Naturally,
there are loyalties which cut across regional or linguistic affiliations and one
can analyse local loyalties and feelings to the detriment of those factors of
national significance already mentioned. One thing that clearly emerges is that the
English-language weekly press, whilst sometimes offering a forum for the exchange
of opinions via their letter columns, rarely offered informed comment and information on the Referendum. Moreover, their letters columns frequently published
letters whose assertions were based on rumour, hearsay, hopes or fears. These were
difficult for either side to combat within the constraints of letters liable to be
edited "for reasons of space".

Straightforward factual reporting of campaign meetings seems to have occurred
without particular emphasis or bias overall, though coverage was by no means uniform. Since many local papers are dependent on a handful of full-time staff, they
rely for the coverage of most events on the submission of information by local
correspondents and interested groups. If a report of a local meeting was not
promptly sent in by the group concerned, it would be unlikely to be printed.

Locally inserted advertisements of the protagonists generally reflected the specific concerns of the national campaigners of "democracy", "costs" and "separatism",
but there were a number which reflected the national and local tendency during the
month of February to put forward emotive, illogical or unsubstantiated arguments.
The *Pontypridd Observer* of February 23, for example, contained an advertisement by
a local No group (based on the New Labour Club, Ystrad Mynach) which, besides
offering the normal national considerations, advised: "Vote No to longer dole
queues; Vote No to playing politics; Vote No to Offa and his Dyke (Who was Offa
anyway?)".

Like most other papers in Wales, the *Pontypridd Observer*, whilst offering factual
reporting of local campaign meetings, had little of the hard information needed to
interpret such contentions as those above. Indeed, during the campaign one of its
rare articles on the issue was written by a person who had changed from Yes to No
and therefore emphasised the latter perspective. One of its neighbours, the
Merthyr Express, contained a neutral pre-Referendum editorial which referred to
the "quality of the letters" it had received on the Referendum but while these had
been the usual cross-section, they hardly added up to an overall debate. This
paper, like most of its rivals, did little to provide its readers with a balanced
assessment of these letters and reports; indeed, one of the few major articles
(1.2.1979), purporting to provide background information, maintained: "If you vote
No it doesn't necessarily mean that you disagree with devolution - simply that the
present plan for an Assembly is a born loser and that Welsh people deserve a better
way of running their affairs".

The Welsh-language Press

The Welsh-language press treated devolution and the Referendum in a very different way. The Welsh-language local newspapers (all weeklies) form a very small grouping - only *Yr Herald Cymraeg* of Caernarfon having an appreciable circulation - but the national weeklies *Y Faner* and *Y Cymro* have an importance well beyond that indicated by circulation figures. In so far as Welsh speakers wish to articulate their interests and exchange opinions on a national basis, these weeklies are often the forums in which issues are developed. Both have a readership considerably beyond their circulation figures. *Y Cymro*, the more popular, ensures family readership by its coverage of almost every topic, from sport to religion and from Parliament to Welsh-language pop music. *Y Faner* relies almost exclusively on contributed articles and like *Y Cymro* has a policy of providing information and opinion on matters of concern to Wales as a whole. *Y Faner* was one of the very few newspapers in Wales to offer a detailed critique of Leo Abse's concept of "Welshness", which seemed to see the specifics of Welsh identity as coming in considerable part from local characteristics - a conglomeration of which in some undefined way created a national identity. As the campaign progressed, largely owing to the success of the No side, in particular the LVN, in emphasising the possibilities of separatism and (Welsh) linguistic domination, it became increasingly difficult to use the idea of national identity, whether linguistically or historically defined, as a reason for voting for an Assembly. Except, that is, in the Welsh-language press.

In this sector of the press it was hardly necessary to argue that Wales had a formidable historical identity. The majority of Welsh speakers would take that as given; they would also emphasise the role of the Welsh language in the creation and sustenance of that identity. Defining and adhering to this model of identity is far easier than explaining the relatively amorphous models put forward by those without the language. But the 70 per cent of people in Wales who speak no Welsh would find this language-based model of identity much more difficult to accept. Thus the ethos of these papers reflects the agreement on the nature of Welsh identity amongst Welsh speakers. That does not mean, as the Referendum results show, that they would support the Assembly *en bloc*, simply that they and their newspapers are rather more likely to support possibilities of sustaining and enhancing national developments.

As it happened, both *Y Faner* and *Y Cymro* supported devolution. *Y Cymro*'s reporting of the campaign emphasised national issues; it ran a series of articles providing background information, its regular Parliamentary column being particularly helpful in isolating issues. Its pre-Referendum editorial gave two main reasons for a Yes vote. The first was to unite the Welsh people, whatever their language and to "end the talk of coupling the South with Bristol and the North with Liverpool". The second was that devolution was already here and that democratic control of its resultant structures should be established. *Y Faner*'s editorial line was broadly similar. Neither newspaper had any doubt that they and their readers supported an Assembly which would help to unite the historical and cultural entity that was Wales, which hitherto had had no formal democratic means of expressing Welsh views in an all-Wales forum.

The letters to these papers rarely questioned the notion of a Welsh identity that was related to language and of a Welsh culture that depended on the survival of the language for its continuance. Nor on the whole did the articles in *Y Faner* seriously question such an emphasis, whatever the political attitudes of their authors. Given these indicators, it is reasonable to hypothesise that the reasons for rejecting or supporting the Assembly by Welsh speakers were, in part at least, different in nature from those of English speakers. The Welsh-language press has always sustained a serious and detailed approach to political, social and cultural issues; they have tended to see Wales as an easily-recognisable national unit. Had such traditions and ethos existed in the English-language press, it could have been possible to have a reasoned debate not only on the question of national consciousness and its expression, but across the whole area of the devolution issue.

Broadcasting

Welsh-language radio and television (the BBC television service in particular) reflected a more positive discussion of the question of Wales's national identity than occurred in the Welsh-language press. Firmly injected into the debates and general coverage of the question were considerations of culture and history. English-language services, on the other hand, tended to consider the more immediate aspects of the Referendum largely in polarised terms and in particular focused on the Act itself. The lack of consistent consideration of Welsh history and culture in the education system militates against those who understand only English gaining a full appreciation of the unique aspects of their own national environment, and this compounds the failures of the English-language media.

Moreover, a large number of television viewers in the populous coastal strip of the South-east are able to receive the programme services of BBC and ITV that are based in Bristol. A glance at the roofs of houses in this area, with aerials mainly pointing to the transmitters across the Bristol Channel, confirms that many people in this area "opt out" of any local programmes (see Pilsworth, 1980, p. 228). It is often argued that they do this to avoid the small amount of Welsh language programmes currently carried on BBC Wales and Harlech Television; but by avoiding these they also miss the English-language news of Wales and cut themselves off from television coverage of Welsh affairs generally.

THE OUTCOME

TABLE 10.2   Wales: The Referendum Results by County

County	Turnout %	Yes votes			No votes		
		Total	(a) %	(b) %	Total	(a) %	(b) %
Gwynedd	64	37,363	34	21	71,157	66	42
Clwyd	52	31,384	21	11	114,119	79	40
Dyfed	65	44,849	28	18	114,947	72	47
Powys	67	9,843	18	12	43,502	82	54
West Glamorgan	58	29,663	19	11	128,834	81	47
Mid-Glamorgan	59	46,747	20	12	184,196	80	47
South Glamorgan	59	21,830	13	7	144,186	87	51
Gwent	56	21,369	12	7	155,389	88	49
WALES	58	243,048	20	12	956,330	80	47

(a)   Percentage of *actual* votes cast

(b)   Percentage of total electorate entitled to vote

Without a detailed breakdown of the results below the county level, one can make only a limited number of tentative generalisations about the Referendum outcome. The rural and more Welsh-speaking areas of the West and North (Gwynedd and Dyfed) clearly gave more support to the proposals; they also had a higher turnout. The

urban and industrialised counties of the South-east recorded the smallest percentage of Yes votes, whilst the linguistically and occupationally mixed county of
Clwyd in the North-east fell between the two. Commentators have suggested that
there is little significance in the differences among the county results and that
the Referendum confirmed the existence of a fast growing process of Anglicisation.
This view was seemingly confirmed by the behaviour of Wales in the subsequent
General Election. Certainly this process is at work and political behaviour reflects it; political behaviour, though, can also interact with its environment.
Since the Referendum, economic conditions in Wales, as elsewhere in the UK, have
deteriorated. The issue of unemployment is often posited in national terms and is
agreed upon by people in Cardiff or Caernarfon as "Welsh people" or as "unemployed".
Also, at the time of writing, there is now considerable controversy over the question of a separate Welsh-language television channel, which is an issue uniting
Welsh speakers and non-Welsh speakers. The "second homes" question is important all
over Wales.

These examples are not given to indicate that Wales has, since the Referendum, discovered that it is a nation. Rather they indicate that issues of importance to
Wales can unite and have united Welsh people across the differences of region,
language, class, status or religious affiliation. However, to the majority of them
devolution was something abstract, largely because of the lack of an autonomous,
indigenous political structure. As a result of the tradition of the Liberal and
then Labour Parties giving "block representation" to the Welsh nation at Westminster, the argument for self-government of any kind had been largely confined to
intellectual and party political circles. The Wales Act, therefore, urgently needed
a powerful campaign of public explanation, but circumstances prevented the creation
of a sophisticated debate.

The Referendum was an interaction of Welsh politics with mainstream UK trends. This
chapter has emphasised the variety of reactions within Wales in order to offer an
alternative and historically-based perspective on the results, which do not themselves possess such a uniformity as an immediate structural analysis would suggest.
UK trends in society and politics influence Wales considerably. Even a nation
relatively weak in indigenous social and political institutions of widespread
public influence and membership does not, however, automatically accept these un-
critically. The Referendum and, indeed, the 1979 General Election may have given
this impression; the political structure in Wales certainly changed considerably
during the 1970's. This change has been more than the breakup of Labour Party domination of the Welsh seats at Westminster. It has involved the breakup of traditional voting loyalties. This process cannot be ascribed simply to the Referendum. The
late 1960's and early 1970's saw significant Plaid Cymru successes in elections in
Wales - in the South-east as well as elsewhere. This was not simply a political
aberration: its origin was in the social fabric of Wales itself, as was the strong
element of Conservative success in the 1979 General Election. Toryism, though, has
little substantial basis in Welsh tradition. Is it possible that Margaret Thatcher's
radicalism appealed to a sector of the radical vote in Wales that had tired of what
may have seemed conservative ideas in the Labour Party at local and national level?
Support for radical Conservatism figured greatly in the General Election; it is
reasonable to say that it also figured in the Referendum in Wales. It is also
plausible to suggest that, owing to its lack of historical attachment to the radical traditions of Wales, the Conservative Party may not continue to gain electoral
benefit from the breakup of the old voting patterns in Wales. During this century
Wales has seen single-party dominance come and go; the chances now for a "one-
party Wales" in the near future seem remote. There is little chance of a national,
cultural identity (with obvious consequences for politics) on the lines of that
obtaining in the 18th and 19th centuries, owing to the decline of religious Non-
conformity and of the Welsh language. The 1980's, however, bring with them considerable possibilities for the development of a political system that recognises
Wales as a political and ethnic unit. In times of austerity mere regions can take

on a political identity of considerable magnitude. Wales has a history of relative deprivation; in the severe years ahead it will be almost impossible for *individual* events to remain unconnected with this history. Perhaps this will give the opportunity for the public attachment to the idea of a pluralistic all-Wales identity of the kind that was needed for a Yes vote on March 1, 1979. The kind of considerations that the Yes campaigners wished to present in 1979 may well be capable of better articulation during the coming years of difficulty. A letter written during February 1979 by Saunders Lewis, one of the best known Welsh nationalists of this century, may just prove to be prophetic in nature:

> Sir, we are asked to tell the Government on St. David's Day whether we want a Welsh Assembly or not. The implied question is: 'Are you a nation or not?' May I point out the probably consequence of a 'No' majority. There will follow a general election. There may be a change of government. The first task of a new Westminster Parliament will be to reduce and master inflation.
>
> In Wales there are coal mines that work at a loss; there are steelworks that are judged superfluous; there are still valleys convenient for submersion. And there will be no Welsh defence. (*Western Mail*, 26.2.1979)

REFERENCES

Carter, H. (1976). Y Fro Gymraeg and the 1975 referendum on Sunday closing of public houses in Wales. *Cambria*, 3(2), 89-101.

Erfyl, G. (1979). Talking about devolution; interview with Leo Abse. *Planet*, 47.

Foulkes, D.L., J.B. Jones and R.A. Wilford (forthcoming). *The Welsh Veto: the Referendum on the Wales Act 1979*. University of Wales Press.

Jones, J.B. (1977). The Welsh Labour Party and the problem of devolution. *U.K. Politics 1977 - Papers of 2nd Annual Conference, Working Group on U.K. Politics*. Centre for the Study of Public Policy, University of Strathclyde.

Madgwick, P., N. Griffiths and V. Walker (1973). *The Politics of Rural Wales*. Hutchinson, London.

Pilsworth, M. (1980). Balanced broadcasting. In D.E. Butler and D. Kavanagh *The British General Election of 1979*. Macmillan, London.

CHAPTER 11

CONCLUSIONS

John Bochel, David Denver and Allan Macartney

The Referendum of March 1, 1979 was undoubtedly a significant event for Scotland and for the British political system as a whole. As a case study it is also of interest for the growing number of students of referendums in general. This chapter does not aim to summarise the foregoing chapters but rather to explore the significance of the Scottish Referendum in three different ways.

SIGNIFICANCE FOR DEMOCRATIC THEORY

Conservative or Progressive?

As the authors of a major study of referendums put it,

> Is the referendum in effect a conservative or a progressive
> device - that is, does it generally produce outcomes pleasing
> to the right or to the left? This is usually the first - and
> often the only - question political activists ask about
> referendums and it is not without interest for scholars as
> well ... our preliminary verdict would be that the referen-
> dum is a politically neutral device that generally produces
> outcomes favored by the current state of public opinion.
> (Butler and Ranney, 1978, p. 224)

The evidence from Scotland in 1979 appears to bear out these findings. On the one hand those who regard the referendum as such as a "conservative device" can point to the swing towards the *status quo* which occurred during the campaign and had the effect of preventing the implementation of the Scotland Act. On the other hand it is equally true that the then "current state of public opinion" in the famous "winter of discontent" was sceptical of governmental ability to solve pressing problems, and there may have been an element of the protest vote against the government of the day. Moreover it was possible, particularly for Conservative supporters who followed Lord Home's lead, to believe that voting No did not mean the end of devolution.

Participation

To judge the Referendum of 1979 a "success" may cause some surprise, given the political crisis which followed it. Moreover the fact cannot be gainsaid that the

Referendum on the Scotland Act, like the EEC referendum, although justifiable (and, by many, justified) by reference to democratic ideology, was in fact held out of expediency because the governing party of the day was deeply divided on the issue at stake. Nevertheless the fact that each referendum originated as a party "life raft" need not detract from the potential of referendums as a means of involving the electorate in the resolution of large and contentious political questions. Thus by many criteria, the Scottish Referendum, like its predecessor, was a "success". Firstly, the people approved of this form of consultation, as is evidenced by the very respectable turnout of voters (higher than in 1975), by the findings of opinion polls and by the (admittedly modest) numbers of previously inactive citizens who became involved in some of the campaign organisations. Secondly, an intensive public debate on the Referendum question did take place and few of the important arguments went unexpressed or unheard. An impressive number of meetings and debates was held in every corner of Scotland, which was awash with leaflets, pamphlets, stickers and posters. The media, despite the qualifications made by several contributors, proved, on the whole, equal to the task of contributing usefully to the debate (the letter columns of newspapers alone providing a much used forum). Thirdly, despite some minor flurries, the polling and counting arrangements worked smoothly. Finally, the question seems to have been decided "on its merits". In saying this we do not wish to imply that the No side had the better case or even that it necessarily won the argument. We are referring to the limited amount of party voting that seems to have taken place in the Referendum. Given the extent of Labour and SNP support in Scotland, a straight party vote on the Scotland Act should have carried the day overwhelmingly for the Yes side. In fact there was in evidence a wide spectrum of party-line solidarity, which broke down increasingly from the SNP through the Conservative Party and the Labour Party to the Liberals. From a partisan point of view defection from the official party line may be embarrassing but, if referendums are to be a genuine means of consultation or decision-making rather than a mere public endorsement of government policy, then one must expect the result to be unpredictable and, on the whole, non-partisan.

To pronounce the Referendum a "success" does not imply that it was an unqualified success, but the exercise has probably enhanced rather than diminished the prospect that the device will continue to be used, albeit very sparingly, in the future, for popular approval of significant constitutional change. It is to the implications of the experience of 1979 for the British constitution that we now turn.

SIGNIFICANCE FOR THE BRITISH CONSTITUTION

There are three possible approaches to the question of assimilating the referendums of the 1970s into British constitutional thought. The first is to adopt a purely *ad hoc*, expedient approach. That is to say, one could view the 1970s as an interesting but possibly unique decade, witnessing as it did three referendums on constitutional matters, caused however only by divisions within the ruling party. According to this view there would be, for instance, no necessity to put to a referendum a major change such as the abolition or transformation of the House of Lords. One senior politician involved in the Scotland Act exercise summed it up by saying "politicians don't need to be consistent". As long as Parliamentary supremacy exists he is technically right.

Many politicians would, however, feel uncomfortable with this position, and would instead argue that relevant precedents should, or would in practice, be followed. The only problem is how to decide which precedents are relevant. This is where the striking differences between the EEC referendum of 1975 and those of 1979 (see Chapter 1) cause problems: where the practice varied, which variant should be taken as precedent?

It may be widely expected that the latest model, i.e. the rules applied in 1979, should be applied in future to any other referendums. The most important question of course concerns the 40 per cent rule. Not to apply it to a future referendum would open Parliament to the (renewed) charge of bending the rules to get the result desired and would surely cause more than eyebrows to be raised in Scotland.

Would the same be true of other rules which were likewise criticised in 1979? Again, to do otherwise would attract the charge of blatant expediency if not "rigging". But if, far from following the 1979 precedents, any further referendums were to revert to the 1975 precedents this might leave sensitive Scots (and Welsh) feeling aggrieved that their devolution referendums were treated differently; but such is the result of the exercise of discretion by MPs who relish the application of Parliamentary sovereignty to constitutional matters.

There is, however, an alternative to expediency or the problematical search among conflicting precedents, and that is codification: the determination *in advance* of detailed rules for any future referendums.

More Referendums?

The first question to be settled is whether the referendum device should ever be used again and, if so, in what circumstances. The unwritten nature of the British constitution has meant that the introduction of referendums in Britain has inevitably been done in an *ad hoc* way, and the rules and conventions covering them have been of this character. Parliament has not at any time decided in principle that major constitutional, or any other, issues should be put to a referendum. As it happens, membership of the EEC and the changes proposed in the Scotland and Wales Acts were defined as major constitutional questions, but this is little guide to the future.

It is by no means inevitable that there will be more referendums. Those who take the traditional view of the British constitution may be expected to oppose the continued use of referendums for two reasons. Firstly, the use of referendums abridges the sovereignty of Parliament and, secondly, conflicts with the doctrine of the mandate. There is some substance in the first argument but British membership of the European Community and of some other international bodies has already eroded the sovereignty of Parliament, with the acquiescence of that institution. At least technically the British referendums have been consultative and, if any held in the future remain so, the doctrine could stay theoretically intact. So long as Parliament decides whether to sanction any referendum and retains the right to accept or reject the result, then its sovereignty would not seem to be seriously impaired. The doctrine of the mandate which implies that governments are deemed to have been given popular approval for their programmes when elected is more controversial. Governments certainly claim this when it suits them. Against this it can be held that parties come to power as much as a result of the perceived failures of their predecessors as because the electorate positively approves every detail of their election manifestos. Whilst most governments would no doubt claim, with some justice, that they have carried out the bulk of their major manifesto commitments, it is easy to point to consequences of some of these commitments that were neither spelled out to the electorate, nor even anticipated (during an election campaign) by the party concerned. Nor do governments feel obliged to confine themselves to legislating or acting upon matters specified in their manifestos.

A further objection resulting from the Parliamentary sovereignty position stems from the perception that judicial review would inevitably follow the adoption of procedures for putting constitutional issues to the electorate in referendums. It goes without saying that judicial review of constitutional issues is as unacceptable to those who cherish the supremacy of Parliament as is the concept of popular sovereignty exercised through referendums. There are two possible responses to this: either judicial review will become acceptable, or a different device for settling disputes concerning referendums could be fashioned.

There is yet another objection but one of a rather different kind. It can be objected that the designation of constitutional questions as suitable subjects for submission to the electorate through referendums implies both acceptance of and a measure of entrenchment for the present British constitution, "warts and all", although it is recognised that the system is the result in part at least of historical accident. This school of thought would point to the anachronistic House of Lords and the sometimes capricious electoral system as two examples of arguably undesirable features of the present constitution.

A final objection is the virtually unsurmountable problem of selecting from an unwritten constitution those features which would require popular approval (expressed in a referendum) to change them.

The difficulty of defining what is constitutional and of distinguishing between major and minor constitutional change is formidable (see Alderson, 1975, pp. 107-109 and *passim*). Parliament, which essentially for this purpose means the party in power, could go on making decisions on this in an *ad hoc* way, but this is clearly unsatisfactory. If, as Balsom, McAllister and others have argued, it has become politically or morally untenable for future Parliaments to effect major constitutional change without majority support in a referendum (Balsom and McAllister, 1979, p. 405), then some agreed means must be found of declaring what is constitutional and of major significance. The hostility of politicians towards any form of judicial review and its incompatibility with the doctrine of the supremacy of Parliament probably excludes giving the judiciary, as such, any part to play in the decision, and similar objections could be made to the involvement of any other extra-Parliamentary body. There is, however, a precedent for "constitutional" declarations in the power of the Speaker of the House of Commons to certify certain bills as money bills and as such to be outside the purview of the House of Lords. It might be felt, however, that the responsibility of judging whether measures are of major constitutional importance is too much for one man, however well-advised. At any rate, if referendums are to continue to be a feature of our political system, a great many more details of rules and procedures need to be defined clearly.

A Referendum Bill?

If, as seems likely, governments cannot or will not find legislative time for a Bill on referendum rules, then some backbench MP might make a name for himself by promoting a Private Member's Bill on the subject. This is not the place to produce a draft of such a Bill but several important areas suggest themselves for legislation (see Baur, 1979).

Determining "major constitutional change". Firstly, Parliament might be asked to agree that major constitutional changes should be put to the electorate for an expression of opinion. The question of what is a major constitutional change need not be defined in such a Bill, but the machinery for making such a decision could be specified. In order for Parliament to retain the final say, but for the matter to be removed from the partisan arena, it might be referred to a Select Committee or a version of a Speaker's Conference with the duty of advising the Speaker. Any other proposals for referendums - and examples suggested in the past include trade union reform and capital punishment - could be similarly referred to such a body.

Referendum status. Secondly, such a Bill might ask Parliament to declare on the status of referendums, that is whether they should be consultative, as hitherto, or binding. If the sovereignty of Parliament is to be protected then the former would obviously be the choice.

Required majority. Thirdly, Parliament could be asked to make a decision about what constitutes a clear result on a referendum question: a simple majority or some kind of weighted majority.

This is obviously a very important question, although attention must be drawn to the paradox of combining provision for a "clear result" with a purely consultative referendum, since the former implicitly makes the result binding. The importance of this issue is twofold. In the first place any weighting, whether of the majority required or as an expression of a proportion of the electorate, undoubtedly increases the conservative nature of the referendum as a device. The second aspect of this question is illustrated graphically by both the campaign preceding and even more the aftermath of the Scottish Referendum of 1979, when spokesmen for both sides claimed victory, and the Labour Government of the day was left impaled on the horns of a painful dilemma.

On the one hand the No side claimed variously that "Scotland's 'Noes' [had reduced] nationalism to a myth" (Adam Fergusson, London *Daily Telegraph*, 9.3.1979), that there was an even, three-way split (John Mackay, MP, "Current Account", BBC1 Scotland, 12.2.1980), that less than a third of Scots wanted devolution, or even that there was a two-thirds majority against devolution. On the other hand devolutionists saw things very differently, as the following statement (representative of others) shows. "On March 1st 1979 the Scottish people voted on the British Government's proposals for an elected assembly in Scotland. It was the first separate, collective and democratic action in their national history ... They said 'yes'." (Editorial *Bulletin of Scottish Politics*, 1980).

It is difficult to forecast how this issue would be resolved if it came to Parliament in the near future. A number of academic writers, including Bogdanor (1980, pp. 261-262), have assumed that in the name of consistency the 40 per cent rule would have to be applied to any future referendums. Yet politicians intimately involved in the 1979 Referendum have variously indicated their dissent from this view. Many on the Yes side did not accept the rule in the first place. John Smith, MP has described it as a "mischievous amendment" which ought never to be repeated and Helen Liddell called it an "inbuilt foul". For his part Tam Dalyell, MP stated after the event that he did not like the provision either, a sentiment shared by a number of Scotland Says No leaders. Even the author of the amendment, George Cunningham, MP has declared his view that it need not necessarily apply in future and would be inappropriate in a referendum on, say, the abolition of the House of Lords. So clearly there would probably be much debate on the principle.

The electorate. The fourth question with which a referendum Bill should deal is who the relevant electorate is. This question arises in two ways. In a referendum covering the governance of one or more parts of the United Kingdom, it should be specified whether, as on this past occasion, only those resident in the respective area should vote, or whether the recent suggestion by Ian Paisley, MP for a referendum in Great Britain on the position of Northern Ireland could be taken up. The question could arise in a different way, namely if the 40 per cent rule, or some variant, was again applied. Much controversy surrounded the question of "eligibility". A radical reform of the system of registration would solve many of the problems; but short of that, some tighter definition of eligibility might be advisable; or perhaps some figure based on previous general election and referendum turnout might provide a formula. Again this matter might be referred to the suggested Select Committee or Speaker's Conference.

Wording of the question. Some attention would have to be given to the wording of
the question upon which electors are asked to vote. It is well-known that question
wording can influence responses and that leading questions can be put quite inno-
cently (see Butler and Kitzinger, 1976, p. 60). As it happens there was no great
controversy about question wording in the referendums of 1975 or 1979, even though
the wording was chosen by the government of the day. Despite this, it might be
deemed prudent in any future referendum to give to a Select Committee or to a referendum commission the task of wording the question.

Timing. Fears have been expressed that the timing of a referendum might influence
the result. It is still an open question whether the unpopularity of the Labour
Government in February 1979 had a decisive influence on the result. But this is not
the kind of thing that most people are worried about. It is rather the danger that
the timing could turn a referendum into a plebiscite on the popularity of the
government of the day. A government returned to power with a safe majority nearly
always enjoys an initial honeymoon period. A referendum held soon after an election
might be expected to go the way that a government wishes. The Scotland Act contained a provision about timing, presumably with this in mind, as well as out of a
desire to prevent the Referendum being synchronised with a general election. A
referendum Bill ought to address itself to this matter, and also to a definition
of the length of the campaign period in relation to the passage of the requisite
legislation for a particular referendum. Some such definition would be necessary
if accounts of receipts and expenditure are to be realistic and if the length of
the campaign period is not to be determined by the broadcasting authorities. A
simple provision that Parliament would decide the beginning of the campaign period
would be the most straightforward method. Alternatively there could be an application of the interpretation of the Representation of the People Act, which suggests
that when a candidate invites electors to vote for him, then his campaign has begun
and his election expenses should be recorded from that date.

Counting areas. One might have thought that the specification of counting areas
for a referendum would be a relatively uncontroversial matter. For a variety of
reasons partisans in the EEC and Scottish referendums advocated counting on a
national or constituency basis. In both cases a compromise was adopted, namely that
the largest local authority areas (in England and Wales, the counties, and in Scotland, for both referendums, the regions) should constitute the counting area. This
compromise seems to have been generally acceptable and its insertion in any con-
solidating referendum Bill could be expected.

A referendum Bill should deal with as many as possible of the complex rules that
are inevitable in any "election" arrangements. Whether this takes the form of
amending the Representation of the People Act or is incorporated in the new Bill
does not matter too much. What is important is that *ad hoc* and inconsistent decisions for particular referendums are reduced to a minimum, and that more or less
informal arrangements for such things as party political broadcasts should be
written into legislation. Some of the rules are relatively minor and could make no
perceptible difference to the result, but if vaguely stated and inconsistently
interpreted they might cause friction that detracts from the main referendum debate.

Recognition of umbrella groups. It rapidly became apparent in connection with the
Referendum on the Scotland Act that the problem of *ad hoc* campaigning groups
bedevilled a number of issues. This is illustrated by a minor issue, the admission
of observers to the Referendum count. The decision to admit only representatives
of political parties and MPs to the count for the Scottish Referendum gave rise to
justified complaints. In some cases parties were minor participants in the campaign
and much of the campaign activity was undertaken by members of *ad hoc* groups, some
of whom had no party connection and were thus excluded from the count, and they
naturally felt a grievance. Even this minor matter would not be an easy one to

resolve. How is a campaign group to be defined so that it could have access to the count? This is a problem that will arise elsewhere in the discussion of rules and it is convenient to enlarge upon it here. There seems to be no reason to exclude from the count representatives of any political parties that can provide evidence of some minimum involvement in the campaign in any given region. In an election, no matter how small an effort or how serious a campaign challenge they make, candidates are entitled to an equal number of observers at an election count. It might make rough justice, but a solution might be provided by a formula based on the number of candidates fielded at the last general election by each party in a region (or for those who did not contest the previous election the number of adopted prospective candidates).

Ad hoc campaign groups are a more difficult problem but some way should be found to accommodate these. The problem of dissenting minorities of political parties (like Labour Vote No) is even more difficult. In the case of the former the Bill would probably have to proceed on the assumption that referendums would be held on single issues and that the alternative votes would be Yes or No. Given this, a further assumption would have to be made, namely, that an umbrella group would be formed for each side of the case. It might not be easy in practice to prescribe for the formation of such groups (for a Quebec precedent see p. 4, above) but the attractions for the protagonists would be considerable. Judgements as to which groups qualified as genuine umbrella groups would certainly have to be delegated by Parliament to some body like a referendum commission, which could also allocate, say, a quota of group observers to each counting area. Dissenting minorities in parties would have to align with or integrate themselves into a group or suffer the penalty of no representation. Some such compromise might well be necessary.

Broadcasting. One of the major procedural issues of the Scottish Referendum, dealt with at length in Chapter 7, was that of broadcasting. It seems unlikely that any challenge would be mounted to the well-established rights of the broadcasting authorities to cover referendum campaigns in their own ways, providing that a broad balance is maintained; but few would dispute that the provision for partisan broadcasts in the Referendum campaign of 1979 was totally unsatisfactory. The undesirability of allowing the purchase of broadcasting time by parties and groups is also probably beyond dispute. The promoter of a referendum Bill should not shrink from attempting to codify and formalise arrangements for partisan campaign broadcasts. Again the problem arises of defining those eligible. Presumably parties would usually play a big part in any referendum campaign, so arrangements would have to be made for them; but this could give rise to complications if there was a serious imbalance in the number and strength of parties on each side in the referendum - as was the case in the Scottish Referendum with the Labour Party, the SNP, the Liberals, the SLP and the Communists ranged against the Conservatives. Only the first three and the last qualified for radio or television time, but it does not require a major exercise in objectivity to admit that, if all had been allowed broadcasts during the campaign, grave imbalance would have been obvious, especially since *ad hoc* groups had been excluded from the allocation of broadcasting time. A referendum Bill would therefore have to address itself to the question of whether, during a referendum campaign, parties should have to mount party political broadcasts, more or less on the same basis as they are allowed now. If parties were to retain this right, the Bill would have to incorporate some formula for equality between the sides and for the participation of umbrella groups. Which groups were eligible could be decided in the same way as were those claiming the right to send observers to the count. Alternatively there could be a ban on PPBs during the campaign period and instead broadcasting time could be made available only to the two recognised umbrella groups, one for each side.

Information policy. A major criticism made of the Scotland Act is that many people did not understand it. This ignorance was not lessened by the failure to provide explanatory leaflets for each household. The contrast with 1975 is stark: on the occasion of the Euro-referendum every household received three leaflets - Yes, No and the Government's own leaflet. Again it seems clear that a referendum Bill would have to make explicit provision for the production and delivery of such literature. A referendum commission could if necessary adjudicate on any questions of the content of such literature but would be greatly aided by the insistence on recognising only one umbrella group on each side.

Public subsidies for campaigners. In addition to the free distribution of Yes and No literature (estimated at the equivalent of £750,000 to £1 million to each side [Butler & Kitzinger, 1976, p. 57]), the state gave each umbrella group a grant of £125,000 in 1975 but nothing at all in 1979. This is a further matter which arguably should be removed from the partisan arena of Parliament by being incorporated in a referendum Bill. Again the details of any subsidy could be left to a referendum commission or could conceivably be index-linked.

Campaign expenditure. There are major difficulties in the way of limiting expenditure on a campaign involving an unknown number of parties and groups. Perhaps the most that could be done would be a requirement that all groups of protagonists submit to Parliament accounts of monies received and disbursed during a defined campaign period; this rule would apply to headquarters and local branches of parties and groups. Such an arrangement was made for the EEC referendum (once public funds had been used), but not for the Scottish Referendum. This may seem like shutting the stable door after the horse had bolted, but if it reduced the likelihood of allegations such as that "foreign money bought the result" it would be worthwhile. Experience from the EEC referendum suggests that some generous upper limit on expenditure should be set, especially for party and group headquarters. Evidence about the efficacy of political advertising in Britain is inconclusive but, if one side can afford to indulge in large-scale advertising in, say, daily newspapers and the other side cannot, there are bound to be recriminations.

Conclusion

Apart from the appeal of tidiness, consistency, predictability and equity, a referendum Act would probably remove many of the impediments to a full-scale and thorough debate on the central issue in any future referendum. On reflection the Yes side in the Scottish Referendum may regret the amount of time, energy and media space devoted to what after all were side issues in the campaign: the size of the eligible electorate, the sources of finance of their opponents and so on. Any fixed and formal rules that can be incorporated in legislation, thus enabling debate to be focused on fundamentals, will well serve those with the best case and thus in the end democracy itself.

POSTSCRIPT: POST-REFERENDUM SCOTLAND

This chapter has been concerned chiefly with drawing lessons from the Referendum experience in 1979 for democratic theory and for the future of the British constitution. But it can be assumed that many of those who read this book in future will do so because of their interest in Scotland. Accordingly it is to Scotland's future that we now turn, and in particular to the prospects for a further referendum should the question of devolution, Home Rule or self-government return to a prominent place on the political agenda.

Another Scottish Referendum?

Even if the above heading causes shudders to run through the disappointed devolutionists of 1979 (who would mutter "never again" through clenched teeth), the
question is worth posing, and in two different ways. Would any substantial (i.e.
legislative) devolution of power to Scotland require a further referendum? There
are strongly divided views on this question. One view is that any such move in
future would by definition be a constitutional change and that this would inevitably require endorsement in a referendum as per the post-1970s British Constitution (see the preceding section for an elaboration of this argument). In this view
Scotland could not be an exception. The opposite view - that a sequence similar to
1978-1979 is not an inevitable stage should Home Rule be proposed again - can be
based on opposition to the principle of referendums (again, see above) or can rely
on a number of other possible courses of action. One school of thought argues that
the mandate for devolution exists in Scotland as demonstrated by the fact that at
no time, in opinion polls or in the Referendum itself, has there been a majority
against devolution: quite the reverse. Shadow Secretary of State for Scotland
Bruce Millan, for instance, left the door open for this interpretation when he
said "I will remind you that we did have a majority of those voting who voted Yes
in the Referendum ... and I think an assembly, something like the Assembly that
was provided for in the Scotland Act would be very good for Scotland" ("Current
Account", BBC1 Scotland, 12.2.1980). A further possibility (discussed by James
Kellas in Chapter 9, above) is the constituent assembly or convention approach:
if such a body was directly elected it might be unnecessary to put its findings
to the people. Yet another suggestion (with which John Smith, MP is associated)
is for a referendum to be held first on the principle of devolution; given endorsement of an outline scheme it would then be very difficult for Parliament to refuse
it and this fact could considerably speed up the passage of a new Scotland Bill
through the Commons.

One thing is clear. If there ever is another referendum in Scotland its result
would be much more likely to command general acceptance if the referendum had been
preceded by the passage of a referendum Bill (as outlined above) which had formu-
lated clear and fair rules governing the conduct of all future referendums.

REFERENCES

Alderson, S. (1975). *Yea or Nay? Referenda in the United Kingdom*. Cassell, London.
Balsom, D. and I. McAllister (1979). The Scottish and Welsh devolution referenda
    of 1979: constitutional change and popular choice. *Parliamentary Affairs*, 32
    (Autumn 1979).
Baur, C. (1979). Time to lay down referendum rules. In H.M. Drucker and N. Drucker
    (Eds), *The Scottish Government Yearbook 1980*. Paul Harris, Edinburgh.
Bogdanor, V. (1980). The 40 per cent rule. *Parliamentary Affairs*, 33, 3.
    (Summer 1980).
Bulletin of Scottish Politics (1980). 1, 1 (Autumn 1980).
Butler, D. and U. Kitzinger (1976). *The 1975 Referendum*. Macmillan, London.
Butler, D. and A. Ranney (1978). *Referendums*. American Enterprise Institute,
    Washington, D.C.

Appendix

IMAGES OF THE CAMPAIGN

Cartoons by courtesy of cartoonists Gall, McCormick, Turnbull, Dewar and Bain; and of The Evening Times, The Glasgow Herald, The Scotsman, The Scots Independent and The Daily Record.

The press cuttings forming the montage on page 197 courtesy of Trustees of the National Library of Scotland.

ASSEMBLY?
AND
LESS POWER
FOR
SCOTLAND
IN
WESTMINSTER

SSN

ASSEMBLY?
MORE
TAXATION
MORE
BUREAUCRACY
MORE
GOVERNMENT

SSN

ASSEMBLY?
DIVIDE
AND
MISRULE

SSN

ASSEMBLY?
AND
BREAK-UP
OF
THE UK
TO FOLLOW

SSN

SCADA

SSN

REFERENDUM MARCH 1ST

NO
THANK YOU!

SCOTLAND SAYS No

SSN

REFERENDUM MARCH 1ST
FOR
SCOTLAND'S SAKE

VOTE **NO**

SCOTLAND SAYS No

SSN

THE
LABOUR VOTE NO
CAMPAIGN
ASKS :—

Will the Assembly create
A Single productive job........ **NO!**

Will it bring Government
Closer to the people .... **NO!**

Do YOU want to see Scotland's
presence at Westminster diminished ... **NO!**

Do YOU want to sell-out
to the Nationalists .... **NO!**

LABOUR SUPPORTERS
ARE URGED TO

VOTE NO

ON 1st MARCH
COME OUT - VOTE 'NO'

Published by A. BIRT, 44 Mathie Crescent, Gourock.   Printed by A. BARR LTD., 14 King Street, Glasgow.

LVN

VOTE NO
TO
BUREAUCRACY
VOTE NO TO DEVOLUTION

SCADA

YFS

VOTE YES!

❌ ON REFERENDUM DAY THURS. 1st MARCH

PUBLISHED by YES FOR SCOTLAND COMM.   printed by HAMPDEN ADVERTISING.

STUC

Scottish Young Liberals

THE SCOTTISH TRADES UNION CONGRESS

AN ASSEMBLY FOR SCOTLAND

ON THURSDAY 1ST MARCH 1979 A REFERENDUM WILL BE HELD TO ASCERTAIN THE DESIRES OF THE SCOTTISH PEOPLE WHETHER OR NOT THEY WANT AN ELECTED ASSEMBLY ESTABLISHED IN EDINBURGH.

THE OUTCOME IS OF VITAL IMPORTANCE TO SCOTLAND.

THE GENERAL COUNCIL OF THE S.T.U.C. CALLS ON ALL TRADE UNIONISTS IN SCOTLAND TO VOTE.

YOUR OBLIGATION IS TO ENSURE EVERY TRADE UNIONIST MUST GIVE SUPPORT TO THIS CALL
TO
VOTE "YES"
ON MARCH 1st ·1979

Published by SCOTTISH TRADE UNION CONGRESS, 16 Woodlands Terrace, Glasgow.
Printed by CIVIC PRESS 26 Civic St Glasgow G4 9RH

SCOTTISH YOUNG LIBERALS SAY

YES MARCH 1st

LMY

YOUR FUTURE –YOU DECIDE

YES
FOR A STRONGER SCOTLAND

LABOUR MOVEMENT CAMPA

SNP

Scotland YES

CYC

TORIES!

"The Responsibility rests on us to find a way whereby those who believe we must move forward on Devolution are able to ensure that we do so."

Rt. Hon. EDWARD HEATH
Former Leader of the Conservative Party

TAKE TED'S ADVICE
VOTE YES

CONSERVATIVE
YES
CAMPAIGN

CPGB

SCOTTISH COMMUNISTS SAY
VOTE YES
On Thur, 1st March.

YFS

YES!

For Scotland

ASSEMBLY means — More Taxes · More Government · More Conflict More Bureaucracy · Less Power for us in Westminster The Start of the Break-up of Britain.

THAT'S WHY **SCOTLAND SAYS NO**

Published by Scotland Says No Campaign
90 West Campbell Street, Glasgow G2 6RU. Tel: 041 226 4705

THE ASSEMBLY.
KNOW YOUR MYTHOLOGY!

The people pushing hardest for a Scottish Assembly are those who hope to profit politically or personally from it. Many see it only as a stepping-stone to separation. Others have made claims for it that do not stand examination. Here are some of the myths that have been put about.

MYTH 1 — That an Assembly would bring government "closer to the people".
Indeed it would! Suffocatingly so. The kind of devolution the Scotland Act proposes means even more government, even more bureaucracy right on our backs, breathing closer down our necks than ever. But is that what "closer to the people" ought to mean?

MYTH 2 — That the Scots would be given "more say in their own affairs".
Who said so? The only Scots with more say in their own affairs would be the 150 new Members of the Assembly, and everyone knows it. And they would only be doing what Scotland's 71 Members of Parliament already do perfectly well on behalf of us all.

MYTH 3 — That an Assembly could improve job prospects in Scotland.
Not a chance. The only guaranteed extra jobs would be for the Assembly Members themselves —and for the hundreds and hundreds of extra Civil Servants the Assembly would mean. Employment and industry are not devolved matters.

MYTH 4 — That the Assembly would control vast sums of money.
It might seem like that. The Block Grant from the British Treasury—the means of financing the Assembly's activities—would be around £2,000 million at 1978 prices. But that is no more than the Scottish Office in Edinburgh handles now. The Assembly would only be able to spend more on education at the expense of housing; or more on roads at the expense of health—and so on. What would be the point?

MYTH 5 — That the Assembly would have no power to tax.
Ah, but it would have the power to withhold the huge subsidies now provided for the Local Authorities by the Treasury. If the Assembly held back only one quarter of these subsidies, the Local Authorities would have to raise rates by an average of £150 per year per household. Either that, or council services would have to be severely cut back.

MYTH 6 — That the Assembly would not need tax powers.
Oh yes, it would. You can't have a democratic government spending money without responsibility for raising it.
Without power to tax, the Assembly would have no real freedom of action, and would perpetually be complaining about it.
Every Government White Paper on the matter has said as much—for the danger of friction and conflict between Edinburgh and Westminster is well understood.
The trouble with tax powers for the Assembly is that they would undermine Britain's constitutional unity— and that they would make the Scots the most highly taxed people in Britain.

MYTH 7 — That Scotland would be better governed.
Rubbish. There is not a scrap of evidence that the Scotland Act was even intended to improve the administration of Scotland.
At best it duplicates expensively what is already being done efficiently either by Scots in Scotland or by Scottish MPs at Westminster.
The Scotland Act, as everyone knows, was a political expedient—an act of appeasement of narrow nationalism—brought forward without the slightest consideration for the real problems of Scotland. Even the separatists say that.

MYTH 8 — That Scotland's voice in Westminster would remain the same.
If you believe that, you will believe anything. The voting rights of Scotland's MPs have already been modified by the Scotland Act. There have been strong parliamentary demands for a reduction of the number of Scottish members.
The powers and duties of the Secretary of State for Scotland would be reduced by three-quarters: so how long could he stay in Cabinet?
Our MPs' chances of providing future British Prime Ministers, Cabinet Ministers or even Junior Ministers must be remote—why should such offices come their way when Scotland has her own Assembly?
Scotland's hard-won power to control her own destiny through Westminster, the place where she most needs influence, would be tragically diminished.

MYTH 9 — That the Scotland Act means a stable constitutional settlement.
Not possible. The two biggest stumbling blocks to devolution discovered by Parliament remain: the question of tax powers for the Assembly, and the future rôle and number of Scottish MPs. Both these must be resolved before "devolution" could be said to be complete.
Both threaten the future unity of Great Britain.

MYTH 10 — That an Assembly is the way to prevent the break-up of Britain.
Then why do the nationalists want it so badly, and say it will be their "springboard" to separation?
The conflict, expense, frustration, over government and disillusion that the Assembly would bring to all of us would make the disintegration of the country unavoidable.

MYTH 11 — That the only alternative to the Assembly is the "status quo".
That is like saying the only alternative to blue is red.
Most people in Scotland are unaware of the present constitutional position.
They are unaware that there are 12,000 Civil Servants already in the Scottish Office in Edinburgh, running our affairs; that four Scottish committees of Scottish MPs scrutinise and process Scottish legislation at Westminster; that we have our own Secretary of State and two Ministers of State and three Junior Ministers to share his burdens; and that there are dozens of governmental agencies based in Scotland and reporting exclusively to the Secretary of State for Scotland.
We already have devolution. Would it not be more sensible to improve what we already have without adding another tier of governmental interference to run our lives for us?

OF COURSE IT WOULD

SSN

So what should we do?

Go out and

Vote No X

on

Thursday 1st March

Its the right answer

for you . . .
for your children
for Scotland

Vote No X

YOU CAN VOTE NO

ON
1st March 1979
Between
7am and 10pm

DURING FEBRUARY YOU WILL RECEIVE AN OFFICIAL POLL CARD TELLING YOU WHERE TO VOTE.

Published by Scottish Conservative Party, 11 Atholl Cres., Edinburgh EH3 8HG
Printed by Peter Henry Printers Ltd., Unit 31, Brownsburn Industrial Estate, Airdrie

THE RIGHT VOTE FOR SCOTLAND

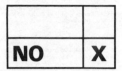

NO	X

Why is a 'no' vote right for Scotland?

Why are the Conservative plans better for Scotland?

We answer *your* questions

Will the Assembly make government more efficient and less expensive?
No. It'll mean higher taxes or poorer services. Official Government estimates show that it will cost the taxpayers an extra £13,000,000 each year and require an extra 1000 civil servants.

Will the Assembly Bring More Jobs?
No. The assembly doesn't have any economic powers. And Scottish industry and commerce is overwhelmingly opposed to the scheme. They feel that top heavy Government and an unstable constitution will mean less investment and fewer jobs.

Will the Assembly Bring More Cash to Scotland?
No. Under the present United Kingdom arrangements Scotland gets about £10 per week per family more in Treasury spending on the services to be devolved than is spent in England. There's no guarantee that this would continue if the assembly was set up and the cash was subject to an annual haggle between London and Edinburgh.

Would the Assembly Bring the Rates Down?
No. But there's a real danger that it could push them up. The only way the assembly could raise revenue, apart from the block grant, would be by reducing grants to local councils.

Would the Assembly Give Scotland a More Powerful Voice?
No. It would mean a weaker voice in Westminster — where the major decisions affecting Scotland would still be made. Scottish MPs in Westminster would be in the ludicrous position of having votes on English Education, English housing, and English law and order but not on Scottish education, Scottish housing and Scottish law and order.

What about those who say that the assembly's the only way of avoiding separation and the break up of the United Kingdom?
If you believe that, ask yourself why the SNP, who want separation, are the keenest supporters of the assembly plan. They know that the scheme is a recipe for non-stop conflict between Westminster and Scotland.

If It's Such a Bad Measure, Why Did Parliament Approve It?
It was approved with a small majority because MPs who opposed the measure said that they'd vote for it only as a means of giving the voters of Scotland a chance, through the referendum, of speaking their own mind.

Is It Only Tories Who Oppose the Assembly Plan?
No. Labour MPs and many active Labour supporters are campaigning just as vigorously as we are. It's not a party issue and shouldn't be.

Isn't the Best Way of Voting 'No' to Stay at Home and not Vote at All?
No. We need to know what all the people of Scotland think.

Parliament may feel it necessary to go ahead with the act even if there is not a 40 per cent vote. So if you think No, vote No.

IT'S 'NO' FOR SCOTLAND

But Isn't a 'No' Vote a Vote Against Devolution?
No. It's a vote only on the Government's costly, bureaucratic and divisive scheme of devolution.

Wouldn't a 'No' vote Mean Killing Any Devolution Plans for Good?
No. If there's a 'No' vote, the Conservatives propose the immediate calling of a constitutional conference to consider practical ways of improving the government of Scotland within the United Kingdom. We've already published the evidence we would put to the committee outlining four workable schemes of devolution which would make Government better — not worse.

Does That Mean Nothing happens at all While the Conference Goes On?
No. We've made it clear that while the talks were going on, we'd put to Parliament proposals to extend the number and scope of Parliamentary select committees. This would mean a greater degree of scrutiny and control of all Government departments including the Giant Scottish Office.

Why Can't We Have One of These Committees Sitting in Scotland?
One of the four options we'd put to the constitutional conference would be a greater role for the Scottish grand committee and the establishment of a Scottish select committee to monitor the activities of the Scottish office and investigate their policies and spending. Such a committee of MPs could, of course, sit in Scotland.

Scottish Conservative Party

But what is the alternative?

To argue for a "No" vote is NOT to say that there is no need for change ... far from it!

In this instance, NO is not negative ...

But we believe that the prospect of a Scottish Assembly offers only the ILLUSION of change — and that more frustration and disappointment would follow when it was discovered that, really, nothing had changed.

REAL change in society will only come through the return of strong Labour governments, on a UNITED KINGDOM basis. We, in Scotland, cannot opt out of the problems — just as severe — in Newcastle, on Merseyside or, for that matter, in the slums of London. We shouldn't even want to try.

If as much energy had gone into legislation on housing . . . the elimination of poverty . . . the plight of low-paid workers . . . then we in the Labour Vote No Campaign would have been the first to cheer.

If there is money to be spent on an Edinburgh Assembly, let it be spent instead on decent housing, new schools, more hospitals, and all the other REAL needs in our society . . .

Forget the red herrings

Who's against it?

You'll be told that if you vote "No" you'll be on the side of the Tories. Well the most enthusiastic campaigners for a YES vote include the Orange Order, the Communists, Ted Heath, and the SNP. So two can play at that game! Make up your own mind — on the basis of FACTS rather than emotion or propaganda.

The 40 per cent rule

You'll be told that it's unfair to insist that 40 per cent must say "Yes" before the result is binding. Rubbish. First, the rule is only advisory. Second, it's a sensible precaution against the chance of a small and noisy minority pushing through a far-reaching change.

Labour loyalty

You'll be told that, at the top of the STUC and Labour Party, the policy is to vote "Yes". That's true — but in a referendum EVERYONE is entitled to make up his or her mind. The Labour Party and STUC leadership have been wrong before — and, by heavens, they're wrong this time.

Published by the Labour Vote No Campaign, 40 St. Enoch Square, Glasgow, and printed by West Highland Publishing Company Ltd., Old School, Breakish, Isle of Skye IV42 8PY, telephone Broadford (04712) 464.

TIME TO COUNT THE COST...

DON'T STAY AT HOME — EVERY VOTE MATTERS
GO OUT ON MARCH 1st AND
VOTE NO
TO THE YES-MEN

This is a Referendum communication published by the

LABOUR VOTE NO CAMPAIGN

LVN

IF YOU ARE...
A Worker in Heavy Industry

The Assembly would be the first huge step towards the separation of Scotland from the United Kingdom. Every such move threatens your livelihood.

Most heavy industry in Scotland relies on Government orders — and they could just as easily be met by the spare capacity south of the Border.

Scotland with her own government — the Assembly — simply would not get the favourable treatment she has today. She would lose orders and jobs.

A separate Scotland would have her home market cut by nine-tenths.

In Light Industry

Political uncertainty has held back investment in Scotland for years. An Assembly would add to that uncertainty.

Even without the endless, damaging conflicts between Edinburgh and London which the Scotland Act must bring, your firm's business would inevitably suffer from having to deal with one more level of governmental interference.

IF YOU ARE...
In Trade or Commerce

You, too, would have to cope with more government, more bureaucracy—and would meet an endless flow of new regulations, restrictions, controls, directives and guidelines from Edinburgh.

And as soon as the Assembly received taxing powers you would become its prime source of new rates and taxes.

A Miner, a Railwayman, or a Steelworker

You would still be working for a nationalised industry, and so (curiously enough) your affairs would not be the Assembly's business. But beware the day when separation comes. Scotland's mines, railways and steel industry would be much less economic on their own. Without the British framework, it is doubtful whether most of them could survive at all.

IF YOU ARE...
A Farmer, or a Farm-worker

Agriculture comes under the Common Market, and would not be devolved. (The Agricultural colleges, on the other hand, come under "Education", and would be devolved.)

Scotland Act is that kind of Act.)

Your interest must be in maintaining to the full the role of your own Member of Parliament at Westminster, and the strength of Britain's united voice in Europe.

An Inshore or Deep-Sea Fisherman

The Assembly would not deal with fisheries outside the three-mile limit: fishery policy is decided by the Common Market.

Fishery limits would remain a matter for the UK Government and their protection and patrolling the business of the Royal Navy.

The strength of Scottish MPs' influence at Westminster, which would be reduced if the Assembly were set up, will always be of the greatest importance to you.

IF YOU ARE...
A Nurse, a Postman, a Policeman, or a Civil Servant

You would be "devolved"—but your unions would still be subject to national agreements. So you won't really be properly devolved at all.

Thus—unless separation came, prompting the whole Scottish economy—you would have to decide who your public employers really were: the Assembly which would pay you, or Parliament which would decide how much you would be paid. Could either of them look after you properly?

A Housewife

Would the Assembly make life cheaper for you? On the contrary: raising and spending money is what all government is about.

You cannot possibly duplicate in Scotland what is already being adequately done by Scottish MPs in London, and then add another 750 Civil Servants to the 12,000 now in Edinburgh, without a massive increase in costs. You, the taxpayer, would have to pay for the bill.

The extra legislation, government and bureaucracy now threatening Scotland would hit the purses and pockets of everyone living there.

IF YOU ARE...
Unemployed

The Assembly could do nothing for you. Industrial and economic policy would remain in Central Government hands.

And once the Assembly was set up those in the South who now steer new business and investment in Scotland's direction would not feel the need to push it so far.

As uncertainty affected the Scottish economy again, the hope of new jobs would melt away.

Could a Scotland separated from the United Kingdom do any better for you? Not a hope. Our economy, now so strongly integrated with all Britain, would have to be entirely restructured over many years—even to provide the level of activity and employment we have now.

And all the oil in the North Sea might not make the slightest difference.

A Ratepayer

The Assembly would have no means of raising its own cash —except by holding back for its own use the huge funds provided by the British Treasury to support the rates. Every householder could find herself paying extra rates of £3 a week, or more.

Either that, or local council services would be drastically cut back, and you would have to pay for them yourself.

SSN

...would be: You would even be able to attack Scott... at Westminster (so many of whose righ... for not extracting more money from th... spend on Scotland.

And of course you would earn a place o... For you would certainly be part of the c... Assembly and Westminster which would... Britain, and to the end of the Union that h... for so long.

SCOTLAND SAYS NO

DEVOLUTION
Equals
SEPARATION

If an Assembly is set up in Edinburgh, it will be the stepping stone to a Separate Scottish State, and the break-up of Britain.

If this is what you want Vote Yes, on Thursday, 1st March.

If not, GO OUT AND VOTE NO!

If you are interested in joining the Labour Vote No Campaign, get in touch with Archie Birt, 44 Mathie Crescent, Gourock. Telephone 34371. Or your local Labour Vote No Campaign branch Secretary.

LVN

HAVE YOU FOUND OUT WHAT THE SCOTTISH ASSEMBLY WOULD REALLY MEAN TO YOU IF YOU ARE...

THE REFERENDUM

Think it out for yourself

THINK of the cost of the Assembly.
THINK of the extra burden on your rates.
THINK of another layer of government.
THINK of a thousand more civil servants in Scotland.
THINK of more controls, laws, regulations and directives.
THINK of how the parliamentary power of Scotland's MPs would shrink.
THINK of the bickering and quarrels between Edinburgh and London.
THINK of the slide to separation.
THINK of the break-up of Britain.

AND THEN TRY TO THINK

of a single certain way in which the Assembly would bring the smallest real benefit either to
the United Kingdom
or to Scotland
or to your region
or to your district
or to your friends
or to your family
or to yourself

AND THEN THINK

WHO are pressing hardest for the Assembly;
WHY they want it; and
WHAT it would do for them

AND THEN

WHEN THE REFERENDUM COMES ON MARCH 1ST MAKE SURE THAT

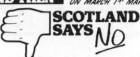

SCOTLAND SAYS NO

SSN

Give us our own Assembly and Scotland will have

MORE
TAXATION
MORE
CIVIL SERVANTS
AND MORE
GOVERNMENT

THAN ANYBODY ELSE!

THAT'S WHY

SCOTLAND SAYS NO

SSN

LABOUR VOTE NO CAMPAIGN

Did **YOU** vote Labour to get an Assembly? No? Then vote against it on 1st March.

Many Labour Party members and supporters are coming out against a policy they believe to be divisive and dangerous for the future of Britain.

Think about it! The only real enthusiasts for the Assembly are the Nationalists. Would THEY support it if they thought it would work?

Say NO to the Yes-Men —an Assembly would be an expensive irrelevance to the real problems of Scotland.

LVN

SCADA

YES!

NOW TAKE THE CHANCE YOU ASKED US FOR!

● Prime Minister James Callaghan sends this personal message to the voters of Scotland.

WILL YOU LET THE NO-MEN BEAT YOU ON A TECHNICAL KNOCKOUT?

Remember to vote YES X on March 1

YES!

And let's all say so!

● This is a unique picture. The man on the balcony is Bruce Millan, Secretary of State for Scotland. Behind him you see the chamber that soon will house the Scottish Assembly.

It is nearly ready, but the finishing touch must come from you, the Scottish people. On this page, Bruce Millan tells you how a vote for the Assembly is a vote for Scotland . . .

By BRUCE MILLAN
Secretary of State for Scotland

THE OFFER THAT MAKES SENSE

Remember to vote YES X on March 1

The powers

The answers

HOW many extra civil servants and staff will be required for the Assembly?

WILL the Assembly make us the most over-governed people in Western Europe?

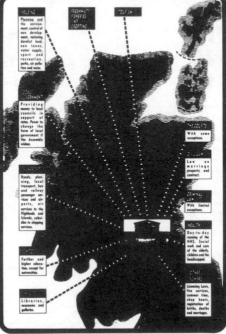

The myths

THEY WANT TO SCARE YOU OFF

WORK IT OUT ON THE SPOT

The history

NO SLIPPERY SLOPE

LMY

The Assembly can...

save money

Under Westminster, 10,000 civil servants in Scotland already spend over £2 billion of your money without real accountability. This bureaucracy will be subject to democratic control and stricter scrutiny from an elected Assembly, and give better value for money. It can SAVE money too.

reform local government

The Assembly can correct the mess Westminster made of local government, by abolishing one unnecessary tier. That means saving LOTS of money.

revitalise essential services

Scotland's shame is to be Europe's worst housed nation. The Assembly can seize initiatives on Housing and take positive action to cure this old sore. The same goes for Education, the key to life for Scottish youngsters. As for Health — how can one Junior Minister at Westminster properly administer Scotland's Health Service while running Police, Fire and the Prison Service as well? He can't. But the Assembly, with its own Ministers, can give Housing, Health and Education undivided attention.

promote jobs

With 190,000 on the dole, Scotland's top priority is to create jobs. The Assembly has authority to develop industrial sites, clear derelict land for new projects, promote tourism and help shape policies for vital bodies like the SDA and the HIDB. The Assembly will be decisive in driving Scotland along the road to full employment. At last!

Remember, it is this assembly or no assembly

YES

YFS

We've fought hard for a Scottish Assembly

Now it's up to you. Only your YES vote can make it happen

Our Assembly

- will **create** the Scotland of the future that you want

  - will **ensure** that purely Scottish issues are decided here in Scotland

- will **strengthen** democratic control over a wide area of Scottish life

  - will **preserve** the economic and political unity of the United Kingdom

IT'S YOUR FUTURE YOU DECIDE

LABOUR MOVEMENT **YES** **CAMPAIGN**
LABOUR
CO-OP
STUC

1 Lynedoch Place,
Glasgow G3
Printed by CWS Ltd., Glasgow G51 4SE

YFS

Referendum 1st March

Vote positively

YES

Now or never. That stark choice faces every Scot. On March 1st we decide for all time whether we have a Scottish Assembly.

All time? That's it. Scotland for over a century has sought some measure of home rule. Now Westminster has ordered a referendum to prove we really want the Assembly.

The vote is unique. If Scotland says "NO" after years spent demanding devolution, we will never be taken seriously again. Scotland will be universally ridiculed. A laughing stock. All bark, no bite.

Our self respect demands that Scotland resumes responsibility for key areas of domestic policy. The Assembly helps us work out our own solutions to make Scotland flourish.

Referendum Day is different. Each of us holds the future of Scotland in our hands. We can make or break — send Scotland surging forward or settle forever for the second rate.

Vote positively. "YES" — it is truly now or never!

Published by the 'Yes for Scotland' Campaign. Printed by J. Geddes, Irvine.

LMY

IT'S YOUR FUTURE

HELP BUILD IT—WITH LABOUR'S SCOTTISH ASSEMBLY

ON MARCH 1

YES

FOR A STRONGER SCOTLAND

LMY

LET SCOTLAND PROSPER

VOTE

YES

Scottish Young Liberals

On March 1st we Scots will make a once in a lifetime decision.
It's a decision that will determine Scotland's future for
generations to come.

On the one hand we can choose to have a much greater say and
control over our own nation and our own lives.   More than
that, we can make a fresh start.   We can begin to really
tackle our country's deplorable levels of poverty and unem-
-ployment.

Alternatively, you can opt for no change, for the status quo,
for Scotland to become more and more a rather insignificant
provincial backwater.

The choice us yours.

But perhaps you are still undecided, one of the don't knows.
Maybe you're totally fed up with the devolution debate and
don't want to know.   Then again you might be in favour of
Home Rule but feel that what is being offered is not good
enough.

So why should you vote YES ?

We, as Scottish Young Liberals wouldn't deny for one moment
that the Government's proposals fall short of what is needed,
but it's this Assembly or no Assembly.   If we vote NO there
will be no second chance.   It's now or never.   And
despite it's shortcomings, the Assembly does offer
Scotland a great deal.   Overleaf we have stated
some of the reasons why you should vote YES.

Scottish Young Liberals

In the national interest

vote YES for Scotland

Printed and published by SNP Publications 100 Main Street West Calder

SNP

SCOTTISH SLP LABOUR PARTY

Scottish Labour Party says YES !

The referendum is not only about an Assembly.
It is also about the nature, character, worth,
and future of the Scottish nation.

Those who urge a No vote betray a sub-
conscious contempt for the people of Scotland.

Our basic right

Implicit in their arguments is the belief that whereas
most other nations in this world can govern themselves
in a competent manner, the Scots cannot.

We believe the Scottish people can and should be
able to run their own Parliament.

The only thing Scots have to fear is the myth of
their own inadequacy. A myth created to frighten,
and keep the Scots from our basic right to a
measure of self-government.

This referendum is at one and the same time
Scotland's first and last chance. It has taken
generations of effort and pressure to come
this far, when an Assembly of modest
dimensions and powers is on offer.

Last chance

If we reject this Assembly, it will be
seen in London as the Scots rejecting
their national birthright to a say in
their own affairs.

This Assembly is Scotland's opportunity to move forward. It must be
grasped. We must vote YES.

Jim Sillars, M.P.
Chairman of S.L.P.

There's no future in a "No" vote

The alternative to the Assembly
is nothing. We will stay as we are,
sunk in a quagmire of despair.

A No vote means accepting:
* Mass unemployment
* No jobs for our young people
* Remaining the worst housed nation in Europe
* Ignored by London and Europe

For Scotland's sake – vote YES

The SLP is fighting for a YES vote, because an Assembly now is
essential if Scotland is to move forward, out of its present poverty
into a better future. A Yes vote is a vote, FOR SCOTLAND.

SLP

YES !   YES !   YES !

Don't be fooled by the people who tell you

"This Assembly / Act isn't good enough"

They are the very people who stopped the Assembly getting more power so that they could use
this excuse to campaign against it !

"The Assembly will add another tier of government"

Actually the Assembly is the only chance we have to cut down the tiers of local government – it
has full power to do this – and get control of Scottish affairs in Scotland. In many
important matters it is Whitehall which is the 'extra tier'.

"The Assembly will cost too much"

With firmer control over the Scottish Office the Assembly can SAVE money if you want it to.

"Devolution is the slippery slope to separation"

Devolution is being offered so as to keep the U.K. together. If it fails because of the anti-
democratic 40% rule the people who wanted separation will still be there and will have a real
grievance at last. Ordinary Scots who just want good government will become more bitter and
militant.

YES = Devolution = Peaceful change

NO = no progress = no end to strife

SCOTTISH LIBERALS SAY YES

Scottish Liberal Party
Telephone: 031-229 7484

Printed and published by Cranston Print, Alva Street, Edinburgh

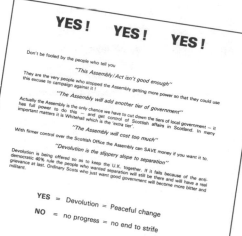

Scottish Liberal Party

STUC

AN ASSEMBLY FOR SCOTLAND

Since the turn of this century, the Scottish Trades Union Congress, acting for and on behalf of, the Scottish working class, have consistently advocated decentralisation of the decision making process and have fought for the conception that the Scottish people have a greater say in governmental process within Scotland.

On Thursday, 1st March, 1979, a Referendum will be held to ascertain the desires of the Scottish people on this principle. The outcome of this will determine whether or not an elected Scottish Legislative Assembly will be established in Edinburgh. At the 1978 Congress in Aberdeen, the Trade Union Movement undertook to campaign for a 'Yes' vote and the General Council now reiterates this call and seeks the participation of all affiliated organisations to ensure the 40 per cent requirement of the Referendum is met beyond all reasonable doubt.

It is, therefore, obvious that an abstention from voting in this Referendum will count as a 'No' vote. The objectives in this campaign must be to ensure a positive and clear 'Yes' to an elected Assembly. This task is not an easy one—it presents a challenge to our Trade Union and Labour Movement—it is our conviction that an elected Assembly for Scotland will enhance and enrich our nation without separation from a United Kingdom structure.

* MAKE SURE
THIS OPPORTUNITY IS TAKEN

* VOTE 'YES' ON 1 MARCH 1979

Published by the S.T.U.C., 16 Woodlands Terrace, Glasgow G3 6DF.
Printed by Civic Press Ltd., 26 Civic Street, Glasgow G4 9RH.

SNP

A voice for Scotland

▶ Say **YES** to the Assembly and we in Scotland will be able to make our own decisions in future

▶ For the first time in 272 years we will be able to make our own laws. The Assembly will control Housing, Education, Local Government etc.

▶ Although it won't have all the powers the SNP seeks for a Scottish Parliament it is still an important step in the right direction

▶ It **will** give you a say in your future

▶ It **will** give us control over the bureaucrats in the Scottish Office.

▶ It **will** give us a chance to streamline the way we · are governed—for example by doing away with the Regions.

▶ Thanks to the hundreds of thousands of Scots who have voted SNP since 1973 you have the chance to vote in the Referendum on 1st March for a Scottish Assembly.

▶ This is our chance to start building a new democracy through an Assembly answerable to the people of Scotland. With your vote it could be a new beginning.   Put your country first.

vote YES

Law. Town and Country Planning, Tourism and the countryside. Passenger and Freight services; roads and bridges.

Control of New Towns. Industrial Kites. Power to shape policies of the Scottish Development Agency and the HIDB and thus help create jobs. And lots more.

Responsibility for major economic and industrial policy stays with Westminster. How, then can the Assembly threaten Scotland's economic and trading prospects within the UK?

That's right. It does not.

The Assembly will work harmoniously with Westminster. But will be a prod and pressure point when necessary.

That is exactly how devolved assemblies work in Commonwealth countries like Canada, Australia and New Zealand. Or in Switzerland and West Germany — all nations with prosperous economies such as Scotland has never known.

So the final fact is: there's no future in a negative 'No' vote. Revitalise Scotland by voting positively.

5 It's this Assembly or no Assembly

SO YOU THOUGHT 40% WOULD FIX THE FIGHT!

40%

Dimples.

Published by the "Yes for Scotland" Campaign
Printed by John Geddes (Printers) Irvine

Get up...and GO!

The Referendum is about life-or-death – for Scotland. A "No" vote means we've chickened out, funked responsibility after years of agitating.

If we vote "No" we hand things over to those who publicly declare there is no Scottish nation. Thumbs down to the Assembly means laying the boot into Scotland.

That happened before. In 1707. The same kind of people, the parcel of rogues that Burns condemned, the rich and influential are at it again.

But in 1707 Scotland's ordinary folk had no vote. Then it was the privileged few. They sold out. They want you to sell out now.

Scotland must vote "Yes" to be sure of its future. To prove we care about our nation have pride and confidence in our future.

Scotland each one-and-a-half million "Yes" votes. When was anything born in Scotland last? Risks taken or triumphs won?

That is the challenge. Rise to the occasion. Stand up and be counted. Vote YES!

As once asked Hugh MacDiarmid, the great poet,

YES
...GET THE FACTS

YFS

YFS

1 It's about 'Devolution'

The first fact is this: Vote "Yes" and you [...] for Devolution. For nothing else.

Not for Separatism. To confuse and [...] you into voting "No", unscrupulous peo[...] pretend the Assembly will put us on whe[...] call the slippery slope to Separatism.

Rubbish! Nowhere in the whole worl[...]

Devolution ever led to Separatism.

Many countries, great and small, have [...] assemblies with domestic powers roughly [...] to the Scottish Assembly. Only last mon[...] Greenland voted for Devolution – but a[...] separating from Denmark.

The big scare story is that Scotland a[...] England will part company – that indus[...] bale out, that your job will disappear.

That's bunkum. Worse, it's a delibera[...] The danger's not in voting "Yes" but in [...] panicked into voting "No".

There's your slippery slope all right, [...] to frustration and resentment when thin[...] worse.

As they will without an Assembly. P[...] recognise what the Assembly's all about.

"We must ask whether there should be devolution. I believe that there must be . . . I support the criterion . . . that there should be better government for Scotland and Wales . . . The responsibility rests on us to find a way whereby those who believe that we must move forward on devolution are able to ensure that we do so . . ."

Rt Hon Edward Heath, former Leader of the Conservative Party, in Parliament, 1976.

"Once the pacesetters on devolution, the Conservative Party are now seen publicly as dragging their heels. It is vitally important that the Conservative Party affirm again and again their commitment to the principle of Devolution as being the logical extension, in constitutional terms, of the economic devolution of power implicit in the free enterprise system."

Young Conservative policy report August 1975.

The Conservative Party was **committed to devolution** as far back as 1968 by the **Rt Hon Edward Heath,** at that time **Leader of the Conservative Party.** Since then the **Conservative Party has ditched devolution** and in consequence many of its **keenest and brightest supporters. Devolution** is consistent with the **freedom of choice and democratic control** inherent in **Conservative principles.** Conservatives should vote **'yes' for a Scottish Assembly,** not only **in support of** the reforming ideas of men like **Edward Heath,** and not **to prevent** the **Labour Party** from **hi-jacking** devolution, **remember** it was the Conservatives who **first proposed it.**

Conservative YES Campaign
VOTE YES FOR FREEDOM!

CYC

Westminster won't listen when we complain that Scotland is being neglected again; that the SDA and HIDB are kept short of cash to implement development plans.

Reject the Assembly now and we're where we deserve to be. Captive, quiescent – in the bag. A second class people in a third rate place. Westminster will waste no time on us. Vote "No" and vote your future away.

3 Assembly controls and saves money

Money. Bureaucracy. Two hard facts. The Assembly will cost £13 million but for that, for the first time ever, you get control of the 10,817 Civil Servants who actually run Scotland now.

The cost scaremongers don't tell you that, don't admit that the Assembly has powers to remove a tier of government. To sweep away the vast bureaucracy spawned by expensive regions like Strathclyde.

That would cut costs with a vengeance. But it's not merely by reforming local government that the Assembly will save money.

Look at Westminster's record. It has proved incredibly weak in preventing disgraceful over-spending by government departments.

Westminster's outmoded system of scrutiny always spots mistakes and rings alarm bells **after** the damage is done.

The Assembly will be smaller and closer to the action. Working under the tight discipline of a block grant, it will firmly control costs. Assess them realistically in good time to **avoid** waste.

That way you get better value – by saving money.

4 Make Scotland a winner!

The most important fact. The Assembly is positively our last chance to get Scotland on its feet.

Vote "Yes" and you win an Assembly with real powers to improve life for us all. No less than 25 groups of "devolved matters" will be transferred from Westminster.

Matters that touch our lives in countless ways. Critical matters. Like Housing, including rents; Health, Education, Social Welfare, Scots

KEEP BRITAIN UNITED
VOTE NO

No Campaign, 90 West Campbell Street, Glasgow G2 6RU TEL 041-226-4705

SSN

SCOTLAND *No's* **BEST**

Issued by the Scotland Says No Campaign, 90 West Campbell Street, Glasgow G2 6RU TEL 041-226-4705

SSN

SCOTTISH DAILY EXPRESS | **SAY NO TO DEVO!**

ASSEMBLY? DIVIDE AND MISRULE  **SCOTLAND SAYS NO**

Issued by the Scotland Says No Campaign, 90 West Campbell Street, Glasgow G2 6RU TEL 041-226 4705

SNP

ASSEMBLY BE DAMNED *KEEP BRITAIN UNITED*

SSN

LMY

SCOTTISH ASSEMBLY— YES

LABOUR PARTY | LABOUR PARTY

LMY

LABOUR MOVEMENT **YES** **CAMPAIGN** **YES** **YES**

LABOUR CO-OP STUC

...CH PLACE, GLASGOW G3 6AB.
...QUARE, EDINBURGH

Scotland YES

SNP

YES FOR SCOTLAND

...land, 148 High Street, Edinburgh.

Printed by Forrest, Hepburn & McDonald, 8 Nicolson Square, Edinburgh.

YFS

LIBERALS SAY YES

 Scottish Liberal Party   Scottish Liberal Party

Scottish Liberal Party

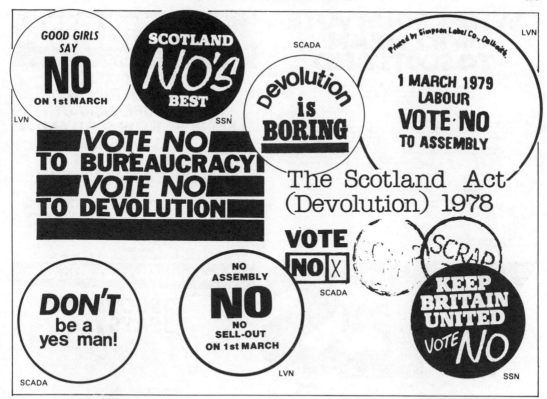

WHAT YOUR VOTE WILL MEAN TO SCOTLAND

March 1st is Scotland's day of decision, the day we can help create a brand new Scottish Assembly. 40% of us must vote **YES** to guarantee its creation. Here's what that **YES** vote will mean to every one in Scotland.

Our Own Assembly
Life here in Scotland is different and our own Assembly will enhance it. Scottish decisions will be taken here, in Scotland — by people we elect. But Scotland will still enjoy the benefits and strengths of being in the U.K. A better deal all round.

Our Children's Education
Scotland's Education system has been a model for the rest of the world. In future we'll decide how to keep it that way.

Our Health and Welfare
The lifeblood of a nation. Again — under full Scottish control.

Our Roads
We'll build them where we need them. Let's by-pass the black-spots — once and for all.

Our Houses
The bricks and mortar and determination to put a decent roof over all our heads. Housing where and when we need it.

Our Countryside
Scotland's countryside is the most beautiful in the world and we want to protect it. The Assembly can take up that challenge.

Law and Order
We all want a more law-abiding society. Bringing control nearer home is a step in the right direction.

In General
We'll be bringing Government closer to the problems. We'll move faster and more positively to solve them as they arise.

The Labour Government under James Callaghan is backing the Scottish Assembly because they believe in its importance to Scotland, a strong Scotland within a strengthened U.K. We are voting for a greater say in the things that matter, the things that affect us every day of our lives — and we'll still have the resources of the United Kingdom behind us.

So go out and vote. That's crucial. No vote counts as a "NO" vote. We need 40% of Scotland to vote "YES" to give us that stronger and louder voice. Let's not miss this opportunity to step into an exciting future in Scotland.

LABOUR MOVEMENT YES CAMPAIGN

YES
FOR A STRONGER SCOTLAND

LMY

ASSEMBLY
MEANS
MORE TAXES
MORE GOVERNMENT
MORE BUREAUCRACY
LESS POWER FOR SCOTLAND IN WESTMINSTER
MORE CONFLICT
POSSIBLE BREAK-UP OF UK

The Assembly proposed in the Scotland Act promises nothing but dangerous and divisive conflict between Edinburgh and London, reduced power for Scotland's MPs in Westminster, the one place where it matters, and more expensive government interference at home for all of us. The SCOTLAND SAYS NO campaign seeks a massive NO vote in the Referendum on March 1st 1979. Please give us your support now by returning the coupon below with whatever donation you can spare, to the Campaign Headquarters, 90 West Campbell Street, Glasgow. If you are willing to help in leaflet distribution, canvassing or help with organisation of meetings please tick appropriate box.

Joint Chairmen:
The Right Hon. Lord Wilson of Langside, Q.C. The Very Rev. Andrew Herron, DD.

Assembly-We can't afford it.

SCOTLAND SAYS NO

If you can help in any way please fill in the coupon and send to address below.

Name

Address and/or telephone

I am/We are willing to: help deliver leaflets☐ canvass☐ help organise meetings☐
I enclose a donation of _____ to assist with funds.
Make cheques or postal orders payable to SCOTLAND SAYS NO, 90 West Campbell Street, Glasgow, G2 6RU.

SSN

SCOTLAND ACT 1978 REFERENDUM
VOTING BY POST

APPLICATIONS MUST ARRIVE BY THURSDAY 15 FEBRUARY

If you cannot vote at your polling station in the Referendum on 1st March, 1979 you may be entitled to vote by post.

The main grounds on which you can apply to do this are:

1 If you have moved to an address in another electoral division since 10th October 1978.

2 If you will be away from your home on polling day because of the general nature of your job (but NOT because you are on holiday).

3 If you are ill, disabled or blind.

Issued by the Scottish Office

Scottish Office

Catalonia

Quebec

ESTATUTO   Greenland

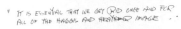

NOTES ON CONTRIBUTORS

J.S. Berridge   Lecturer in Political Science, University of Dundee

J.M. Bochel   Senior Lecturer in Political Science, University of Dundee

M. Brown   Journalist; Research Student, University of Dundee

Dr D.E. Butler   Fellow of Nuffield College, Oxford

Mrs M.A. Clark   Lecturer in Social Sciences, Duncan of Jordanstone College
                       of Art, Dundee

D.T. Denver   Lecturer in Politics, University of Lancaster

Dr M.C. Dyer   Lecturer in Politics, University of Aberdeen

P. Fotheringham   Lecturer in Politics, University of Glasgow

J.P. Fowler   Lecturer in Politics, University of Glasgow

A.D. Grant   Assistant Librarian, University of Dundee

Dr C.T. Harvie   Professor of British Studies, University of Tübingen

I. Hume   Staff Tutor in Politics, The Open University in Wales

Dr J.G. Kellas   Reader in Politics, University of Glasgow

Dr W.J.A. Macartney   Staff Tutor in Politics, The Open University in Scotland

W.A.R. Mullin   Lecturer in Industrial Studies, Centre for Industrial Studies,
                       Glenrothes

SUBJECT INDEX

This index has been compiled so as to give several alternative access points to each topic. For example Press advertising may be found under that heading but also under party or group names and place names.

"See" references are made from unused to used headings. "See also" references are made from general headings to more specific headings: for example, "Leaflets, see also under names of parties and groups". In such cases the headings referred to will not all produce entries as most groups only indulged in selected activities.

Key to letters in brackets after certain entries: (S) - in Scotland; (W) - in Wales; (N) - footnote; (and ill.) - see also illustrations. A full list of abbreviations can be found at the beginning of the book.

INDEX OF NAMES

The status accorded to persons in this index is that which they held at the time
of the Scotland Act and Wales Act Referendums.